TENNESSEE WILDCAT

On the Trail of Laura Ingalls Wilder's Mr. Edwards

Practical Pioneer Press

PRAISE FOR TENNESSEE WILDCAT

"I finished this book in one long and one short session. Not because it is a quick read, but because I wanted to keep reading! The level of research is impressive, but the analysis of the records unearthed is what makes this book an extraordinary read.

"Miller looked at the data from every angle, and while she could have made some leaps of logic, she stayed grounded to say, 'this is what the data does and does not show us.' I very much appreciated this aspect of the work; it can be very fun to speculate, but unless the facts are conclusive, it is best to stick to possibilities instead of declarations.

"*Tennessee Wildcat* is a must-have addition to the library of anyone who wants to learn more about the history behind and within the *Little House* books.

—Cindy Wilson, author of
The Beautiful Snow: The Ingalls Family, the Railroads, and the Hard Winter of 1880-81

Tennessee Wildcat

On the Trail of
Laura Ingalls Wilder's
Mr. Edwards

Robynne Elizabeth Miller
J.D. Rushmore

TENNESSEE WILDCAT

Paperback ISBN 978-1-947370-06-7
Hardback ISBN 978-1-947370-07-4

Library of Congress Control Number: 2023915930

Photograph of Isaac T Gibson, Che-To-Pah, and Sam Bevenue, courtesy of Gateway to Oklahoma History, Oklahoma Historical Society.
Satellite image of section 36, Rutland Twp., used with permission of Google. Imagery ©2023 CNES / Airbus, Maxar Technologies, USDA/FFPAC/GEO, Map data ©2023.
Photograph of Colmans Farm, Lifton ©2023 Roger Mounce. Used with permission.
The photograph of the Washing Reser Store at Preston, Hickory County, MO is in the public domain (*See* Ihrig, 1970, p. 186)

"… the light we throw upon them …" quote by Laura Ingalls Wilder was published in the "As a Farm Woman Thinks" column in *The Missouri Ruralist*, February 1, 1922, p.26 under the byline, Mrs. A. J. Wilder. Public Domain.

The following photographs are from the authors' personal collections: *Grave of Robert B. Gilmour, Gravestone of Edmund Mason, Walnut Creek flowing through Edmund Mason's land.*

Interior design and layout by Author Digital Services
Cover Design by miblart
Published by Practical Pioneer Press (Portland, OR)

VISIT WWW.TENNESSEEWILDCAT.COM
for additional resources and background material.

... persons appear to us according to the light we throw upon them from our own minds.

—LAURA INGALLS WILDER

A wholly fictitious character is created, not remembered.

—ROBYNNE ELIZABETH MILLER

Dedication

I can't begin to express how privileged I feel to have worked on this project at all, let alone with some of the finest researchers and writers and editors in the industry. Although J.D. and Ian get top billing for their contributions to this project, the fact is, it was a collaborative effort by historians, record-keepers, and researchers from across the country . . . as well as from Australia!

So, this is dedicated, with deepest appreciation, to every person who brought this book into being. Thank you . . . for everything.

It's also dedicated to my sweet Noah James. You put up with (among other things) my road trips and rummaging through archives and frequent stops at graveyards for the several years this project required. Your support means the world to me, Noah James. I love you.

~Robynne Elizabeth Miller

To Robynne, I am so thankful for the privilege of getting to work alongside such a gifted writer, especially one with as much knowledge of the "Little House" world as you. Your passion for all things "Laura"... and your skill as a writer are inspiring. Thank you.

I also dedicate this book to the pioneering settlers of Montgomery County, Kansas and to the Osage Nation, whom they displaced . . . and to Laura Ingalls Wilder fans everywhere – especially those that love historical mysteries.

~J.D. Rushmore

Contents

Table of Figures

Acknowledgments

J.D., it has been a pleasure and an honor to work with someone who cares so deeply about meticulous research, respecting our subject matter, and honoring the legacy of Laura Ingalls Wilder. You are the epitome of excellence in all you do. I can't express my gratitude enough for your collaboration on this project.

Ian Feavearyear, if ever there was a hidden hero, it's you. Painstaking research, attention to detail, refusal to accept dead ends, and your genuine heart for the work we do is appreciated more than I can say. And the way you keep me focused and laughing is nothing short of miraculous. Already looking forward to our next project together!

~Robynne Elizabeth Miller

Robynne, thank you for bringing so much life into this manuscript and making this entire work so much more readable than it could ever have been without your expert craftsmanship. Your skill as a writer and your deep love and knowledge of all things Laura Ingalls Wilder have brought so much to this project. It has been a privilege to work with you.

~J.D. Rushmore

We would also both like to thank the following for their help while researching this book: **Craig G. Wright**, Supervisory Archivist at the Herbert Hoover Presidential Library in Iowa, for supplying the original manuscripts of *Pioneer Girl* and the *Little House on the Prairie* background material; **Tatyana N. Shinn**, Ph.D., Assistant Director at the Center for Missouri Studies in The State Historical Society of Missouri, for supplying original early manuscripts of *Little House on the Prairie;* **Tina Swyers & Susan Kniffen**, for their research in the Montgomery County courthouse in Independence, Kansas; **Lin Fredericksen** (retired) of the State Archives

Division of the Kansas Historical Society, who was extremely helpful in supplying several documents related to Edmund Mason's land in Montgomery County, Kansas—and for hunting for other documents that proved elusive; **Elizabeth Burnes**, Archivist at the National Archives at Kansas City, MO, for searching for declaratory statements in the depths of the archives; **Lauren Gray**, Head of Reference at the Kansas Historical Society, for searching for declaratory statements; **Wade Popp**, Archives Specialist at the National Archives at Kansas City, MO, for searching for the relinquishment record of William VanWinkle; **Lori Cox-Paul**, Director of Archival Operations at the National Archives at Kansas City, MO, for searching for declaratory statements and relinquishment records of William VanWinkle; **Stephen Spence**, Archives Specialist at the National Archives at Kansas City, MO, for searching for the declaratory statement of Charles M. Thompson; **Andrea Israel**, Archives Technician at the Bureau of Land Management, for deciphering some of the writing in tract books.

Thanks are also due to **Andy Taylor** and **Mike Maxton**, members of the *Kansas History Geeks* group on Facebook, for the information they provided on the lost town of St. Paul, KS.

We are also especially grateful to **Roger Mounce** of Lifton, England for supplying photos of Colmans farm, birthplace of Edmund Mason, and to **Kelly Passauer**, City Manager at the City of Independence, Kansas, for permission to use the portrait of former mayor, William E. Brown.

We would like to give a special shout-out to **Sharon Easley née Mason** for supplying an abundance of information on the Mason family and whose encouragement and support in the early days of this project were invaluable. This book would almost never have been written without Sharon's enthusiastic assistance. Thank you, Sharon!

We would also like to offer a very special thank you to **Geoffrey Standing Bear**, Principal Chief of the Osage Nation, for his advice, assistance, and input.

Note to Readers

Certain commonly-used sources are referred to as follows:

The 1881 Atlas - Edwards, John P. Historical Atlas of Montgomery County, Kansas. 1881, https://www.kansasmemory.org/item/224026. Kansas Memory.

Wilson's History - Wilson, Ebenezer E. "History of Montgomery County, Kansas" in *The 1881 Atlas*, pp. 7–9.

The 1903 History - Duncan, L. Wallace. History of Montgomery County, Kansas. By Its Own People. Press of Iola Register, 1903. archive.org, Internet Archive, http://archive.org/details/historyofmontgom00dunc.

BLM GLO Database – The Bureau of Land Management's General Land Office Records search database, https://glorecords.blm.gov/search/

BLM Tract Books – Digital Copies of the Bureau of Land Management's original tract books, available at https://www.familysearch.org/search/collection/2074276. The most commonly referenced volume is Kansas Vol. 41.

We abbreviated the book title "Little House on the Prairie" to *LHOTP* throughout this work. When referring to Laura Ingalls Wilder's published novel, we cited the "newly illustrated uniform edition," Harper & Row, 1953.

Most Kansas newspaper articles referenced in this work are available for viewing online free-of-charge via the *Kansas Open Historical Content* project, at: kansashistoricalopencontent.newspapers.com.

The drafts and fragments of *Pioneer Girl* by Laura Ingalls Wilder, housed in the Rose Wilder Lane Papers at the Herbert Hoover Presidential Library, have now been published by the South Dakota Historical Society Press in a single volume under the title: *Pioneer Girl: The Revised Texts* (2021), edited by Nancy Tystad Koupal.

The Location of the Ingalls Cabin

Much of the hunt for Mr. Edwards centers on the location of the Ingalls family during their time in Kansas. The exact location of their land is critical because so many of the clues Laura left us require a clear understanding of who was in the immediate vicinity. For our search to be relevant, pinpointing their Kansas homesite accurately ensured our resulting investigation was accurate, and our final conclusions sound. After all, if we were looking in an inaccurate area, we'd be looking at a completely erroneous cast of suspects.

The incredible, and painstaking, research of Margaret Clement was our starting point . . . but it wasn't something we took at face value. You'll note throughout our hunt that we examined primary sources to glean our own clues and substantiate our own opinions. It wouldn't do to start our hunt for Mr. Edwards with our foundational premise laid upon someone else's work.

But Margaret did a wonderful job on the initial legwork of locating the Ingallses' cabin site in Rutland Township, Montgomery County. What's more, she did a thorough job of substantiating and documenting her methods, facts, and conclusions.

As a result, her research was easy to corroborate, and we are confident that our assessment of the data renders the same result hers did: the Ingallses settled in section 36 of Rutland Township.

Terminology

Homestead

Throughout this work, the term *homestead* was used in the general sense of "the home and adjoining land occupied by a family" or in its verb form "to acquire or occupy as a homestead" ("Homestead." Merriam-Webster.com Dictionary) in addition to the more technical meaning of public land obtained under the Homestead Act of 1862.

Osage Indians

We primarily used the term *Osage Indians* throughout this work rather than "Native American" or "American Indians" on the advice of Geoffrey Standing Bear, Principal Chief of the Osage Nation.

TENNESSEE
WILDCAT

Rutland Township
Montgomery County, KS
July 10, 2017

Bumping off-road through rolling prairie in an SUV, it was exciting to see the land, and two now-in-ruins homesites, once owned by Edmund Mason. After stopping near a cluster of trees and stepping into the long grass, we moved carefully, unsure of what was underfoot. An afternoon of exploring revealed the remains of Mason's homestead: long-forgotten wells without covers, ramshackle cellar entrances, rocks from foundations and walls, historic bricks, and odd bits of metal and debris. A *Little House* archeologist's dream.

We returned to the vehicle and looked toward the *Little House on the Prairie Museum*—the site of Laura's second "little house"—which connected at the corners with Mason's land. The *Little House* site boasted a well hand-dug by Pa and was the location of the birth of Carrie, Laura's younger sister. It wasn't far away. In fact, it was very, very close.

After a moment of gazing across the prairie, something didn't feel right. What had Laura written about the location of Mr. Edward's home? Ah, yes . . . *"it was a long way back to Mr. Edwards' camp."* Two miles, if Laura's memory and words were accurate. And on the other side of woods and a creek.

Scanning the silent, rolling grassland, imagining it was 1869, things started clicking into place. It was too close!

Mason's land was just too close . . .

Introduction

Fans of Laura Ingalls Wilder are intrigued by many things, including her vivid descriptions of the western landscapes she traveled across and lived in. And though she beautifully rendered the grandeur of the wild, open prairie, it's her characters we tend to remember most. Iconic villainess, Nellie Oleson, manly heartthrob, Almanzo Wilder, and the Ingallses' own much-loved Pa brought the frontier into sharp focus and drew us into its story. Laura's rich characters and brilliant depictions of the land they inhabited brought pioneer history to life.

The combination was magical.

Of all the incredible characters Laura introduced her readers to, however, one remained something of a mystery: that beloved Tennessee Wildcat, Mr. Edwards.

You can find almost all the people Laura mentioned in her *Little House* series by searching censuses, land documents, and other historical records. If you care to, you can visit many of their graves, a few of their still-standing homes and businesses, or even the parcels of land they worked first as homestead claims, and then as "proved-up" farms. They were real, live, verifiable humans with documentary proof of their existence and descendants proud of their pioneer and literary connections.

But Mr. Edwards? The exact person described in Laura's books? He was nowhere to be found in historical records . . . at least not in the person of a single homesteader identical in name, location, and various character traits to the man Laura depicted. And that made him the biggest enigma of the entire *Little House* series.

We know Laura gave a few of her characters fictitious names, such as the Brewsters (whose real name was Bouchie), with whom she boarded during the first term of school she taught. Another exception is Nellie

Oleson, who wasn't just given a fictitious name. She was actually a composite character constructed from three girls Laura knew in her youth: Nellie Owens, Genevieve Masters, and Estella Gilbert.

Beyond having their names changed, however, the Bouchies and the Nellies had something else in common—Laura didn't like them. At all. But she was a decent person, who knew her literary depiction of them wasn't exactly favorable. So, in assigning false names, she was likely trying to protect their identities from potential gossip or scandal. And no wonder. Nellie and the Bouchies were the central characters in the only truly negative stories Laura intentionally published.

Of course, Laura couldn't foresee the vast and enduring world-wide popularity of her books, the eventual publication of her earliest notes, letters, and drafts, or the advent of the internet. She had no idea how thoroughly future fans would search for the places, people, and details Laura wrote about. Nor how very much people would care.

But we are living in an age of information. And so, through modern avenues, as well as access to her personal letters, notes, and drafts, we have ringside seats to her decision-making process in masking both the Bouchies' and the Nellies' actual identities, as well as endless other bits of information about other people and places she wrote about.

But what about Mr. Edwards?

No researcher or historian has ever been able to find an actual "Mr. Edwards" who perfectly matches Laura's detailed description. And, unlike her explanation of the formation of the composite Nellie Oleson, there are no known letters or other writings in which Laura discusses the origin of Mr. Edwards as some sort of created character. There is one letter in which she admits the *story* in which he helped Pa file his De Smet homestead claim was complete fiction (Wilder, 2016, pp. 210–211), but nothing telling us how Mr. Edwards as a character came to be. There are some mentions throughout her notes and letters that give us hints, of course. But nothing clearly identifying the real Mr. Edwards, if he even existed at all.

In the context of all Laura's notes and drafts, and what we know about how she chose to craft her stories, this is odd. She wrote about hundreds of people throughout her *Little House* series, and the vast majority of the characters Laura wrote about are verifiably real . . . there's plenty of historical documentation to prove they all lived. So, surely, there had to be an actual person as a basis for Mr. Edwards. After all, Mr. Edwards couldn't possibly be the only character made up entirely from Laura's imagination, could he?

If Mr. Edwards wasn't fiction, however, his name proved to be a problem. There are plenty of records, from land deeds to newspapers to censuses and more, that should establish his existence and match the details Laura gave us. But even a thorough search of the available period data didn't seem to solve the mystery.

Of course, Laura could have changed his name. She did so in two other instances. But "Nellie" was a rather nasty piece of work. And the Bouchies, specifically Mrs. Bouchie, were the main players in a particularly unpleasant experience in young Laura's life (Laura's first teaching contract in which she boarded during the week with the Bouchies). It made sense for new names to be given to characters attached to negative stories.

But, unlike dodgier folks, Mr. Edwards was a hero to Laura, much like her own Pa. As such, she had no reason or motivation to hide his true identity. If she actually knew it, that is.

So, maybe Mr. Edwards was a composite of her heroes ... men that really existed and interacted with the Ingalls family. Nellie was a composite of negative characters in Laura's life, so it's not a stretch to imagine Laura could have employed the same literary technique to craft a kind of composite hero character in the same fashion.

And there was always the possibility we were overthinking things, too. Laura was a very young child during her family's time in Kansas. A toddler, really. So, it could have been she just she didn't remember exactly who did what on the prairie, or she merely muddled names, details, and stories she'd heard through the years until there was no teasing out which fact belonged with which person.

In the interest of coming at this investigation in as unbiased a manner as possible, however, we couldn't take any option off the table. Until some hard evidence proved otherwise, and to be open to whatever truth might be uncovered, our own suspicions had to be ignored. So, our beginning premise included all possibilities: Mr. Edwards could have been a real man, a composite of several men, a loose collection of memory fragments, or pure fiction.

Whatever the origin of the Mr. Edwards character, however, the uncertainty and elusiveness surrounding his identity added a rather exciting dimension to the already-intriguing man. From our first literary "meeting" with him, we had wanted to know more about this quirky, endearing man. And that desire only intensified over time.

Finally, decades after we first opened *LHOTP* and discovered Mr. Edwards, with whom we instantly fell in love, the opportunity to hunt him down arrived. The process has been as intensive and thorough as it has been exciting and just plain fun. As we've sifted through known details and searched for new clues, we've uncovered fascinating people, wonderful stories, long-concealed data, and even some significant errors in the previously available body of *Little House* knowledge. In short, it's been a bit of a wild ride.

So, if you'd like to join the hunt for the true Mr. Edwards, just slip on your boots and saddle up.

We're hot on the trail of the Wildcat from Tennessee.

– 1 –

The Starting Line

ALL GOOD MYSTERIES start with an examination of the scene where the body was found, the jewel got stolen, or the action took place. Our hunt for Mr. Edwards was no exception. Our first task was to study the Kansas environment Laura wrote about . . . via her own words, previously known data, and new information gleaned from multiple historic sources. Understanding the 1869 Kansas landscape in which *LHOTP* was set, including information Laura *didn't* incorporate into her published descriptions and stories, was a critical first step in uncovering the potential identity of Mr. Edwards. Visualizing the actual setting in which the Ingallses lived changed our perspective and had a profound impact right from the very start: it reset the previously acknowledged search area.

When all pertinent information was laid out on our research board (à la stereotypical television detectives), an important truth was revealed: Laura's description of the area surrounding her family's Kansas homestead, and the distinct lack of near neighbors she described, simply wasn't accurate. The land the Ingallses settled on wasn't a remote, sparsely populated speck on the vast, empty prairie. In fact, the territory was almost teeming with a variety of settlers and inhabitants, whose numbers swelled significantly during the Ingallses' short time in Kansas. As we uncovered a more accurate picture of the Kansas landscape Laura's family lived in between 1869 and 1871, more and more of their suddenly discovered neighbors became potential suspects in our hunt.

Whether Laura's inaccuracy about Kansas, and the people in the area, was a result of her very young age at the time she arrived, or because she was intent on imbuing her stories with strong themes of independence and self-reliance, we may never know. Laura did intentionally alter details in other books to emphasize the idea that the family relied primarily on themselves as they forged new lives in the west. So, it's likely her omissions and errors regarding much of the surrounding population were intentional. She omitted three lodgers in *The Long Winter*, for example, to underscore how "alone" the family was during those seven months of blizzards (Wilder, 2014, p. 205, 2016, pp. 166–167). So, it's likely that reducing the number of settlers in Kansas was at least a partially intentional choice in her bid to paint the west as isolated and fit for only the most prepared and hardy of pioneers.

We also can't forget Laura's age when she lived in Kansas, nor the fact she took quite a bit of literary license in fiddling with timelines in her initial books, when considering the clues she left us. We know Laura rearranged some details, including ages, intentionally for the sake of narrative arc, literary flow, and to avoid having to document the time the family "back-trailed" to Pepin. Back-trailing was a somewhat negative term given to those who had headed west and found themselves re-tracing their steps back east . . . often because they simply couldn't make it on the rough and unforgiving frontier.

She probably also rearranged details, or got them outright wrong, unintentionally. Laura was a mere toddler during her time in Kansas, after all, despite the age she assigned herself in *LHOTP*. So at least some errors in conveying exact details were inevitable.

The Ingallses left their little house in the big woods near Pepin, Wisconsin, in 1869 when Laura was two years old. They returned from Kansas to that same little house in Wisconsin in the spring of 1871, when Laura was barely four. So, during her whole time in Montgomery County, she was a very little girl . . . one who wasn't likely to remember many facts accurately.

Because Laura wrote *Little House in the Big Woods* about the second time her family lived near Pepin, she simply adjusted the order of their overall journey to Kansas, as well as her corresponding age, when she wrote about leaving Wisconsin. By writing the story as if they'd gone to Kansas *after* they'd been in Pepin the second time, instead of before, Laura eliminated the appearance of back-trailing and offered a smoother narrative flow. The real timeline was:

- Laura was born February 7, 1867, in Wisconsin, where she lived until she was two.
- In late winter or very early spring of 1869, the family move to Missouri, to a piece of previously unseen land Pa had purchased.
- In the fall of 1869, the Ingallses moved to Montgomery County, Kansas, and lived there until the spring of 1871. Laura would have been between two-and-a-half and just-turned-four years of age during those Kansas years.
- After leaving Kansas in the spring of 1871, the family moved back to Wisconsin and the Little House in the Big Woods, where they resided for a few more years. Laura was four to seven during this period.
- In February of 1874, they sold the house and land again and moved west, settling near Walnut Grove, Minnesota. Laura had just turned seven.

The literary timeline adjustment Laura made to her age was significant. Laura turned five in *Little House in the Big Woods* and was almost seven when she arrived at Plum Creek. So, she effectively depicted herself as being five and six during the time she lived on the Kansas prairie. Because Laura was actually between two and four years old during that time period, she couldn't really be considered reliable as a firsthand witness. Toddlers usually aren't.

Since Laura wasn't five when she rolled into Kansas, which is already pretty young, our understanding of the first portion of *LHOTP* must be viewed through that lens. According to the story, Mr. Edwards was one of the first people the Ingallses met when they arrived in Rutland Township. As Laura was only two at this time, she couldn't possibly have remembered those first days of their acquaintance, nor what was said or done. She probably wasn't even out of diapers!

That doesn't necessarily mean she made Mr. Edwards up, however. The family likely spoke about their time in Kansas over the years, and the people they had known and spent time with. One of the blessings of growing up in a household without electricity, gadgets, the internet, or close neighbors is that the inhabitants would have spent a lot of time just talking together. So, it's reasonable to presume the people the Ingallses lived among during their Kanas adventure would have come up in conversation from time to time. We know that, in later books, the family did reminisce about Mr. Edwards and the time he brought Christmas gifts from Independence. So, he was certainly someone who made an impression and was talked about through the years.

In addition to information Laura could have acquired from family storytelling, however, she probably had some sparse personal recollections of her own. By the end of their time in Montgomery County, Laura was four. Barely out of the toddler years, yes, but old enough that she might have had a few early personal memories, or at least impressions, mingled with her family's recollections.

Some family lore and a few fuzzy memories re-shaped into stories made for engaging reading, it's true. Laura was an enormously gifted storyteller. But the unfortunate sum of all her tales about this time in her life wasn't really enough for us to definitively identify an actual, historical Mr. Edwards.

But this is where her own notes and drafts, along with intensive historical research, came into play. After all, we were on the trail of his real identity, so we needed to look at early drafts, contemporary records, and other hard evidence. Fifty years ago, we might have taken Laura at her word that Mr. Edwards existed, and that her portrayal of him was accurate. Even knowing she intentionally and unintentionally rearranged details due to lack of first-hand memories and her own admitted occasional literary license wouldn't necessarily give us cause to doubt the man was who she said he was.

But phones, email, and the internet now give us the means to substantiate claims, information, and details like never before. That's particularly crucial as Laura simply wasn't old enough to be a reliable witness when she lived in Kansas. And this is not an educated guess, either. We know Laura didn't give us an accurate depiction of Mr. Edwards simply because no man in any historical record perfectly matches Laura's description.

We also know this because the area the Ingallses settled in wasn't anywhere near as empty or remote as Laura led us to believe.

– 2 –

Lay of the Land

THERE ARE TWO kinds of Laura fans:

- Those who simply enjoy her stories and the pioneer life she portrayed without their minds wandering outside *Little House* pages.
- And those who want to understand every detail, fact, and nuance of her life, the people she knew, and the places she lived.

If you're the second kind of person, which you probably are if you're reading this book, you'll be thrilled with what we've compiled at the end of this manuscript: hundreds of period references and sources, as well as a thorough explanation of how townships and maps were defined and rendered in the 1800's (see Appendix). It's a little technical in places, but imperative to really grasp how many of Laura's clues fit together. Learning how the land was organized and laid out helped us understand the environment and community in which the Ingallses settled during their time in Kansas. To even begin to unravel who Mr. Edwards might have been, getting the lay of the land was absolutely critical.

Why? Because one of the biggest mistakes previous researchers had made was that they didn't pay enough attention to the Kansas landscape as a *whole* when considering candidates. Most *Little House* historians seem to have lifted Rutland Township, the Township in which the Ingallses settled, right out of the prairie and examined it as if nothing existed beyond its borders.

But the Ingallses' part of Rutland Township, within Montgomery County, *didn't* exist in a sea of nothingness. Despite Laura's assertions that their Kansas little house was in the middle of wild, unsettled land and far from civilization, that actually wasn't true. When the Ingallses arrived in 1869, they found themselves in something of a small, but established, neighborhood. And it rapidly swelled to a respectable settlement, numbering about eight thousand people, by the time they left almost two years later. This fact was fundamentally significant to our search. Widening our scope to beyond Rutland Township's borders revealed there were a whole lot more folks meandering about on the prairie than Laura described in *LHOTP*.

If you merely looked at Rutland Township, where Laura resided, as if all potential "Mr. Edwards" suspects were contained there, you'd be missing something very important. And we'll explain just what that is in a moment. First, however, we need to start with a simple breakdown of how Kansas land was laid out during the late 1860's.

As the Appendix describes in great detail, the territory was divided into grids. Surveyors separated land into *townships, sections,* and *quarter sections.* A *township* (twp.) was a six-by-six mile grid (a total of thirty-six square miles). Townships were then divided into *sections,* which were one-mile-by-one-mile squared, or 640 acres. There were thirty-six sections in each township.

Sections were further subdivided into *half-sections* and *quarter-sections.* A quarter-section was 160 acres, and that was the amount of land a homesteader could claim under the Homestead Act of 1862. Accounting for some set-aside sections we'll discuss in a moment, there were approximately 142 potential quarter-section homesteads in each township.

On a map, sections in each township were numbered, starting in the northeast corner, then zig-zagging down as follows:

6	5	4	3	2	1
7	8	9	10	11	12
18	17	16	15	14	13
19	20	21	22	23	24
30	29	28	27	26	25
31	32	33	34	35	36

Figure 1 - Order of section numbers within a township

The land could, of course, be divided even further, into eighth-sections (eighty acres), sixteenth sections (forty acres), and so on. But the important thing to understand is that the land was segmented like one huge waffle . . . rows and rows of little squares, all numbered in the same way, no matter where the township was.

Considering how orderly that seems, it would have been nice if all counties had been comprised of even numbers of townships. Or if the term *township* had only one meaning. But county lines were drawn willy-nilly right through the middle of those neatly drawn grids. And the word *township,* for whatever reason, had three distinct meanings.

The first definition of a *township* is the thirty-six-square-mile grid we've already described. A second usage was to define a position north-south of a baseline. (A full explanation of what a baseline is, as well as further township descriptions, can be found in that amazing Appendix). If you've always wanted to read land records and know exactly what that means (and, perhaps, be able to find old homesteads across the U.S.), the Appendix is your new best friend.

The third usage of *township* is "a named subdivision of a county."

Confusing, isn't it? Why whoever was in charge didn't adopt three separate terms for these distinct definitions at the beginning of America's westward expansion is a puzzle. To have a township that is a subdivision of a county, made up of a smaller area also called a township, located at a specific township in relation to a baseline, is an obvious recipe for confusion. Worse still, sometimes a township (subdivision) was the same as a township (thirty-six-square-miles). Sometimes it wasn't. We can't fathom what the designers of this system were thinking.

To help you navigate this confusion, however, we'll use a lower-case *township* (twp.) when referring to a thirty-six-square-mile area, and a capitalized *Township* (Twp.) when referring to a named subdivision of a county, sort of like capitalizing a village or modern town name. The north-south of a baseline usage would also use a lower-case "t," but that's the term we'll use least. If it does appear, we'll make sure to clarify.

Montgomery County, where our hunt for Mr. Edwards is focused, is comprised of twelve Townships (remember, these are the subdivisions within a larger county): Louisburg, Sycamore, West Cherry, Cherry, Independence, Drum Creek, Liberty, Caney, Fawn Creek, Parker, Cherokee, and Rutland Township, where the Ingalls homestead was. Those twelve Townships were comprised of twelve townships (lower-case "t": thirty-six-square-mile grids) and thirteen partial townships. See the following illustration, taking particular note of Rutland Township's location, as well as the city of Independence:

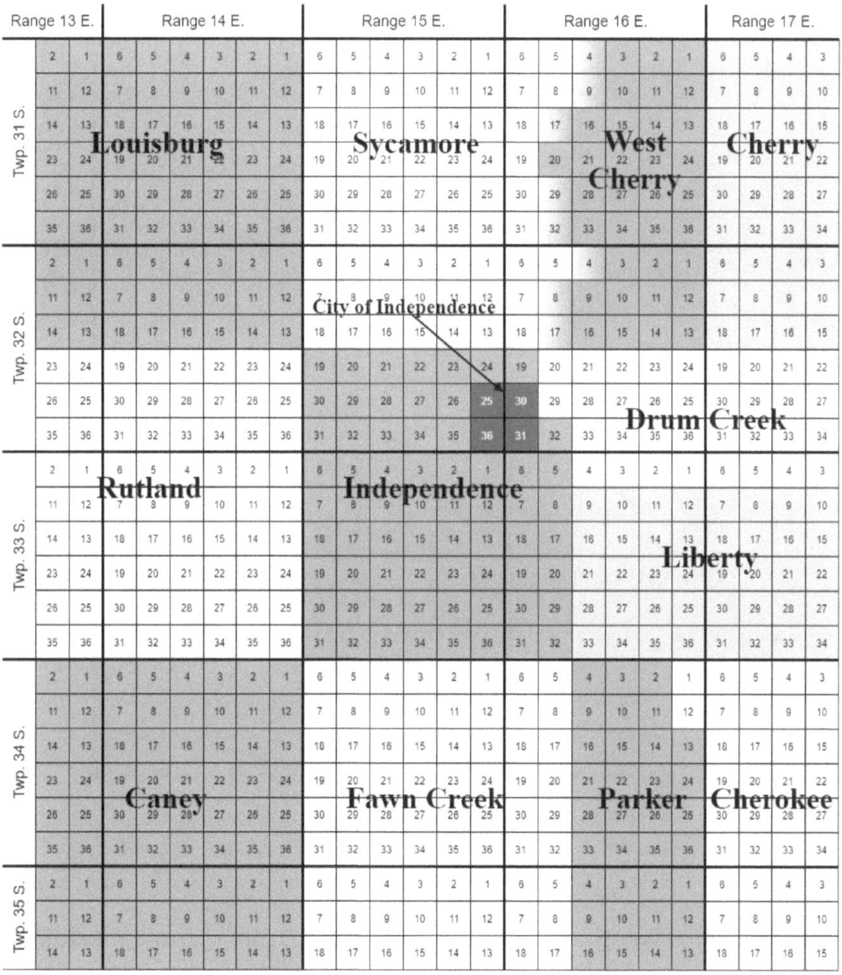

Figure 2 - Schematic map of Montgomery County showing townships and section numbers

See Figure 3 for a closer look at Rutland Township (note section 36 in the lower right corner of the shaded area). What are you looking at there in that shaded section 36? The site of the Ingalls homestead.

Although, technically, there are four "section 36s" in Rutland Township (because three other (lower case) townships are part of that (upper case) Township), we're going to simplify things as much as possible. So, when we refer to "section 36 of Rutland Twp.," what we mean is the Ingallses' "section 36" unless otherwise noted.

	Range 13 E.		Range 14 E.					
	23	24	19	20	21	22	23	24
Twp. 32S	26	25	30	29	28	27	26	25
	35	36	31	32	33	34	35	36
	2	1	6	5	4	3	2	1
	11	12	7	8	9	10	11	12
Twp. 33S	14	13	18	17	16	15	14	13
	23	24	19	20	21	22	23	24
	26	25	30	26	28	27	26	25
	35	36	31	32	33	34	35	36

Figure 3 - Schematic diagram of Rutland Twp., showing townships, ranges, and section numbers, with the Ingalls homesite in the shaded section 36

Are we done being confusing yet? Not quite . . . though we are close to pulling this all together, so stick with us a little longer and it will all make sense.

In the original 1785 act, the Public Land Survey System (PLSS) designated section 16 in every township as school land. The reasoning was that if a school was built in the southeast corner of that section, it would be centrally located within the township. Eventually, as settlement increased, both sections 16 and 36 were specifically reserved to be used for school land, while the other sections in a township were available for regular homesteading.

This had a significant impact in our search for Mr. Edwards because the method by which a homesteader obtained land in sections 16 and 36 was different to other, regular homestead sections and, therefore, impacted the type of historical land records kept. As pointed out above, the Ingalls family, and some of their neighbors, settled in section 36 of Rutland Twp. This was a "school section," which meant rules were a little different there. As if that complicating factor wasn't enough, Montgomery County was located almost entirely within a portion of Osage land, known as the Osage Diminished Reserve. And *that* fact meant that other regulations and methods of acquiring and recording land in that area were unique, as well.

So, not only were there regular rules of settlement in play, but there were also school section rules, *and* Osage Diminished Reserve considerations in the mix. Add in different record-keeping methods for each, and you can see why figuring out the lay of the land was challenging . . . and why previous researchers had a difficult time creating a cohesive picture of the territory at the time the Ingallses lived in Kansas.

But here is where we begin to pull things all together. If, when doing *Little House* research, you only looked at Rutland Township, you'd be missing something huge. You wouldn't be alone, however. Several reputable historians have made this exact mistake. Isolating Rutland Township as the boundaries of a *Little House* research area dismisses everything, and *everyone,* else in the picture at that time.

Take a look again at Figure 2 on page 17, remembering this is the entirety of Montgomery County. Find the Ingallses' section 36 of Rutland Township. Now, ask yourself: Where is that section in relation to the rest of Rutland Township? And where is it in relation to Independence, Fawn Creek, and Caney Townships?

See it?

The Ingalls homestead is almost exactly in the middle of a square made up of Rutland, Independence, Fawn Creek, and Caney Townships. This means that most of the land, and its inhabitants, in the three Townships *adjoining* Rutland were far closer to the Ingallses than most of Rutland Township, itself.

With this knowledge in hand, we shifted the Ingalls homestead into the center of a new search grid and *that* became the area of interest in our hunt for Mr. Edwards, leaving much of Rutland Township beyond logical consideration. After all, it is unlikely that Pa would consider folks "neighbors" if they lived several miles away, and it's just as unlikely they would be willing to help if they lived several miles from the Ingallses. In fact, it would be unlikely that such distant settlers would even be known to Pa.

But if you shift Pa's section 36 in Rutland Township into the center of the search area, the land and the folks of the three adjoining Townships come logically into play. So, within that newly defined search area were settlers we needed to investigate.

Several historians had not only limited their research to Rutland Township, which mostly lies northwest of the Ingallses' section, but had also limited their sources to traditional land records. For our hunt, we readjusted the search perimeter to put Pa's chosen homestead into the exact middle of a search grid containing portions of Rutland, Caney, Independence, and Fawn Creek Townships. Correspondingly, we expanded our research via a plethora of historical records to accommodate that more accurate search area and the complicated nature of the land Pa had built on.

The good news? We secured the correct area of interest and identified a collection of untapped period records in which to hunt for Mr. Edwards.

The bad news? When we put a whole lot more land into play, that meant *many* more people to investigate.

– 3 –

Setting the Scene

Settling in Montgomery County on the Osage Diminished Reserve

BEYOND UNDERSTANDING the physical lay of the land, and the Ingallses' location within its larger landscape when they settled in Kansas, we had to step back a little further to understand where America, as a whole, was at during this period.

When Charles and Caroline, along with Mary and Laura, arrived in Rutland Twp., Montgomery County, in the fall of 1869, the United States was still recovering from four years of civil war. Many travelers to Kansas were Civil War veterans—battle-hardened, and often displaced, young men recovering from one of the most traumatic events in U.S. history. They sought a new home and a new start in Kansas, just like the Ingallses.

Ulysses S. Grant, who had led the Union army to victory, was less than a year into his first term as president when he oversaw the driving in of the golden spike, marking the completion of the transcontinental railway at Promontory Summit, Utah Territory on May 10th, 1869. What better symbol of the hoped-for reunification of the country?

But as healing, industrialization, and modern culture progressed in the east, typified by the railroad expansion, publications such as Louisa May Alcott's *Little Women,* and the formation of the National Woman Suffrage Association by Susan B. Anthony and Elizabeth Cady Stanton (May 15, 1869), the pioneers of Montgomery County were in a very different environment. When you think of the stereotypical "wild west," this was it. It was the golden, chaotic, often lawless era of the American frontier.

Kit Carson, the famous explorer and frontiersman had died the year before, at fifty-eight. Mark Twain was then thirty-four and had already completed his adventures in Nevada and California, though it would be another seven years before he published *The Adventures of Tom Sawyer*. The first story of Buffalo Bill's adventures (when he was just twenty-three) would be published in December of 1869 on the front page of the *Chicago Tribune*. And Wild Bill Hickok had just been elected city marshal of Hays, KS and sheriff of Ellis County, KS.

Just before the Ingalls family's first Christmas in Kansas, twenty-two-year-old outlaw Jesse James committed his first confirmed bank robbery in Gallatin, Missouri, a state that borders Kansas. Butch Cassidy and the Sundance Kid were still just toddlers and living 2,000 miles apart. It would be another seven years before General Custer's death at the Battle of Little Bighorn, twelve years before the gunfight at the O.K. Corral, and twenty-one years before the massacre of the Lakota Sioux at Wounded Knee.

The Ingallses were smack dab in the middle of a rough-and-ready period of history. They were smack dab in the middle of a wild, wild frontier.

Kansas

In the middle of this period of westward movement and expansion, and all its associated drama and lawlessness, Charles Ingalls was continually drawn to the frontier. Pa was far more a pioneer and adventurer than a farmer, and his longing to travel is evidenced by the surprisingly large number of miles the Ingallses traveled, in a simple covered wagon, throughout their many journeys. Laura mentioned in various writings that she and Pa were alike and would have both loved to continue west if they could. One such place was in *By the Shores of Silver Lake*, chapter 12, "Wings Over Silver Lake," when Laura wanted to follow her relatives west:

> "Let's go West," she said one night after supper. "Pa, can't we go West when Uncle Henry does?"
>
> . . . .
>
> "I know, little Half-pint," said Pa, and his voice was very kind. "You and I want to fly like the birds. But long ago I promised your Ma that you girls should go to school."

Kansas, which had only become an official U.S. territory in May of 1854 and admitted as a state on January 29, 1861, was on the very edge of the western frontier Pa so longed to explore.

Figure 4 - Map showing Kansas' position as a state on the edge of "the West"

To the west, Colorado Territory wouldn't achieve statehood until 1876. To the far north, Dakota would remain a territory until 1889. And Wyoming, in the northwest, would become a state the following year, in 1890. Directly to the south lay Indian Territory (and No Man's Land), which wouldn't be admitted to the Union as Oklahoma until November 1907, thirty-six years after the Ingalls family left Kansas and five years after Charles Ingalls' death.

Montgomery County was located in the very southern part of Kansas, where Kansas shared a border with Indian Territory. Rutland Township, where Laura would first meet Mr. Edwards, was just nine miles north of that border.

Montgomery County

Montgomery County was only a few months old when Pa decided to stop the wagon and build the little house, having been organized by proclamation of Governor James M. Harvey on June 3, 1869. The first official newspaper, the *Register*, which was published by E. R. Trask in Oswego, a town directly east of Independence, recorded an account of the westward travel in its very first edition:

> COVERED WAGONS.--The streets were filled with immigrant wagons yesterday, so thick that it was almost impossible to drive through them with a team, it was no easy matter, indeed, for pedestrians to crowd through. . . . So they come, every day, and still there is room. (*The Oswego Weekly Register*, 13 May 1869, p.2)

Figure 5 – Illustration of prairie schooners crossing the prairie

Even though Laura painted a picture of relative isolation in *LHOTP*, about the time they arrived, there was a rush of immigration into the county, resulting in over 8,000 settlers by March of 1870. Though the town of Lawrence was about 120 miles from where the Ingallses settled, the paper referred to Montgomery County in this story:

> Immigrants are pouring in in large numbers, and taking claims in every direction. (*The Daily Kansas Tribune*, Lawrence, KS, 18 Jun 1869, Fri, p 2).

The rush of immigration was echoed in a story from Independence itself, just a few months later:

> Immigration still continues to pour in. As many as twenty claims have been taken in this vicinity in one day. At that rate, every quarter will have an occupant by spring. (*Independence Pioneer*, Independence KS, 13 Nov 1869, Sat. p.2).

Initially, settlers stayed on the eastern, "Independence" side of the Verdigris River, which wound north-south in the eastern half of the county. Then they began to move further west, crossing the river early in 1869. However, it took a few months for settlers to teem across the Verdigris in any significant numbers.

> . . . [i]t was not until late in the Summer of '69 that the rush became general, and in the fall of that year there was a grand charge along the whole line. . . . they came pell mell, and came to stay, bringing with them their families and all their household goods. Train after train of Prairie Schooners were sailing through the grass, and there was no halt until a claim of 160 acres had been staked off for every member of the family, . . . All over the County families were camped in wagons, while log or hay shanties were being built. (Edwards, 1881, p. 7)

The rush to settle this part of Kansas was problematic, however. Even though Montgomery County had become an official, organized county in June of 1869, the land had not yet been formally surveyed. Without proper, legally established property lines, settlers took things into their own hands, wild west style:

> There was the preliminary surveyor with his compass and chain, making measurements and establishing corners with as much ceremony and apparent authority as though deputized for the purpose by the General Government, and with as much accuracy as though he had shut both eyes and stepped it off. And then the claimant would change the corners so as to be sure of enough land, or to include some stream or choice piece of Valley land. There were claim speculators or jobbers in claims, who pretended to own claims and would victimize the "tenderfeet." (Edwards, 1881, p. 7)

Because settlers, at this time, couldn't officially register claims at the local Land Office, there was a serious and ever-present risk of having their land unfairly reshaped or even stolen, especially by the more intimidating and rough among the homesteaders. To resolve this problem . . .

> . . . there was organized the "Claim Protection Clubs." The laws of these clubs required the member to be entitled to homestead entry on Government land, to make a specified amount of improvement on his claim in a limited time, and in turn pledged him protection from that class of adverse claimants known as "jumpers." They were legislative, judicial and executive in their functions, and sometimes enforced their decrees with promptness and severity. . . . A decision of the club always passed title. Settlers in most new counties have short methods of dispensing justice that lack the tedium and expense of civil courts, and the pioneers of Montgomery Co. were not altogether an exception to the rule. (Edwards, 1881, p. 7)

Sounds a little like chaos, doesn't it? No proper land surveys. No way to formally file your claim. Residents re-drawing corners and property lines to suit themselves. Claim jumpers, intimidation, and "Claim Protection Clubs." (Which seems like a fancy term for vigilantes to us!)

It was into this scene that thirty-three-year-old Charles Ingalls arrived with one thing on his mind—land. Of course, land is what drew most settlers from across the country. Some were recovering Civil War soldiers, as we've said. But many more were simply bachelors and families looking for cheap, fertile land to farm. And possibly a bit of adventure along the way. Kansas was a perfect spot for both.

The Land Act of April 1820 had authorized the sale of public lands in half-quarter sections (eighty acres), which hadn't been previously permitted, and reduced the price from $2.00 per acre to just $1.25. A supplementary act in 1832 authorized the sale of quarter-quarter (forty acre) tracts. Cheaper cost per acre, and smaller sections, meant that more folks could afford to own large enough parcels of the rich prairie soil to have a shot at viably farming.

To sweeten the appeal of settling in Kansas, the Preemption Act of 1841 permitted "squatters" who were living on federal government-owned land to purchase up to 160 acres at a very low price (not less than $1.25 per acre). They could do so before the land was formally surveyed and offered for sale to the general public, so, if they had already been squatting there, they got first shot at prime real estate. To qualify under the law, the "squatter" had to be: "the head of a family, or widow, or single man, over the age of twenty-one years, and . . . a citizen of the United States (or intending to become naturalized)" (U.S. Congress, 1856, p. 455). The preemptor also had to have settled on, inhabited and improved the land, and built a dwelling on it.

So, folks rushed in to claim the best land, banking on being able to meet the requirements of the Preemption Act of 1841 and purchase prime real estate for a mere $1.25 per acre.

Not all settlers had enough money even for a smaller parcel of land at the new, lower per-acre price, however. And Charles Ingalls likely fell into this category. While he'd sold his home and land in Pepin, Wisconsin, before traveling to Kansas, he didn't receive full payment before he left. We know from Laura's drafts and letters that the family left Pepin in late winter or early spring of 1869 and returned to the same home and property in 1871. The original buyer hadn't been able to complete payments, so the little cabin in the Big Woods returned to Charles because the buyer defaulted on the purchase.

Between those two events, Charles had purchased property in Missouri, sight unseen. After only a brief stay there, he sold that piece of land and continued on to Kansas the following fall. Given his short time in Missouri, it's unlikely he had time to cultivate much acreage, let alone harvest a significant crop, before he brought the family to Kansas.

Since Charles didn't arrive in Kansas with the money from the Pepin sale in his pocket, and, likely, he'd spent much of what cash money he had sustaining the family throughout the Missouri months, it's unlikely that outright purchasing Kansas land, at least a parcel enough to profitably farm, and all the required farm equipment and tools, was within his reach. Especially as the family arrived in autumn, and needed to sustain themselves through a whole winter, spring, and summer before a cash crop could be made. Laura noted in chapter 21, "Indian Jamboree," of *LHOTP*, that Pa had to take all the furs he'd trapped over winter to trade for a plow and seed. A year-and-a-half was a long time to sustain a family without any crops or consistent form of income. But Charles had a plan.

The Homestead Act of February 1862 offered 160 acres to anyone prepared to settle public land for a small filing fee, which amounted to a total cost of just $18. The escape clause to that, just in case the requirements for proving up on a claim under the Homestead Act weren't met, noted that the land could also be purchased for $1.25 per acre following six months of proven residency. This meant that Charles had a decent shot at a free farm or, at the very least, cheap land. And he was banking on it.

There was only one, and fairly large, problem with this plan. Not only had Montgomery County not yet been surveyed, which would have permitted settlement under the Preemption Act, it wasn't even public land. Except for a narrow strip along its eastern edge, the entire county was completely within the Osage Diminished Reserve.

It was *Osage Indian* land.

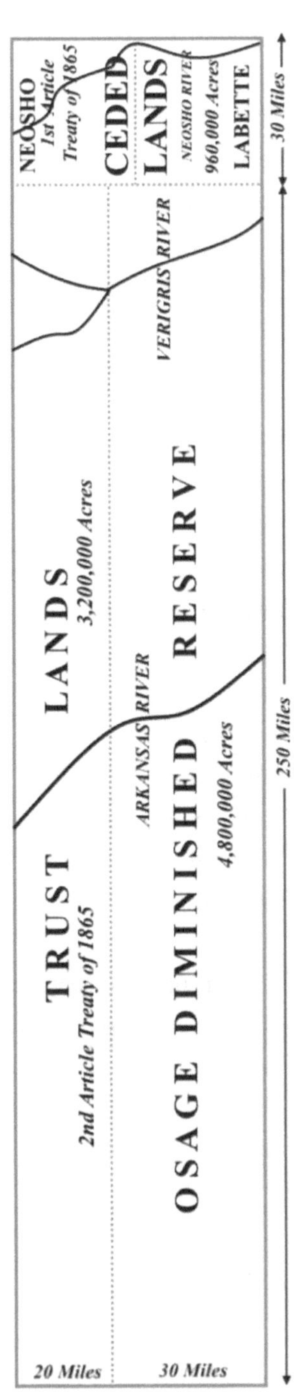

The Osage Diminished Reserve

From an original land mass of over 100 million acres, and through a succession of treaties during the first half of the 1800s, the Great and Little Osage tribes gave up vast swaths of land in the Great Plains to the government of the United States. Under the Osage Treaty of November 1808, they relinquished 52.5 million acres of land in Arkansas and Missouri. Another 1.8 million acres were ceded under the treaty of 1818. Under a third treaty, signed in 1825, they were forced to cede all their remaining land and to move to a reservation along Kansas' southern border. These three treaties resulted in the Osage Indians losing a total of about 96.8 million acres in return for just $166,000. That works out to $.0071488 per acre, or 100 acres for just over 17¢.

Their reservation was "diminished" even further by the Canville Treaty of September 1865 (ratified the following year), which the Osage agreed to because they "now [had] more lands than [were] necessary for their occupation, and all payments from the Government to them under former treaties [had] ceased, leaving them greatly impoverished, and [] desirous of improving their condition by disposing of their surplus lands . . ." (Fitzpatrick, 1895, p. 20).

Figure 6 - Schematic map of Osage lands in Kansas

In the first two articles of this treaty, they ceded two additional strips of land from their reservation to the United States. One was a 960,000-acre strip, thirty miles east-west by fifty miles north-south, comprising all of Neosho and Labette counties, and a small strip along the eastern side of Montgomery and Wilson counties. In return for this parcel, known as the Osage Ceded Lands, the U.S. government agreed to pay $300,000. With this land, they intended to survey and sell it "on the most advantageous terms, for cash, as public lands are surveyed and sold under existing laws . . . but no pre-emption claim or homestead settlement [would] be recognized" (Fitzpatrick, 1895, p. 21).

In addition, the Osage Indians entered into a separate agreement for a strip twenty miles wide along the entire northern border of the remaining reserve. This section, which comprised about 3.2 million acres, was to be held in trust for them. It would be surveyed and sold for not less than $1.25 an acre. The proceeds from the sale of the "Osage Trust Lands" were to be spent on "building houses, purchasing agricultural implements and stock animals, and for the employment of a physician and mechanics" and other necessary requirements for the Osage Indians "to commence agricultural pursuits under favorable circumstances" (Fitzpatrick, 1895, p. 22).

The treaty also allowed "squatters" who had already "made settlements and improvements" on these ceded lands to buy a quarter section at the cost of $1.25 per acre, once surveyed, within a year of the ratification of the treaty (Fitzpatrick, 1895, p. 23).

The resulting Osage Diminished Reserve was a long, narrow strip of land of about 4.8 million acres along the southern border of Kansas, with Montgomery County in its southeasternmost corner.

After full ratification and proclamation of the treaty, which didn't occur until January 21, 1867, it didn't take long for a steady stream of settlers to begin moving beyond the legal boundaries of that treaty and into the off-limits Diminished Reserve to the south. This movement was described in detail in a local newspaper at the time, which also portrayed a typical, and appalling, view of the Osage Indians by white settlers:

> All eyes are now turned towards the Osage diminished reserve. The tide of emigration is beginning to flow that way. Already farms may be seen along the valley of the Verdigris, and towns are springing up on its banks. The importance of removing the Osages from this land, and throwing it open to actual settlement, cannot be overestimated—it would add millions to the wealth of the State in a few years, and would furnish thousands of homeless emigrants with homes, while now it is occupied by a small band of lazy, worthless Indians (*The Daily Kansas Tribune* [Lawrence, Kansas], June 20, 1869, p.2).

The Osage Indians, even though they frequently allowed settlers to reside within the Reserve for a small rent or "tax," were also unhappy with the increasing numbers of intruders on their theoretically protected land. The result? A corresponding increase in tension between the Osages and the settlers.

This tension was exacerbated by the terms of another treaty, concluded at the Osage council ground on Drum Creek in Montgomery County, May 27, 1868. Under the terms of the "Drum Creek Treaty" (aka "Sturges Treaty"), the Osages agreed to sell all their remaining land in Kansas, including the Diminished Reserve, to the Leavenworth, Lawrence & Galveston Railroad Company for only about twenty cents per acre. This meant title to the land did not pass to the U.S. Government and the ceded lands did not become "public lands."

Although the Drum Creek Treaty made provision for the purchase of the land by settlers, there was no provision for existing settlers on the Diminished Reserve and no provision for schools, as had been in place with the lands ceded to the government by prior treaties.

But it wasn't just these issues concerning the interests of already-there settlers that raised objections. Sidney Clarke, Kansas' only congressman expressed his concerns to Congress that the Osages were "improperly influenced to consent to the signing of [the] treaty; that they were very reluctant to execute it and [that they were not] satisfied to sell their lands at such a price . . ." (Clarke, 1868, p. 3257).

Over the ensuing months, the treaty aroused a great deal of passion and controversy (*The Osage Mission Journal*, 1869, p. 2; McVicar and Kansas State Hist'l Soc., 1896, pp. 70–71; Mack, 2009, pp. 27–29). Eventually, due primarily to Clarke's opposition, and at his request, as well as the efforts of Rev. Schoenmakers of the Osage Mission, the Drum Creek treaty was withdrawn from the Senate in February of 1870 by Ulysses S. Grant, shortly after he became President (Graves, 1916, pp. 203–204, 1928, pp. 118–120). Therefore, it was never ratified. Almost immediately afterward, a bill to remove the Osage Indians from Kansas was introduced in the Senate under somewhat better terms. It wasn't ideal, but it was mildly better than what the Drum Creek Treaty had offered them.

Contemporary Kansas newspapers frequently published updates, and sometimes quite forceful opinions and discussion, on the subject . . . as well as the ongoing conflicts between the Osage and the settlers, who continued to increase in numbers on the Diminished Reserve that still belonged to the Osage Indians.

Isaac T. Gibson, the Indian Agent who represented the Osages' interests, described the progression of these issues in his report to the Office of Indian Affairs in October 1871, which covered the period the Ingalls family was living in Rutland Township:

> In the spring of 1867 [my predecessor] asks for the assistance of the military to remove the settlers that have intruded on the Osage diminished reserve, and otherwise enforce the laws for the protection of the Indians. In [October 1867] he states: "Their horses are constantly being driven off by the white men. . . . Immigration is still crowding on their lands. . . . They seem determined to occupy the best of the Osage diminished reservation. By the time the Indians are in next spring all their camping grounds on the Verdigris River will be occupied by whites. This should not be allowed by the Government, and I cannot check this settlement without a small armed force."
>
> From succeeding reports to [June], 1868: "The people on and near these lands are made to believe, by speeches delivered by so-called leading men and newspaper articles,

that those Indians have no rights which should be respected by white men. They have had, to my certain knowledge, over 100 of their best horses stolen since the 1st of May last. . . . The Indians dare not follow their stock five miles into the white settlements; and those thieves have always managed to baffle the officers sent in pursuit, and not one of them have as yet been brought to justice, or one in a hundred of the Indians' horses returned to them." In [March 1869] he states: "Men are taking claims, building houses and mills on the diminished reserve, which disturbs the peace of the Indians very much." He again asks, later in the spring, for military assistance, to remove the settlers and enforce the laws, and adds: "If this is not done, there will be much trouble, and the Indians will be driven from their homes. The settlers are preparing to organize a county, entirely on the Indian lands, and they have applied to the governor of the State for protection. I can do nothing in the matter without instructions from the Government, which I will await with great anxiety." His next and last report, in [June], 1869, says: "More than 500 families have settled on the eastern part of the Osage diminished reserve; have built their cabins near the Indian camps, taken possession of their cornfields, and forbidden them cutting fire-wood on their claims" (Gibson, 1872, pp. 484–485).

Figure 7 - Isaac T Gibson, Che-To-Pah, and Sam Bevenue, a Quaker interpreter, c. 1868–1872. Credit: Gateway to Oklahoma History, Oklahoma Historical Society. Used with permission.

It was just a few months later, in the fall of 1869, and in this same eastern part of the Osage Diminished Reserve, that the Ingalls family settled . . . and about the same time that Agent Gibson took charge of the local Indian Agency. At the time, he stated, "The condition of affairs, so well presented by my predecessor, was unchanged, save that aggressions upon the Indians were more frequent and more aggravated. Increasing numbers had given boldness to the aggressors." (Gibson, 1872, p. 485) He also described the impact of the Claim Protection Clubs and these squatters on the Osages:

> The settlers were generally associated in clubs, pledged to defend each other in the occupation of claims, without regard to the improvements, possession, or rights of the Indians. Many of the latter were turned out of their homes, and threatened with death if they persisted in claiming them. Others were made homeless by cunning and fraud. While absent on their winter hunt, cribs of corn, and other provisions, so hardly earned by their women's toil were robbed. Their principal village was pillaged of a large amount of puncheons, and wagon-loads of matting hauled away and used by the settlers in building and finishing houses for themselves. Even new-made graves were plundered, with the view of finding treasures, which the Indians often bury with their dead. (Gibson, 1872, p. 485)

This was the situation that surrounded the Ingalls family and their neighbors in Montgomery County as they arrived to settle in the area. Because Laura's prairie wasn't public land, the settlers there weren't "squatters" as defined by the Preemption Act; they had no claim to the land at all, not even under the Homestead Act. This fact was recognized in the 1870 Census for the county by census enumerator, Asa Hairgrove. In one of the columns on the census form, he was supposed to write the value of each family's land. Instead, he left it blank but added the annotation:

> N.B. The reason no value was [entered] . . . is that the Lands belonged to the Osage Indians and settlers had no title to Said Lands (Hairgrove, 1870).

However, on July 15, 1870, twenty-nine days before Asa Hairgrove visited the Ingallses' cabin, Congress passed their annual Indian Appropriation Bill, which was supposed to provide funds and resources for American Indians. In this 1870 bill, the entire Diminished Reserve was ceded to the United States and opened for settlement "*. . . whenever the Great and Little Osage Indians shall agree thereto*, in such manner as the President shall prescribe . . . [And it will also be] the duty of the President to remove said Indians from the State of Kansas to lands provided or to be provided for them for a permanent home in the Indian Territory" (U.S. Congress, 1870, p. 362) (Authors' emphasis in italics).

The most pertinent points in this piece of legislation were:

- The land would be sold to actual settlers only, who were heads of families or over twenty-one years of age
- In quantities not exceeding one hundred and sixty acres
- The land had to be sold "in square form"
- The price would be $1.25 per acre—to be paid in cash within one year from the date of settlement or of the passage of the Act
- The sixteenth and thirty-sixth sections would be reserved to the State of Kansas for school purposes
- The land would only be available for settlement after being surveyed "under the direction of the Secretary of the Interior as other public lands are surveyed, as soon as the consent of said Indians is obtained."

The agreement came in September 1870 by a full council of the Osage Indians who had gathered at the old council grounds on Drum Creek. All but one band of the Osages signed the agreement on September 10th, with the remaining band signing two days later when "Watanka [Wah-tun-ka], head councilor of the Claymore band, arrived at the council grounds, and, after having fully asserted his dignity and right to be consulted, signed the act" (*Independence Pioneer*, 1870; Chapman, 1938, p. 297).

The agreement was communicated to the army responsible for monitoring the situation in the area by First Lieutenant D.H. Murdock in a letter dated September 17, 1870:

> Camp on Drum Creek - near Liberty, Kas. September 17, 1870
> Adjutant Post of S.E. Kas.
> Fort Scott, Kas.
>
> Sir,
>
> I have the honor to report, that the Osage Indians in Council at this place, have consented to Sec. 15. and 16. of the Indian Appropriation Bill, which provides for the sale of all their lands in this State, and their removal to the Indian Territory.
>
> Very respectfully,
> Your obedt. servt.
> (Sgd.) D.H. Murdock
> 1st Lieut. 6' U.S. Infy. (Murdock, 1870)

Once the Osages had agreed to these terms, their agreement was still needed to begin the survey of the reservation, which:

> . . . was obtained on the 22d October [1870], and on the same day the surveyor general was telegraphed to close contracts for surveying the same. The work has been vigorously prosecuted, and returns of survey have been received to the extent of 4,792,789.73 acres. (U.S. Gen. Land Off., 1871, p. 16)

Following completion of the survey, approved plats were transmitted to the Land Office at Humboldt on June 16th, 1871, and it opened for filings three days later.

The following week, the *South Kansas Tribune* reported "there ha[d] been 2,493 filings received . . . and 1,012 entries made, and about $200,000 received [with] about two-thirds of the entries . . . from Montgomery County" (*South Kansas Tribune*, 1871b, p. 3).

And within a month, the same newspaper published notices of contested land claims under the provisions of the Act of July 15, 1870 (*South Kansas Tribune,* 1871d, p. 3). The land rush was on.

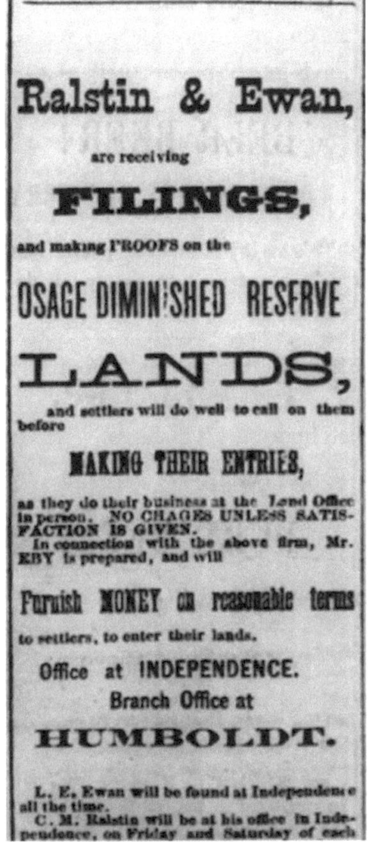

Figure 8 - Advertisement for land on the Osage Diminished Reserve

Local newspapers expressed in their editorials a great deal of dissatisfaction that settlers had such a long and costly journey to get to the town of Humboldt, resulting in an order to move the District's land office to Independence on September 20, 1871, but the order was suspended (*South Kansas Tribune,* 1871c). Shortly after this initial order, a lawsuit was initiated against the Registrar and Receiver of the Humboldt Land Office, accusing them of "charging illegal fees to the settlers who have entered lands in that office" (*South Kansas Tribune,* 1871a).

Instead, the District Land Office first moved to Neodesha on December 8, 1871, and was finally moved to Independence on March 26, 1872, where it remained until 1889, before being transferred to Topeka (U.S. Dept. of the Interior and Kansas State Hist'l Soc., no date).

It's within this setting of unsurveyed Osage land, claim protection clubs, squatters, conflict between settlers and the Osage Indians, calls for military intervention to enforce the rights of American Indians, and concern for them being driven yet again from their rightful homes, that we began our search for Mr. Edwards. All these settlers and issues, particularly the surveying, sale, and purchase of land within the Diminished Reserve (which was within Montgomery County), had a surprising impact on our quest.

The Removal of the Osage Indians and the Ingalls Family

The events surrounding the final removal of the Osage Indians all occurred in the middle of the Ingalls family's residence in Kansas (mid-1870). By the time Pa decided to return to the "big woods," the Osage Indians had already agreed to move to Indian Territory and the Diminished Reserve was almost completely surveyed. It is probable that Pa witnessed the surveying. Rutland Twp. was surveyed Feb 14-19, 1871, Caney Feb 21-25, Fawn Creek Feb 26-Mar 3, & Independence Twp. Mar 5-9, 1871.

In chapter 25, "Soldiers," of *LHOTP*, Pa told Ma, they were leaving Kansas because "the government is sending soldiers to take all us settlers out of Indian Territory." This was entirely fictitious. In reality, as Pa must have known, the land was opening up for settlement and many of the Ingallses' neighbors stayed in Rutland and the neighboring Townships.

– 4 –

Gathering Clues

Looking in *Little House on the Prairie*

WE FIRST ENCOUNTERED Mr. Edwards in Laura Ingalls Wilder's *LHOTP* when he and Pa met on the prairie. And it was there, through Laura's own stories, that we began to develop our character sketch of the Tennessee Wildcat. After traveling to Kansas via wagon, the Ingallses found a piece of land they liked, located in Rutland Township, Montgomery County. Pa scouted the land for resources, decided the piece he found held all the family needed, and began the process of building a small cabin from logs gleaned from trees in the creek bottoms.

Figure 9 - Illustration of a pioneer cabin

According to Laura's version of events, Ma had to help Pa lift and fit the heavy logs, but suffered a serious ankle sprain when one slipped and nearly crushed her foot. No more work could be done on their house until she healed, they reasoned, so Pa did a little scouting of the surrounding area while he hunted and Ma rested. One day he rode back into camp with the good news he'd found a neighbor. In chapter 5, "The House on the Prairie," of *LHOTP*, Laura wrote:

> They had a neighbor, only two miles away on the other side of the creek. Pa had met him in the woods. They were going to trade work and that would make it easier for everyone.
>
> 'He's a bachelor,' said Pa, 'and he says he can get along without a house better than you and the girls can. So he's going to help me first. Then as soon as he gets his logs ready, I'll go over and help him.'

When Mr. Edwards came to work with Pa on the cabin, Laura wove in physical details about this man she came to love:

> He was lean and tall and brown. He bowed to Ma and called her 'Ma'am' politely. But he told Laura that he was a wild-cat from Tennessee. He wore tall boots and a ragged jumper, and a coon-skin cap, and he could spit tobacco juice farther than Laura had ever imagined that anyone could spit tobacco juice.

Continuing to write about him, she provided more crucial information:

> Mr. Edwards said he must go. It was a long way back to his camp on the other side of the woods and the creek. . . . He said a bachelor got mighty lonesome, and he surely had enjoyed this evening of home life.

And, finally, she provided one of the most endearing facts about Mr. Edwards: he could sing a rousing western song of the day!

> 'Play, Ingalls!' he said. 'Play me down the road.' So while he went down the creek road and out of sight, Pa played, and Pa and Mr. Edwards and Laura sang with all their might.

> 'Old Dan tucker was a fine old man; He washed his face in the frying pan . . .'

When we pulled all these details together, we got a fairly detailed description of Mr. Edwards:

- Tall
- Lean
- Brown
- Wildcat (slang for a rough, uncultured person)
- From Tennessee
- Had decent manners (bowed to Ma and called her "ma'am")
- Wore a coon skin cap, tall boots, and a ragged jumper
- Could spit tobacco juice (so he used chewing tobacco)
- Bachelor
- Got lonesome
- Lived on the other side of the woods
- Lived on the other side of a creek
- Was two miles away
- Had carpentry skills/knew how to build a log cabin
- Could sing, and he knew "Old Dan Tucker"

Once the log cabin was finished, Mr. Edwards slipped into the background of the story, but made a few more appearances throughout the book.

One of those later mentions provided another significant detail about Mr. Edwards. It's found in chapter 17 of *LHOTP*, "Pa Goes to Town":

> On his way to town [Independence] that morning, Pa had stopped at Mr. Edwards' house and asked him to come over every day to see that everything was all right.

Because Pa stopped at Mr. Edward's house *on the way* to Independence, we could gather the general direction of his property in relation to the Ingallses' land. As Independence was closer to ten miles (rather than the forty Laura claimed in the book) northeast of their house, Mr. Edwards must have lived somewhere roughly northeast of the Ingallses. Pa brought back glass windowpanes and supplies, and the trip was icy cold, which implies the trip was taken in late fall/early winter. Because of the probable timeframe of the trip, it was likely taken to lay in the family's winter supplies and get the house ready for cold weather. This became significant when we looked at our suspects later in our search.

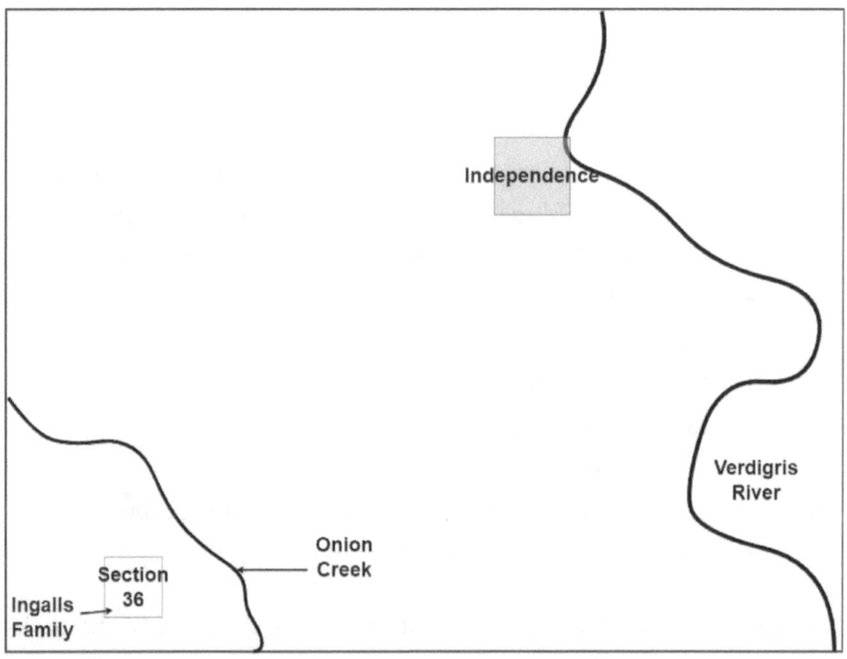

Figure 10 - Map showing location of the Ingalls family, Onion Creek, Independence, and the Verdigris River

It's important to note here that *LHOTP* reads like the Ingallses left the Big Woods of Wisconsin and went straight to Kansas. And *On the Banks of Plum Creek* reads as if the family just came from Kansas. Most *Little House* fans already know that this timeline is incorrect. As we mentioned early on, the Ingallses moved to Kansas, then back to Wisconsin, before leaving for Plum Creek.

But there was another important stop in there, too, and it affected our hunt for Mr. Edwards. In late winter or early spring of 1869, after leaving the Big Woods and crossing the still-iced-over Mississippi, but before arriving in Kansas, the Ingallses went to Missouri. They settled on a piece of land Pa had purchased sight-unseen in Chariton County . . . and they were there for a while before going on to Kansas. There is proof that Pa was there in 1869, as he executed a power of attorney in Chariton County in August. And there is proof that the Ingallses were in Kansas by at least February of 1870, as that's when the family was listed as living in Montgomery County during the sale of the Missouri property back to its original owner.

Pa and Ma had traveled to Missouri with Henry and Polly Quiner, settling near each other when they arrived. Henry was Ma's brother, and Polly was Pa's sister . . . so their children were double cousins to the Ingalls girls. By at least November of 1869, however, the Quiners had moved back north to Wisconsin and the Ingallses had moved south-southwest to Kansas.

We'd always wondered why, if *LHOTP* starts with the family leaving in late winter so they can safely cross the Mississippi River, why the book seems to begin with them arriving in Kansas during the fall. There is no mention of planting crops, nor harvesting, before the first Christmas Laura wrote about, which there should have been if they'd rolled into Rutland Township in the spring. But the Missouri months account for that confusion.

Leaving in late winter/very early spring when the ice was still thick enough on the Mississippi to support a loaded wagon and team, meant leaving in early March at the very latest. The trip from Pepin, Wisconsin to Montgomery County, Kansas was about 620 miles. Teams of horses could, on average, travel about ten to fifteen miles per day. So, at a pace of around twelve miles per day, that would have taken approximately fifty-two days. Throw in a week or more for days of rest or bad weather, and it was about a two-month journey by wagon.

Had the Ingallses gone straight there, this would have put them in Montgomery County by early May at the latest. Plenty of time to plant at least some kinds of crops. But *LHOTP* seems to start with them arriving in the fall. Laura wrote that they arrived when the Osages were away from their camps . . . and the Osage Indians had long buffalo hunts during autumn. With that stop in Chariton County, likely for several months, the timeline works.

But, in *LHOTP*, the Missouri months aren't accounted for. When writing the book, Laura effectively condensed their time in Kansas from the approximately year and a half they actually resided in Montgomery County, and two years they were gone from Pepin in total, to much less than a year. And she left out their stop in Chariton County altogether.

Besides being a little confusing, it also condensed all the Kansas stories Laura remembered, or was told, into an abbreviated timeline. And this created a little havoc with our Mr. Edwards clues. That trip Pa took to Independence, when he stopped to ask Mr. Edwards to look in on the family, wasn't likely before their first Christmas, just after the family had arrived.

Contextually, we can surmise this for two reasons . . . one is that Pa wouldn't have made a crop that year, and so wouldn't have likely had the money to buy the glass windowpanes he purchased on that trip. Also, Laura would have only been two, and not likely old enough to remember Pa's going. The other, and more telling clue, however, is that Carrie was present. This trip came after they had visited the Osage camp and gathered beads, which they strung together for Carrie. But Carrie was born in August of 1870, so this trip couldn't be the first trip into town after the Ingallses had arrived in Kansas.

The next significant encounter with Mr. Edwards that Laura described in *LHOTP* occurred at Christmas and appeared in chapter 19: "Mr. Edwards Meets Santa Claus":

> . . . she heard Mr Edwards say he had carried his clothes on his head when he swam the creek. His teeth rattled and his voice quivered. He would be all right, he said, as soon as he got warm. . . . 'Your little ones had to have a Christmas,' Mr Edwards replied. 'No creek could stop me, after I fetched them their gifts from Independence.'
>
> . . . .

> So Santa Claus said, 'Hello Edwards! Last time I saw you, you were sleeping on a corn-shuck bed in Tennessee.' And Mr. Edwards well remembered the little pair of red-yarn mittens that Santa Claus had left for him that time.

As the story progressed, Laura described how Mr. Edwards also brought some sweet potatoes from Independence, how he stayed for dinner, and, along with Ma and Pa, "sat by the fire and talked about Christmas times back in Tennessee and up north in the Big Woods."

Between these two stories, we added the following details to our list of clues:

- Mr. Edwards lived northeast of the Ingallses
- He had to cross a significant creek to get to their home
- Santa Claus referred to him by his last name
- There are also more Tennessee details (corn shuck bed, red mittens, and Christmases in Tennessee)
- And he spent Christmas with the Ingallses (reinforcing that he was alone/a bachelor)

Laura's final meeting with Mr. Edwards in *LHOTP* was recounted in chapter 25: "Soldiers." This scene depicts the moment Pa decided to leave Kansas rather than being forced to leave by soldiers:

> Mr Scott started to speak, but Pa stopped him. 'Save your breath, Scott. It's no use to say another word. You can stay till the soldiers come if you want to. I'm going out now.
>
> Mr Edwards said he was going too. He would not stay to be driven across the line like an ornery yellow hound.
>
> 'Ride out to Independence with us, Edwards,' Pa said. But Mr Edwards answered that he didn't care to go north. He would make a boat and go on down the river to some settlement farther south.
>
> 'Better come with us,' Pa urged him, 'and go down on foot through Missouri ...
>
> But Mr Edwards said he had already seen Missouri . . .

. . . .

> Mary said politely, 'Good-bye, Mr Edwards.' But Laura forgot to be polite. She said: 'Oh, Mr Edwards, I wish you wouldn't go away! Oh, Mr Edwards, thank you, thank you for going all the way to Independence to find Santa Claus for us.'
>
> Mr Edwards' eyes shone very bright, and he went away without saying another word.

This scene added our final selection of clues . . . well, those we could glean from within the text of *LHOTP,* that is. They included:

- Mr. Edwards left Kansas at the same time as the Ingallses
- He used phrases like "ornery yellow hound"
- He had already seen Missouri
- Went south, by boat
- He was the same person in this scene who had brought the Christmas presents from Independence
- And, Pa referred to him as "Edwards"

When we collected all those descriptors into one final list, it ended up quite specific and detailed, didn't it? Laura gave us a healthy twenty-five identifiers to help track down the real Mr. Edwards. But as promising as this list appeared at first, there was a large problem with it. It's not a police report based on corroborating evidence and witnesses . . . it came from a work of semi-fiction, written by a woman late in life about a period of time in which she was a toddler.

LHOTP was the third book of a very naturally gifted writer and story-teller, whose own daughter, Rose Wilder Lane, also an accomplished author, helped Laura learn and implement the concepts of narrative arc and literary license. So, while we certainly needed to consider all the details and information Laura wrote into her novel, we also had to hold that information lightly. It could have been one hundred percent fact. It could have been one hundred percent fiction.

Likelier, though, it was somewhere in between.

Clues from Laura's *Pioneer Girl* Manuscript

To attempt to establish which of her novel's facts were true, which were likely fiction, and which we could add any further detail to, we turned our attention to Laura's original writings, starting with the draft of her first unpublished manuscript, *Pioneer Girl.* This autobiography was finished in 1930 and became the source material for her subsequent novels.

Before her beloved *Little House* books were written as novels for children, Laura had hoped to publish her autobiography, which included her family's stories about their experiences as pioneers. Realizing she had lived through an important, and pivotal, time in American history, she wanted to preserve both her family's narrative, as well as that of the American pioneer. Laura's lifetime spanned a period from buggies, hand-dug wells, and hand-plows through to four years short of the first man in space. In her time, the telegraph, telephone, electricity, trains, radios, television, cars, and airplanes came into existence.

She knew that if her family's travels and experiences on the prairie weren't chronicled, they would be lost to future generations. After all, by the time she started writing her autobiography, the last in her branch of the Ingalls family, her daughter Rose Wilder Lane, was divorced and in her forties, with no children. Laura knew their family line was going to end with Rose. So, Laura's motivation to preserve her family's stories was acute. She began writing them down on simple drugstore tablets, and the resulting manuscript was *Pioneer Girl.*

This first draft of Laura's autobiography was important for many reasons. One was that it documented the earliest examples of Laura's long-form writing ... before she smoothed out her storylines and perfected narratives. It's raw and a little bit rough, but a wonderful example of her thought processes as she pulled her memories together. It also showcased her natural artistry, something many mistook as Rose's later influence on her writing. While Rose did help her to learn much about writing and publishing, Laura's own beautiful narrative voice was present even in those earliest drafts, proving the natural skills she possessed.

That first draft also chronicled her process of trying to remember and reconstruct details from a period of time she couldn't have had many, if any, clear, firsthand memories. As such, the draft is full of information, sometimes conflicting, about the people and stories that later made their way into her finished novels.

So, of course comparing our list of Mr. Edwards stories and descriptors with Laura's first manuscript was a great way to identify additional details, as well as potential red herrings.

Christmas in the Little House

The *LHOTP* story about Mr. Edwards bringing the Ingalls family their Christmas presents from Independence after bravely swimming across a deep creek is a heartwarming fan favorite. But Laura told a slightly different version of this story, with a differently-named main character, in *Pioneer Girl*:

> . . . when we waked on Christmas morning our stockings were hanging on the back of a chair by our bed and out of the top of each showed a bright shining new tin cup. Farther down was a long, flat stick of red and white striped peppermint candy all beautifully notched along each edge.
>
> Mr Brown the neighbor from across the creek stood looking at us. He said Santa Clause [*sic*] couldn't cross the creek the night before so left the presents with him and he swam over that morning. (Wilder, 2014, p. 16)

In her annotation to this story, Pamela Smith Hill, the editor of *Pioneer Girl*, wrote:

> Wilder transformed Mr. Brown of *Pioneer Girl* into Mr. Edwards, the "wildcat from Tennessee," . . . (t)he 1870 census of Rutland Township does not include a listing for anyone named Brown or Edwards. (Wilder, 2014, p. 16 n. 36)

We have enormous respect for Ms. Hill and her team, who tackled the gargantuan task of annotating *Pioneer Girl*, and its thousands of minute details and facts, brilliantly. It was a massive, important undertaking, and the work and effort put into that project is nothing short of breathtaking. But here, in this statement, we found a bit of an error. Her assertion that there were no Mr. Browns in the 1870 census was inaccurate.

There were two "Mr. Browns" listed in the 1870 census of Rutland Township. More than that, however, is something we mentioned earlier . . . since the Ingallses lived in the very southeast corner of Rutland Township, their section bordered three other Townships: Independence was to the east, Caney was to the south, and Fawn Creek was to the southeast. Because of this near-the-center-of-a-square-of-four-townships location of the Ingallses' land, our search area for Mr. Brown was in all four Townships, not just Rutland. Therefore, the Christmas story's "Mr. Brown" could have resided in any one of those Townships.

Pioneer Girl does corroborate that the "Mr. Brown" Christmas was the first one after Carrie was born, which means it must be referring to Christmas 1870, as we've mentioned that Carrie was born on August 3, 1870.

Interestingly, in relation to the 1870 census, Carrie's birthdate was a bit of a puzzle. It lists her as having been born in April, which is incorrect, and the census publication date is actually *before* Carrie's birth, which means it shouldn't have been possible for her to even be listed. Given the rather shoddy way census data was often gathered and rendered in those days, along with the inherent errors resulting from poor human record-keeping, these curious and conflicting entries were not unheard of. (But they are frustrating from a researcher's perspective!)

From the weird timeline jiggling we see in the 1870 census, which likely resulted from the census taker not collecting all required data by the due date and then back-dating entries to when it was supposed to have been collected by, we could surmise a couple of things. One is that, since Carrie was listed as two months old in that census, yet was born in August, the census taker was probably gathering information sometime around the first of October, 1870. This was *months* after the census was supposed to have taken place.

So, if Carrie shouldn't have appeared on the census, but was, indeed, listed, it's also possible that a new neighbor had moved into the area between the published date of the census and the true date that information was collected. This means there could conceivably be settlers listed as living in Rutland County months before they actually arrived. And, conversely, there could have been settlers living contemporaneously with the Ingallses, but had already left before the census taker had managed to make it to their neighborhood.

At any rate, we *can* surmise something important from a combination of the 1870 census data noting Carrie's birth and Laura's *Pioneer Girl* notation of when the "Mr. Brown" Christmas story happened . . . Laura had to have been referring to their second Christmas in Kansas: December 1870.

Leaving the Little House

When Laura first described her family leaving Kansas in *Pioneer Girl*, she gave quite a different account than the one which ended up in *LHOTP*. In *Pioneer Girl* she didn't mention Mr. Edwards (or any other "Mr.") by name at all. Though she did briefly mention soldiers, she didn't elaborate. She simply said they left and then provided the reason for returning to Wisconsin: the sale of Pa's land in Pepin had fallen through, and the property had been returned to him.

> Soon after this Pa put the cover on the wagon again and hitched Pet and Patty to it. Then he and Ma took everything out of the house and put it in the wagon. Then we all got in the wagon and . . . drove away leaving our little house standing empty and lonely on the prairie. The soldiers were taking all the white people off the Indian's land.
>
> . . . .
>
> All the neighbors went with us for awhile, then they scattered but we went on into Missouri.
>
> . . . .

> After driving for days and days . . . we came at last to the place we had left when we went west. The land was Pa's again because the man who bought it from him had not paid for it. (Wilder, 2014, pp. 18–22)

Beside the interesting omission of any mention of Mr. Edwards—or of a Mr. Brown—there was one other detail of note in these passages. Despite her novel implying there were few settlers around them, and the few there were lived miles away, Laura noted that "all the neighbors went with" them. Why would "neighbors," who, if the Ingallses were largely isolated as Laura intimated, leave with the Ingallses? Unless those neighbors were both plentiful and far closer to their land than she portrayed, this statement wouldn't have made sense.

Clues from Early Manuscripts of *Little House on the Prairie*

After *Pioneer Girl* didn't sell, Laura's daughter, Rose, convinced her to adapt her autobiography into semi-autobiographical novels for children. The result was *Little House in the Big Woods*, published in 1932. It was followed in 1933 by *Farmer Boy*, which detailed the New York childhood of her husband, Almanzo James Wilder. Two years later, in 1935, *LHOTP* joined Laura's first two books.

When Laura was drafting *LHOTP*, she was already a competent writer. After all, she'd been a professional for some time. First as a columnist for the *Missouri Ruralist*, beginning in 1911, then writing for other publications. Her *Pioneer Girl* autobiography, finished by 1930, came after nearly two decades of article-writing, followed by her first two published novels by 1933.

By the time Laura sat down to write her third novel, she'd been able to marry her natural narrative abilities with honed writing craft. In short, she knew what she was doing. So, the problem with producing her third novel wasn't *how* to write it . . . but what to actually write *about*. *Little House in the Big Woods* had been set when Laura was four to seven years old. Young, but old enough to have had first-hand memories. *Farmer Boy* was formed from Almanzo's own first-hand memories of his childhood.

But *LHOTP*, despite her stated age in the book, covered a period of time in which she was merely a toddler . . . from just-turned-two to just-turned-four, though the actual story is condensed into under a year. So, pulling together accurate fragments of her own personal memories, as well as memories of her family's stories about that time, had to be the most challenging of all her books.

Because of that, her early drafts were riddled with revisions and corrections and contradictions. These early drafts should have been one of our best sources of clues regarding Mr. Edwards' true identity. But, often, they only added confusion.

For example, Daniel Zochert, in his biography, *Laura: The Life of Laura Ingalls Wilder*, lists various characters that appear in early versions of *LHOTP*:

> . . . Mr. Edwards, Mr. Scott, the black doctor—although she doesn't tell us his name—Mr. Brown . . . Mr. Thompson, who was a bachelor, who lived across the creek, and who helped Pa build the little house. (Zochert, 1976, pp. 33–34)

In one early manuscript, in which Laura described Pa's first meeting with a neighbor, the man is referred to as "an old batchelor [*sic*] and alone." Laura names this neighbor "Mr. Thompson" and it is he who helped Pa build the little house (Wilder, no date a, pp. 44–46).

Though this draft indicated clearly that it was a Mr. Thompson who actually helped Pa build their cabin, he was described similarly to two other men, a Mr. Edwards and a Mr. Brown, in other versions. At one point or another, Laura described them all as bachelors who lived across the creek from the Ingallses.

Later in this same early manuscript, Laura recounted that Mr. Scott helped Pa dig the well, and it is he who mentioned another person . . . Mr. Edwards. Mr. Scott speaking:

> Edwards fell over, working in his well yesterday and when Stover, who was helping him, went down to see what the trouble was, he keeled over too. Before Mrs Edwards could get help and they could get them out, Edwards was dead and they barely saved Stover. (Wilder, no date a, p. 122)

So, in that draft, Mr. Edwards isn't a bachelor at all. Moreover, he even died digging his own well. However, in another unpublished manuscript, Laura told the same story but, that time, it was Mr. Thompson who collapsed and died in the well. Other details, such as there being a Mrs. Thompson and Stover nearly dying, are identical to the version in which a Mr. Edwards died, so it appears to be the same story . . . just with a different main character.

In another early manuscript, Mr. Edwards didn't leave when the Ingalls family left, or even say he would leave. Rather, "Mr. Edwards said he'd stay a few days and see what happened" (Wilder, no date a, p. 196).

What Does it all Mean?

When we put all these conflicting mentions together, the results didn't appear encouraging. Instead of solidifying facts, and narrowing down suspects, it seemed we were further from discovering who Mr. Edwards really was. After all, if Laura didn't know who was who on the Kansas prairie, and who did what in regard to all the various stories Mr. Edwards appeared in, how were we supposed to figure it all out?

But reading her earliest drafts actually did confirm one important thing. Since we knew, through her early notes and drafts, that Laura was teasing memories and fragments of family lore out of the recesses of her mind, she'd inadvertently given us a large piece of the puzzle.

It took us a while to see it, but we finally did.

Laura was trying to remember *facts* about Mr. Edwards, even if she got them muddled and wrong sometimes. If Mr. Edwards was a completely made-up character, she wouldn't have gone through this process. She'd just have assigned him a name, a history, and a few scenes to move along the greater Ingalls family narrative. But she didn't do that.

That gave us a huge step forward in our investigation: One of the four options we had for the Mr. Edwards character could be taken off the table.

Mr. Edwards almost certainly wasn't pure fiction.

– 5 –
With Facts in Hand

UP UNTIL THIS POINT, we'd gathered information. We had looked at the cultural landscape of America, Kansas, and the Osage Diminished Reserve. We'd discovered how land was divided, what various period Acts laid out as rules and requirements for settlement, and established how the Ingallses just happened to choose a unique homestead to settle on: located on a "school section," at the point where four Townships met, and on Osage Indian land.

We'd learned, too, that the country was actually full of settlers, with the direct area around the Ingallses' section swelling to a population of approximately 8,000 in the short year and a half they lived there. That fact, combined with our newly focused, and expanded, area of interest, put a lot of previously unknown suspects on our radar.

And there was another important clue we'd discovered. From looking at some of Laura's earliest writings, we'd surmised two things: Mr. Edwards was, at the very least, based on a real person, or persons; and Laura's toddler memories, wrenched out of her late-sixties brain, weren't the most accurate or reliable. Her details, stories, and facts shifted and changed.

And, of course, we'd gleaned twenty-five descriptors of and clues about Mr. Edwards from *LHOTP*. Though it's a novel, and therefore semi-fictional at best, it was more than probable Laura's assignment of personal traits, physical characteristics, and nuggets of backstory to Mr. Edwards was at least based on her best recollections or her family's remembrances. Laura, herself, said "All I have told is true, but it is not the whole truth" (Koupal, 2017, p. 15). So, to the best of her ability, Laura was clearly trying to accurately tell her family's story.

To refresh your memory, here are those Mr. Edwards descriptors again:

- Tall
- Lean
- Brown (tanned/Caucasian)
- Wildcat (rough, uncultured person)
- From Tennessee
- Had decent manners (bowed to Ma and called her "ma'am")
- Wore a coon skin cap, tall boots, and a ragged jumper
- Could spit tobacco juice (used chewing tobacco)
- Bachelor
- Got lonesome
- Lived on the other side of woods
- Lived two miles away
- Had carpentry skills
- Could sing, and he knew "Old Dan Tucker"
- Lived northeast of the Ingallses
- Had to cross a significant creek to get to their home
- Santa Claus referred to him by his last name
- Slept on a corn shuck bed, got red mittens, and spent Christmases in Tennessee)
- Spent Christmas with the Ingallses
- Left Kansas at the same time as the Ingallses
- He used phrases like "ornery yellow hound"
- He had already seen Missouri
- After leaving the area, he went south by boat

- The person who brought Christmas presents was the same one Laura hugged when leaving Kansas
- And, Pa referred to him as "Edwards"

Since many of these descriptors aren't "searchable," or verifiable, however, we condensed a short list of traits and clues we could, potentially, substantiate. It's this list we used as a sort of litmus test for our suspects. The fourteen descriptors were:

- Tanned (Caucasian)
- Wildcat (rough, uncultured)
- From Tennessee
- Bachelor
- Alone/lonely
- Lived beyond woods
- Lived two miles away
- Lived northeast of the Ingallses
- Lived across a significant creek
- Had carpentry skills
- Spent Christmas with the Ingallses
- Left Kansas, same time
- Had already seen Missouri
- After Kansas, went south by boat

With all that background, and all those clues, in hand, as well as our pared down list of searchable characteristics, it was time to line up the suspects and see whether any of them measured up as the Tennessee Wildcat.

– 6 –
Mr. Edwards

It was obvious and logical to start looking at suspects with the name, "Edwards," so that was our first stop. If there happened to be a bachelor Tennessean with that moniker in our area of interest, especially who liked to swim across raging winter creeks and lived near the Ingallses, our investigation would have been short and sweet.

There were actually very few men who had the surname "Edwards" living in Montgomery County at the time the Ingallses were there, however. But we crossed our fingers for an early win and to the archives we went.

The Bureau of Land Management's GLO (General Land Office) website has a searchable online database (*BLM GLO Database*), organized by state and county, containing over five million federal land title records that have been issued since 1788. Specific to our investigation, this database has an exhaustive set of records from Montgomery County which allowed us to locate individuals within specific townships and sections with amazing accuracy. It contains three noteworthy men with the last name of "Edwards." We also had another resource: online copies of the BLM's original tract books found on the FamilySearch website (Bur. of Land Mgmt., 2023). Between these two sources, we were ready to begin.

Edward E. Edwards

Edward Edwards received a land patent for the southeast quarter of S19-T32S-R14E on December 15, 1873. (See? We told you all that information about how land was divided and how to read section names would be important! If you haven't yet perused our amazing Appendix, now might be a good time. You'll be able to pinpoint this exact tract of land on any plat map.)

The Declaratory Statement for this tract indicated he entered the land (in this source, this meant he officially arrived on the land) in October of 1871 and the date of sale was April 5, 1873 (Bur. of Land Mgmt., no date, p. 33). This section was just inside Rutland Twp., on the northern border, next to Louisburg Twp., approximately ten miles from the Ingalls family. Given the date in the Declaratory Statement, it's unlikely that Edward Edwards was in Montgomery County during any significant period of the Ingalls family's time there. And the distance of his land from the Ingallses' section was just too far. So, it's unlikely he was our Mr. Edwards, despite having the perfect name.

John Edwards

John Edwards received his patent for the eastern half of the southeast quarter S7-T32S-R15E on October 1, 1873. The Declaratory Statement for this land indicated he settled there in February 1872 and the date of sale was January 20, 1873 (Bur. of Land Mgmt., no date, p. 135). This section was on the western edge of Sycamore Twp., northeast of Rutland Twp. and about eleven miles away from the Ingalls family. Given the location and the dates recorded in the tract book, it is also unlikely that John is Laura's Mr. Edwards.

Joshua Edwards

The third and final person recorded in the land records just happened to be the most likely candidate for our Mr. Edwards of the three possibilities we found. Although the patent for Joshua Edwards' land, the southwest quarter of S8-T32S-R15E, wasn't issued until August 1, 1873, his Declaratory Statement indicated he initially settled the land in October of 1869. This was about the same time the Ingalls family also arrived in Montgomery County, so they would have been building their homes at the same time. The date of sale for his land was July 6, 1871, one of the earliest recorded sales in the area (Bur. of Land Mgmt., no date, p. 135).

Joshua was a widower who, at the age of fifty, married Sarah A. Auldridge on July 11, 1874, in Radical City, which was relatively close to his home. Joshua, Sarah, and the children from his first marriage are listed in the 1875 Kansas state census. (It also looks like he died just a year later, in 1875).

Although Joshua Edwards was almost certainly in Montgomery County at the same time as the Ingalls family and was unmarried at that time, he wasn't a bachelor (or alone . . . he was a widower with children) and his location was about twelve miles away, in Sycamore Twp. So, though the only real possible "Mr. Edwards" as he was contemporary with the Ingallses and unmarried, Joshua was unlikely who we're looking for.

The 1870 Federal Census listed a few other candidates, too, but they were easily discounted for a variety of reasons.

O. M. Edwards

O.M. Edwards was a thirty-seven-year-old Swedish boot and shoemaker, living in the city of Independence, with another boot and shoemaker (F.A. Leyfos), between a tin smith (Edward Adams) and a blacksmith (Mr. Morrison).

Although he was possibly a bachelor, his location and occupation made it unlikely he was Mr. Edwards.

H. Edwards

H. Edwards was an eighteen-year-old African American man (though the census entry is unclear, so he was possibly 13) living in Parker Twp. with the family of William Colwell, a carpenter from Ireland. H. Edwards was located anywhere from nine to fourteen miles away from the Ingalls family and, even though unmarried, and likely with enough carpenter skills to help Pa build the cabin, it is unlikely he was Mr. Edwards as Dr. Tann was the first black man Laura had met.

So, our previous three options (Edward, John, and Joshua Edwards) really were the only mildly potential candidates. But none of them stacked up particularly well.

Without an actual "Mr. Edwards" as our possible *Little House* "Mr. Edwards," the next step in our search meant looking at some of the other names and descriptors Laura used in her drafts and notes. These include the names "Mr. Thompson" and "Mr. Brown," as well as Tennesseans, bachelors, and other close neighbors.

It would have been easy to assume a "real" Mr. Edwards didn't exist simply because there was no one in the area who matched Laura's physical and character description, who also had the "Edwards" name, and was living in close enough proximity to the Ingallses to fit the bill. But it was too early to draw that conclusion. Just because a very young child can't remember the exact name of a person doesn't mean he didn't exist, after all. So, for the time being, we had to keep our remaining options—real person, composite character, or someone based on a loose collection of Laura's memory fragments—on the table.

– 7 –
Mr. Thompson

AS WE NOTED EARLIER, Zochert mentioned in his biography about Laura that, in an early version of *LHOTP*, she described a Mr. Thompson, a bachelor from across the creek, as the person who helped Pa build the family cabin. So, that was our next point of investigation.

Historical records show there had been at least one Mr. Thompson in Montgomery County since the first settlers arrived. *The 1903 History* recalls, "[t]he following names are remembered as being among those who came to this corner of the county in 1868: . . . Jack Thompson" (Duncan, 1903, p. 112). Another notation, probably of the same settler, though with another name variation, was made in *Wilson's History*. He recalled settlers that arrived in 1868, stating "In Elk River Valley in Sycamore Twp. was Jacob Thompson . . ." (Edwards, 1881, p. 7).

While Jack/John/Jacob Thompson was/were the first Thompson/s on the scene, there were a succession of men with that same surname in the area who came soon afterward. Because of this, many more potential "Thompson" suspects appeared than we had with the surname "Edwards." But were any of those we found potential candidates for our beloved Mr. Edwards? And could any of them have been *the* "Mr. Thompson" Laura mentioned as having helped Pa build the cabin?

John Thompson of Independence

John Thompson (born June 3, 1818, according to his gravestone inscription) arrived in Montgomery County in 1868 from Iowa after having served as a Union soldier in the Civil War, where he was a Private in Company K 35th Regiment Iowa Voluntary Infantry. John enlisted on August 14, 1862, but was discharged for disability seven months later, on March 19, 1863, in Cairo, Illinois.

He is almost certainly both the "Jack" and the "Jacob" Thompson referred to in the two histories of Montgomery County. We believe this because the sources that chronicle the very early settlers of the area only ever list one J. Thompson. And this Thompson was clearly already in the county when the Ingallses arrived.

The list of patrons of *The 1881 Atlas* informed us John Thompson arrived in Montgomery County in 1868, was born in Pennsylvania, worked as a farmer and stock raiser, and lived in S19-T32S-R15E on 160 acres, for which he received a patent in May of 1873. This land lies just inside the border of Independence Township adjacent to Sycamore Township with the Elk River running through it. This further supports the belief that John and Jack Thompson are the same person because of that entry we noted a moment ago in Wilson's history of Montgomery County. In that history, when discussing the year 1868, was this statement: "In Elk River Valley in Sycamore Twp. was Jacob Thompson . . ." (Wilson, 1881, p. 7).

However, that was not the land he was living on in the 1870 federal census. In that record, his household was the last one listed in Sycamore Township and with him was M. (Thompson), aged 69. In later records, we learned that "M." was Margret Ropp Thompson, and was John's mother. By reviewing the households immediately preceding John's in the census and searching the *BLM GLO Database* for those households, we learned that, at the time, he was located along the northern edges of T32S-R15E, which is well inside Sycamore Township, close to sections 2-4 and 9-11, and about three and a half to four miles away from his land in section 19. This homestead was across Onion Creek from the Ingallses, which was one of our clues, but well more than two miles away.

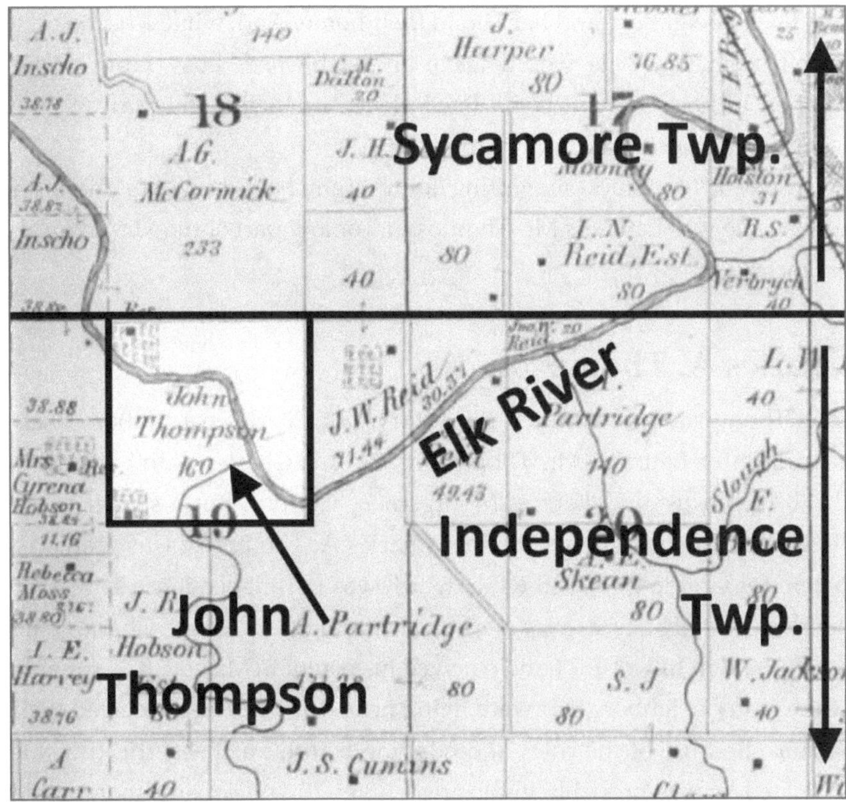

Figure 11 - Portion of map from The 1881 Atlas showing the location of John Thompson's land on the Elk River on the border of Sycamore Twp.

The 1875 Kansas state census told us John came to Kansas from Iowa (though he'd been born in Pennsylvania) and he was still residing with his mother, Margret. The lack of a wife on any document remained the case until the 1880 census, when a wife appears. Interestingly, she is only nineteen and John is in his early sixties. The more than forty-year age difference, and the fact that his new wife, Julia, gave birth to a child in the same month they were married is odd. Whether they conceived a child out of wedlock and then got married, or he agreed to marry an unwed, pregnant girl to help her avoid scandal is a mystery. But it does confirm something: he was a bachelor the entire time the Ingallses were in Kansas.

But even with those details confirmed, nothing else really fits. He wasn't from Tennessee, and he didn't live close enough to be considered the

Ingallses' "neighbor" and help build their home. And, while a bachelor, it didn't seem likely he would leave an established, busy farm, or his mother, to help someone who lived eleven or twelve miles away. Nor leave his mother alone on Christmas.

Despite a few clues suggesting John might have been our man, it's unlikely he was Laura's "Mr. Thompson," or any part of the Mr. Edwards character.

Charles A. Thompson

John Thompson had an interesting story, but Charles was a more likely candidate for Laura's "Mr. Thompson." Oddly, Charles didn't appear in the 1870 census anywhere in Montgomery County. But a search of the *BLM GLO Database* showed us that Charles A. Thompson was granted a patent for land in S17-T33S-R15E, which was in Independence Township and located only a few miles away from the Ingallses' cabin. Charles paid for the land in July of 1871 and received his patent in May of 1873, roughly when many neighbors that were living nearby in 1870 also received their patents. Because of the rules of occupying before purchase, this timeline indicated he was probably in the area c.1869–70. In fact, an annotation in the BLM's tract book indicated he had been in the area since at least March of 1870. That notation was after the Ingallses would have built their cabin, but, because settlers had to wait until land was surveyed to file as having entered land, Charles could have been there in time to help.

If Charles had been living on his land by the fall of 1869, he would have been living on the far side of Onion Creek, between the creek and the Verdigris River. Interestingly, however, and another example of how *not* empty the prairie really was at the time, there were several other male neighbors living between Charles Thompson and the Ingallses—Oliver Carrow, Alonzo Hopson, George W. Menagh, and Benton Goal, as well as two pioneering women, Sarah Hunt (who we'll come back to a little later) and Elizabeth Allen.

However, as Charles wasn't listed in the 1870 census, which would have been after Pa had finished the cabin, this Mr. Thompson probably isn't our man.

There were a couple of "Mr. Thompsons" enumerated in the 1870 federal census and noted as living in the City of Independence, rather than the rural areas of Independence Township, close to the Ingallses. You'd think that would completely preclude them from consideration, but there was one particularly worth looking at.

C. M. Thompson

C. M. Thompson was a twenty-two-year-old carpenter from Illinois who resided in the same household as Fred Brown, a twenty-three-year-old Illinois carpenter, in the home of Mr. Ellis. The fact the names Thompson and Brown are connected here, we mused, could be significant. In her early drafts and notes, Laura stated it was Mr. Thompson who helped Pa build the house and Mr. Brown who brought Christmas gifts. In other places, she used three separate names (Mr. Thompson, Mr. Brown, and Mr. Edwards) to describe almost identical men: bachelors who lived across the creek. As Thompson and Brown were listed on the 1870 census as carpenters, either man would have had the skills to help in housebuilding. If Thompson actually was the person who helped the Ingallses, his friend and housemate, Mr. Brown, could easily have been connected with the Ingallses, too.

But there was a rather large problem. How could we get around the fact the census listed C.M. Thompson as living in Independence? Ten miles from the Ingallses would have been too far to presume any connection, and it certainly wasn't an easy commute even if there had been a friendship between Thompson and Pa. To arrive from Independence before sunup and leave after sundown to return would have been all but impossible if C.M. lived ten miles from the Ingallses. But, at that time, many people who lived in town also filed on homesteads, often for purely practical reasons. For those just starting out, holding a town job was the only way to earn enough money to buy farm tools, seeds, animals, and building materials, etc. Unless a settler came with a pocket full of cash, he had to work until he'd accrued the starting capital he'd need to farm. And most money-making jobs were found in towns. Especially booming ones like Independence at that time.

Do you remember the town dressmaker, Mrs. McKee, in *These Happy Golden Years*? Laura sewed for her and, later, when Mrs. McKee and her daughter, Mattie, had to go live on their claim in order to fulfill the law, Laura came along to keep them company. Mr. McKee couldn't afford to farm yet, but someone in his family needed to live on the claim for six months of each year to fulfill the Homestead Act's residency requirement. Mr. McKee stayed in town to keep working at the lumbermill, and Laura moved to the claim, earning one dollar per week just to stay with the McKees as family. So, it's no stretch to surmise that C.M. Thompson could have been enumerated on the census as living in Independence, but also have had a homestead he was in the process of establishing near the Ingallses.

If he was, the Ingallses could, indeed, have been C.M. Thompson's neighbor.

Charles M. Thompson

There was a very interesting piece of information hiding in the depths of the BLM's tract book for Kansas in volume 41, p. 45, beneath the main entry for S.A. James in S26-T33S-R14E. The section in which Mr. James' land was located was immediately northwest and kitty-corner to the section where the Ingallses settled, so a very close neighbor. This small, handwritten tract book annotation reads:

> D.S. 2909 – Charles M. Thompson – N½ SW¼ - Aug 12–14 '-71.

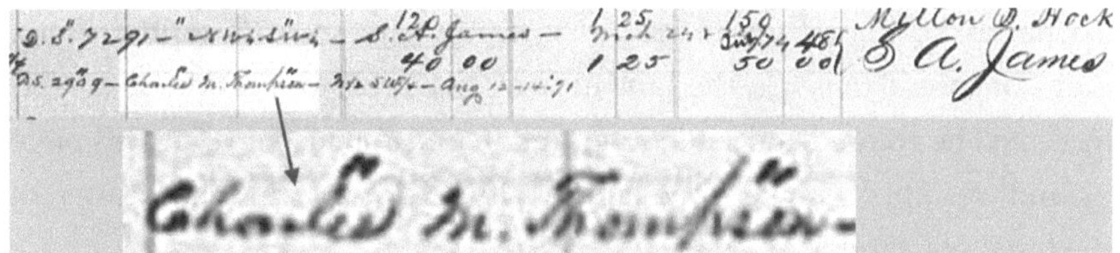

Figure 12 - Charles M. Thompson in an annotation to the BLM General Land Office's tract book entry for S.A. James

This placed a person with the same initials as the previous Thompson we looked at (C.M. Thompson) in close proximity to the Ingallses. Do we know if C.M. Thompson and Charles M. Thompson were the same person? Not for certain. But the clues were more than suspicious: Same last name, same first and middle initials, both in the same area, and both there at the correct time. Also, that one is listed in the Federal census, and the other in a BLM tract book, but neither are in both, is also of note. And, of course, we have Laura's own words that a Mr. Thompson helped Pa build their cabin.

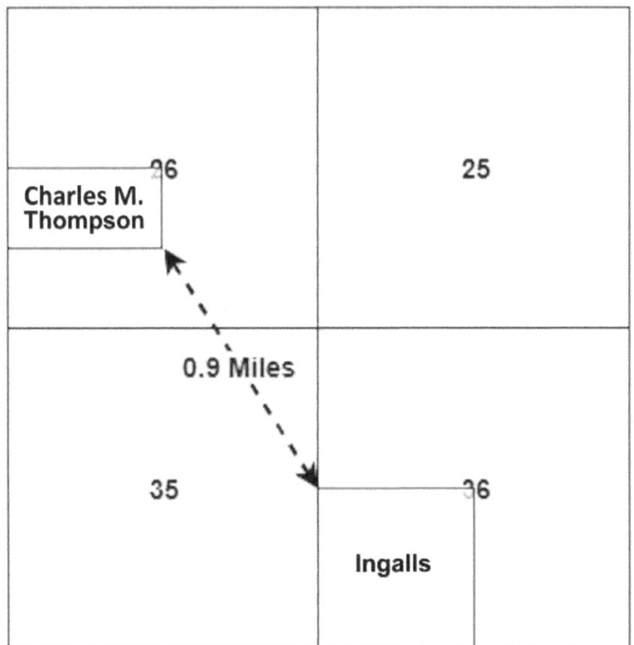

Figure 13 - Schematic diagram showing the relative positions of Charles M. Thompson and the Ingalls family

Charles M. Thompson made a declaratory statement (a written statement of intent to settle the land) for eighty acres of section 26 which indicated he entered and settled the land in mid-August of 1871. This piece of land was approximately one-and-a-half miles away from the location of the Ingallses' land.

Though the date of entry and settlement in the declaratory statement was August of 1871, this didn't mean Charles didn't enter the land earlier. That sounds contradictory, but there was no way for a declaratory statement to be filed until the land was formally surveyed, which didn't happen in Rutland Township until February of 1871. So, no matter when a settler arrived and started living in the area, there was no way to record it until the surveying was complete. Therefore, it's perfectly possible, and even very likely, that Charles M. Thompson was on land very close to the Ingalls property when they arrived.

But was the C.M. Thompson who was listed on the 1870 census the same as Charles M. Thompson who settled near the Ingallses? The one who lived with a Mr. Brown, both of whom were carpenters? Charles was by far the most common name beginning with "C" for a boy in the 1850 U.S. census (over sixteen times more common than the next most common "C" name, Calvin), just two years after C.M. Thompson was born (Buckner, 2004). So, it was highly likely that C.M.'s first name was also Charles and, therefore, very possible, and even likely, that C.M. and Charles M. *were the same person*. If so, C.M./Charles M. ticked all the boxes for the Mr. Thompson who helped Pa: carpenter, bachelor, close neighbor, *and* he had the correct last name.

But even if C.M. and Charles weren't the same person, Charles M. Thompson was perfectly located to be the Mr. Thompson Laura said helped Pa build the house.

In fact, when you read through the *Mr. Brown* section, you'll learn a bonus reason we think C.M. and Charles M. were the same man . . . and very likely to be our correct Mr. Thompson.

There were a few more Thompsons listed in various documents, but either their distance, or their timeframes, excluded them as suspects. So, we were left with a couple of strong candidates, interestingly both with the first initial "C," a middle initial of "M," and a last name of "Thompson."

And this discovery did place a Mr. Thompson (who may have had woodworking/carpentry skills) relatively close to the Ingalls family . . . and who was possibly settling his piece of land at the same time the Ingallses were settling theirs on section 36.

Zochert, in his biography of Laura, also explained that Mr. Thompson was a bachelor, as was C.M. Thompson, and that he lived "across the creek." Walnut Creek, which is a tributary of Onion Creek, flowed between the Ingalls property and Charles M. Thompson's.

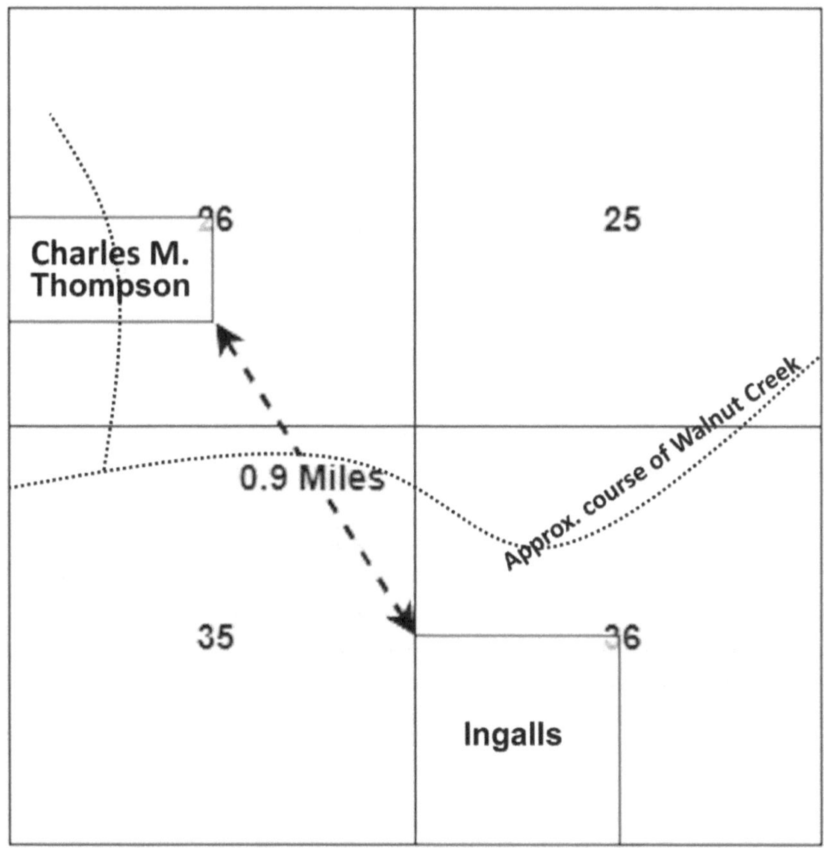

Figure 14 - Schematic diagram showing the approximate course of Walnut Creek between Charles M. Thompson's land the Ingallses' land

Conclusion

If we sliced off the bit of Mr. Edwards that was supposed to have helped Pa build the family cabin, it seemed like we had a strong contender in Charles M. Thompson. He was certainly in the right location, at the right time, and was a bachelor with the correct name who, Zochert noted, lived across a creek (which would have been Walnut Creek, a tributary of Onion Creek) from the Ingallses' land. And, if he was one and the same as C.M. Thompson, the case got even stronger. C.M. was a carpenter, and closely associated with a Mr. Brown, a name Laura noted in an early draft of the Christmas story.

Before we closed the case, however, there were a few things to consider. One was that C.M./Charles M. really only fit one portion of our "Mr. Edwards" descriptors. For example, C.M. was from Illinois. And Walnut Creek was placed such that it didn't absolutely have to be crossed in order get to the Ingalls cabin, which was a crucial detail in the Christmas story. Also, his land lay northwest of the Ingallses . . . not northeast, which was the direction of Independence, so, while it was possible Pa could have swung in that direction when he asked "Mr. Edwards" to look in on Ma and the girls, it wasn't a direct route by any means.

So, if this was our Mr. Thompson, he was a strong and likely candidate for having helped Pa build the cabin, but he certainly didn't fit every detail Laura used to describe the full Mr. Edwards.

Carpenters and Farmers

It is of interest to note the Charles Ingalls was also listed as a carpenter in the 1870 census, rather than a farmer, despite being on a rural claim rather than in Independence. It was also not uncommon for people to have a home in town and another on a claim. So, the fact C.M. Thompson was listed as a carpenter in the census doesn't preclude him from also having a claim near the Ingalls family at all.

– 8 –

Mr. Brown

ANOTHER NAME WE see in early drafts of *LHOTP* is "Mr. Brown." In the novel, it's Mr. Edwards who brought the Ingallses their Christmas presents from Independence, after bravely swimming across an icy and raging creek. But Edwards was not the name Laura used in all drafts of her *Pioneer Girl* manuscript when relating this treasured story. In early versions, she called their Christmas benefactor by a different, and consistent, name. So, on the hunt for "Mr. Browns" we went.

As we noted earlier, in her annotation to the Christmas story in *Pioneer Girl: the Annotated Autobiography*, Pamela Smith Hill wrote:

> Wilder transformed Mr. Brown of *Pioneer Girl* into Mr. Edwards, the "wildcat from Tennessee," . . . (t)he 1870 census of Rutland Township does not include a listing for anyone named Brown or Edwards. (Wilder, 2014, p. 16, n. 36)

This statement, unfortunately, wasn't accurate. There were actually two "Mr. Browns," one of whom was a bachelor, in the 1870 census of Rutland Township. Also, Ms. Hill's statement assumed any "Mr. Browns" needed to be located within Rutland Township in order to be up for consideration as our Mr. Edwards. And that just wasn't the case.

Earlier, we explained the location of the Ingallses' section of land. They lived in the very southeast corner of Rutland Township in section 36. And that section bordered on three other townships: Independence, to the east; Caney, to the south; and Fawn Creek, to the southeast. So, all those Townships had settlers close enough to be included in the search. Ms. Hill and her research team, we believe, may have overlooked that point.

Doing primary research (research that you conduct yourself, rather than relying on others' documentation, assertions, and conclusions) is always critical. So, as a first step to pursuing the name Brown, we started hunting in the 1870 census for Rutland Township, and then expanded our readjusted search area to include all the area within likely reach of the Ingallses.

The trouble with our expanded search border was that the name *Brown* was as common in the mid-1800's as it is now. There may have been only two men by that name listed on the 1870 census in Rutland Township, but there was a whole passel of Browns in the surrounding land included in our search area.

Thankfully, based on a reading of *Pioneer Girl*, we had clues to help us pare down the list of suspects, including the timeframe of the Christmas story. Laura clearly stated the "Mr. Edwards" Christmas was the first Christmas after Carrie was born, which could only have meant 1870, as Carrie's birthdate was in August of that year. Given that Laura would have been nearly four at this Christmas, it's possible this memory was firsthand, rather than handed down, which adds to its credibility.

So, our Mr. Brown must have been from the nearby area, a decently close friend to have done such a kindness for the Ingallses, and a bachelor at that time in order to be considered. After all, it's hardly plausible that a virtual stranger or a married man would choose to go to all that trouble, or spend a Christmas with neighbors if he didn't really know the Ingalls family well and/or he had a family of his own at home!

Frederick Brown (Fred Brown of Rutland Twp.)

In the 1870 federal census for Rutland Township, household 29, the census-taker listed a bachelor: Fred Brown, aged thirty-nine, born in Alabama. It appears Fred (full name "Frederick") must have been one of the earlier settlers in the area because the agricultural schedule of the 1870 census indicated he already had twenty acres of improved land, fifty acres of woodland, and ninety acres of other unimproved land. He also had two horses and three working oxen. All of that spoke to someone who was at least mildly established on his farm which, of course, took time.

Frederick died on March 30, 1878, and remained a bachelor until his death. He left "considerable property" but had no known living relatives and left no will. His obituary indicated he arrived in Montgomery County in 1869 (*The Independence Kansan*, 1878, p. 3).

By reviewing the households listed close to Frederick in the 1870 census (D.H. Good, W. Hamilton, J. Beal, W.M. Lattimore, Wm. Hammond, David Ellis), and reviewing land patents granted to those neighbors, we determined he was, at that time, located in the northernmost area of Rutland Township. He may have been in, or close to, section 1 or 2 of T33S-R14E, or even in the southern edges of the neighboring township to the north (T32S-R14E, but still part of Rutland Twp.). That area was five to seven miles away from the Ingalls family, and beyond several other neighbors. This location made it unlikely Frederick Brown was the Mr. Brown described in *Pioneer Girl*.

However, he had the correct last name, was a bachelor, was born in a state that borders on Tennessee, and appeared in the 1870 census in the same Township as the Ingallses. While he was further away than Laura described Mr. Edwards as being, he *was* on the far side of Onion Creek (and several other smaller creeks), which kept him (barely) in the running as our Christmas Mr. Edwards.

But as for being our full Mr. Edwards—who helped build the cabin, watched over the family while Pa was in Independence, *and* fetched the Christmas gifts—he simply didn't fit the bill. His property was too far away to have been considered a neighbor and, therefore, to have helped with the cabin building. His land would have been almost due north of the Ingallses, too, so he wasn't "on the way" to Independence as Laura stated he was, nor close enough for daily checks on Ma and the girls. And, though his home state was near Tennessee, he wasn't actually born there.

More on the Location of Fred Brown

Fred ended up patenting land in S20-T32S-R15E, (right next to John Thompson), which is just inside the northern edge of Independence Twp. and about eight to nine miles NNE of the Ingalls property. His other neighbors, except his friend, William Jackson, were all enumerated in Independence Twp. in the 1870 federal census, whereas those enumerated close to Fred in the census were mostly located in Rutland Twp.

Thomas J. Brown of Rutland Twp.

The family of Thomas J. Brown appeared as household 32 of the 1870 federal census for Rutland Township, just three households down from Fred Brown, and on the same page. The family consisted of:

- T. J. Brown, aged 29, a farmer, from England
- Francis Brown, aged 28, keeping house, from Virginia
- R. Brown, aged 4, born in Tennessee
- C. Brown, aged 2, born in Nebraska
- Willie, aged 5 months, born in Nebraska

By June 1880, Thomas and family were living in Independence. In the interim, it appeared Willie had died but two more children, George H. and Carrie V., had been born. According to the 1885 Kansas state census, the family then moved to Neodesha, Wilson County, KS, and Mr. Brown was listed as a "carpenter." Eventually, the family settled in Joplin, Missouri, where Thomas died on September 30, 1900, and was buried in Fairview Cemetery, Joplin, MO.

This Mr. Brown checked several of our boxes: his name, he lived in Rutland Township, the fact that he was in the vicinity by 1870, he was a carpenter, and he had a connection to Tennessee as one of his children was born there.

But for one glaring problem, he might have been a strong candidate for the Mr. Brown who fetched Christmas presents for the Ingallses: he was very much married . . . and the father of young children. It's all but inconceivable that Thomas would leave his wife and three youngsters on Christmas to spend the day with the Ingallses. As a father, he certainly would have understood how Mary and Laura might have felt if they didn't receive anything from Santa, and he may have felt compassionate enough to do something dramatic to make sure they didn't go without. But Laura was very clear that Mr. Brown spent the day with the Ingallses, after risking his life crossing a raging creek. Would even the kindest of men have taken that risk and neglected his own family to spend Christmas day with the Ingallses? Probably not.

Also, though his daughter, Rosie, was listed as having been born in Tennessee, Mr. Brown wasn't. And, given his proximity to Fred Brown in the census, he was almost certainly living on the northern edges of Rutland Township, which was somewhere in the region of five to seven miles away from the Ingallses. That's just too far.

While this Mr. Brown had another "Mr. Edwards" trait—he was listed as a carpenter on the 1870 census—there's more than distance and his family to take him off the list as a full Mr. Edwards. In the chapter where Laura says goodbye to Mr. Edwards and thanks him for bringing their Christmas gifts from Independence, she wrote he didn't want to go to Missouri, having already seen it. Instead, was going to head south by river.

Thomas J. Brown, on the other hand, ended up moving to Missouri, though that was several years later. In the meantime, he remained relatively close to Rutland Township until he eventually moved north. In 1880 he had relocated to Independence, and by 1885 he had moved a further fifteen-sixteen miles north to Neodesha before finally settling in Joplin, MO.

There was one further point, which all but precluded him being our full Mr. Edwards: it's hard to imagine a man born in England being compared to any sort of wildcat. From Tennessee or any other place!

So, while it was possible Thomas could have fetched gifts for the family, it's unlikely he delivered them on Christmas or stayed to celebrate the holiday with the Ingallses. So, this Mr. Brown is unlikely to be either our whole Mr. Edwards, or the Christmas portion of the character.

John Brown of Caney Township

With our two Rutland Township "Mr. Browns" addressed, and dismissed, we then had to turn to those Mr. Browns who were in our realigned search area ... the area within reach of the Ingallses' land. There, we found several possibilities.

For example, a land patent was granted to John Brown in April 1875 in section 2 of T34S-R14E (Caney Township), the date of sale being February 6, 1872. The patent was for the southern half of the SW1/4, which would place it just under one and a half miles away, to the southwest, from the Ingallses' cabin.

John didn't appear in the 1870 Federal census, or the 1875 Kansas state census, and, unfortunately, we couldn't find any additional records pertaining to this particular Mr. Brown. Since his patent was granted two years after many of the original neighbors of the Ingallses received theirs, and was purchased nearly a year after they left Kansas, it's possible John wasn't living on the land at the correct time. If he had been on the land, it's curious why he wasn't found on the 1870 census. Could he have moved to the area just after the census was completed, but before Christmas? If so, it's at least possible he was our Christmas hero.

One point in his favor is that John Brown's land was close to Walnut Creek, a tributary of Onion Creek. As Walnut Creek was small, and such creeks changed over time, it's unclear if he would have had to cross it to get to the Ingalls property. The current run of the creek suggests he wouldn't have, but creeks do change over time. And they do flood, changing small, calm waterways into raging torrents.

John Brown did potentially check several Christmas boxes: his name, he lived close enough to be considered a neighbor, lived across a creek, and it's possible he was on his land at the right time. As we had no census data for him, we didn't know where he was born or whether he was a bachelor, so we couldn't rule him out on those points, either.

And there was another possible argument supporting John as our Christmas Mr. Edwards . . . he would have passed close to the Ingalls property if traveling to Independence and would have had to cross Onion Creek to do so. One interpretation of Laura's clue that Mr. Edwards crossed a creek to fetch the Ingallses' presents from Independence is that he must have lived on the other side of a creek from the Ingallses . . . on the Independence side. This would have meant he would have crossed the creek in the *delivery* of the presents, not when he went to get them.

However, Laura could have misunderstood that portion of her family's story. She was clear that a creek had been crossed, but what if it had been between Mr. Brown and Independence, not between him and the Ingallses? If that interpretation is the more accurate one, John certainly could have been the Mr. Brown who saved the Ingallses' 1870 Christmas.

But without census data or other records to give us more information about John Brown, we couldn't definitively say whether he was the true, full Mr. Edwards or not. We just didn't have enough information.

There was one strong argument against him as a possibility, however. In *LHOTP*, it was Pa who passed by Mr. Edwards' land on the way to Independence, not the other way around. In the absence of any other evidence, and on that point alone, it seemed safe to say that John was only a candidate for the Christmas portion of the character, at best.

George A. Brown & William P. Brown of Independence & Fawn Creek Townships

George Andrew Brown and William Perry Brown were brothers, close in age, and sons of William E. and Eliza Brown. Their father, William, was born in Flemingsbury, KY, in December of 1809, but spent most of his younger years in Madison, Jefferson County, Indiana, where he worked as an engineer. This is also where both George and William Jr. were born.

In 1850, the family relocated to Illinois, living in Ashmore Twp, Coles County, where they all farmed, until the outbreak of the Civil War. George and William Jr. were listed there in the 1860 federal census, along with two older, and five younger, siblings. Their father, William Sr., was listed as a farmer with real estate valued at $4,500. William Jr. and George, along with their oldest brother, James A. Brown, were working as farm laborers, probably on the family farm.

Several members of the Brown family arrived in Independence in 1872, where they became prominent figures in the town. William Sr. was mayor of Independence 1875–1876, as well as a member of the school board and justice of the peace. He also built the first three-story building in town. William Sr. died in April of 1890 and was buried in Mount Hope cemetery in Independence, along with several other members of the Brown family.

Figure 15 - William E. Brown, former mayor of Independence. Courtesy of the collection of the City of Independence, Kansas.

Because most of the Brown family arrived in 1872, after the Ingallses had left the area, it appeared easy to cross the Brown brothers off the list of possible Mr. Edwards suspects. But the brothers came *before* the rest of their family. In fact, George and William Jr. were in the area in 1869 and played a role in establishing both Montgomery County as well as the town of Independence.

George Andrew Brown

George A. Brown was one of the earliest settlers in Montgomery County, having arrived in Clymore (close to present-day Coffeyville) in 1868 (Drake, 1943). George appeared in both Independence and Fawn Creek Townships in the 1870 census, presumably because he toggled between two households in the town job/country farm circumstance we've already described. On July 11, 1870, he was enumerated by census-taker Asa Hairgrove in Independence and described as a twenty-six-year-old surveyor from Indiana in the household of J. M. and Eliza Wilson, who were farmers from Pennsylvania.

On July 30th of that same year, Asa listed him again as living in Fawn Creek, but this time he was noted as "alone" in household #127 and described as a twenty-five-year-old surveyor from Indiana. The age discrepancy appeared easy to explain as George turned twenty-six between those two visits with Mr. Hairgrove, as his birthdate and place was July 29, 1844, in Madison, Jefferson County, Indiana. But the switching of his correct ages is a puzzle. Asa surely couldn't have forgotten George as the entries were less than three weeks apart. Nor would George have noted himself as a year older than was accurate on the first entry, and a year younger on the second. Our guess is that Mr. Hairgrove took notes and then transcribed them into the Census forms later, and made the age error (switching them) when he did so.

George, both in and out of his professional capacity, played a very significant role in the founding of Independence, as this story entitled "Let Us Celebrate" from *The Weekly Star and Kansan* of August 20, 1886, recounts:

> Seventeen years ago to-morrow, the 21st of August, 1869, the city of Independence was located by L. T. Stephenson and Geo. A. Brown, who drove a stake at the intersection of Main street and Pennsylvania avenue. (p.3)

The August 27, 1897, edition of the same newspaper provided more details on its front page:

> The site of Independence was selected August 19 or 20, 1869, by a company of men from Oswego. . . . Geo. A. Brown, who had laid off Colfax one and a half miles north-west, was persuaded to abandon his town and join them. Capt. Hamer, of Oswego, run the outer lines of the town, and Geo. A. Brown the inner ones. On the 11th of September, they had a celebration and barbecue. The refreshments, consisting of the ox, four kegs of beer and two barrels of bread, were brought from Oswego with J. N. Bruler's ox team. In crossing the Verdigris river, the team became unmanageable and dumped the whole outfit into the river. Of course it was all fished out—especially the beer.

After processing the new-to-us fact that people had barbecues in 1869, and called them such, we noticed something else. The newspapers failed to mention that George had purchased the land on which Independence was built from the Osage Indians in September of 1869 for the sum of $50. Thus, Independence was founded on a portion of the Osage Diminished Reserve. As part of his agreement with the Osage:

> Each party bound itself to promote peace between the two races. Brown was to build all the houses he wanted, and Chetopa, the Indian chief who took the part of grantor, was to have free pasturage for his ponies. (Duncan, 1903, p. 85)

When he saw the large number of houses being built, however, Chief Chetopa decided Brown had swindled him, so:

> [Chetopa] asked Brown for a new council to rescind the treaty. Brown was equal to the occasion and pictured in glowing terms what the immaculate word and unstained honor of a great Indian warrior required in the observance of such sacred and binding obligations, demanding, if it

> were possible, that he would forever disgrace himself and his tribe by going back on his plighted word. (Duncan, 1903, p. 85)

Although this tactic largely calmed Chetopa, and despite Brown having no interests or say regarding the lands on the Osage Diminished Reserve outside of the Independence town limits, he helped negotiate an agreement: settlers outside the boundaries of the actual town of Independence would pay Chetopa $3.00 per claim. This seemed to appease the chief, despite the very minor sum involved.

In addition to buying the land on which Independence was built, surveying the city, and negotiating with the Osage Indians, George was the town's first civil engineer. He also played an active role in the formation of Montgomery County and appeared on the County's first ever grand jury, in 1870. William G. Cutler's "History of the State of Kansas" recounted:

> Prior to its incorporation. Montgomery was attached to Wilson County for judicial purposes . . . Montgomery County was made a part of the Eleventh Judicial District, and by the authority vested in the County Commissioners, the District Court for and in the county was ordered to be held at Independence on the 9th day of May, 1870. . . . The session was held in the school building, and . . . [t]hose reported on the grand jury were: . . . George A. Brown . . . .
>
> The grand jury at this sitting returned six indictments, one for murder in the first degree, three for murder in the second degree, and two for assault with intent to kill. (Cutler, 1883, p. 1565)

Thus, George was a very active participant in the first ever murder indictments in Montgomery County.

In April of 1872, the same year his parents arrived, George married Minnie Catherine Bowman in Independence. In September, they moved to the historic mining town of Central City, Colorado.

Figure 16 - The first courthouse in Independence, built in 1870

George's popularity in Independence was evidenced by a short comment that appeared on the third page of the *South Kansas Tribune*, April 21, 1875:

> Mr. Geo. A. Brown and wife have returned from Colorado, and will we understand again locate in our city. That's right, George, Independence is the best place after all, and we welcome you back.

But their second stay in Independence was shortlived. George and Minnie's first child, Fred, was born back in Colorado just a few months later, in July of 1875. Their only other child, Ethel, was also born in Colorado in December of 1877. The 1880 census listed George's family in Ophir, Ouray County, Colorado, where George was working as a carpenter and civil engineer. Ophir was another remote mining location, in the San Juan mountains of southwest Colorado, not far from Telluride.

By March of 1894, George, along with Minnie and their children, had moved to Boise, Idaho, where George again worked as a civil engineer. He remained there until his death on May 17th, 1922 and was buried there in Pioneer Cemetery, alongside his wife, who died in 1920.

This Mr. Brown obviously had an incredibly interesting, and important, role in the development of the area the Ingallses settled in, especially Independence. And he did check a few of our "Mr. Edwards" boxes. He was in the area before the Ingallses arrived. He was a bachelor at that time and a major creek lay between him and the Ingallses. His obvious prominence in the area would have likely resulted in Pa and George crossing paths at some point, too.

But not enough other markers existed to consider him as the complete Mr. Edwards. He wasn't born in Tennessee, he wasn't a close neighbor—though his farmland was closer to the Ingallses than Independence was—and he wasn't on the *way to* Independence, so he likely wasn't the portion of Mr. Edwards who Pa asked to watch over his family when he went to Independence or the one who helped build the cabin.

But could he have been Laura's "Mr. Brown" who delivered those Christmas presents at Christmas 1870? He was certainly in the region at the right time and would have had to cross a creek to get to the Ingallses' home. Plus, his bachelorhood would have left him free on the holiday, though that would have meant leaving his brother to celebrate alone. It's not possible to ascertain exactly where George's land was located at the time of the 1870 census because he never received his patent. But, by examining his neighbors in the census, and comparing the land patents they did receive, we know he was probably located across Onion Creek in Fawn Creek Township and only a couple miles from the Ingallses.

As George also had a home in Independence, and such strong ties to it, his going there to fetch gifts wouldn't have been improbable. He could have easily just picked them when he went into town for other reasons. If he did, he might have felt compelled to deliver them to the Ingallses at Christmas, raging creek or not. Did he know the family well enough to risk his life to deliver some tin cups, sweet potatoes, and Christmas candy? Maybe. But we were not convinced.

William Perry Brown

William Perry Brown was listed as "W. P. Brown," household #126, in the 1870 census for Fawn Creek Township, right next to his brother, George. His entry in the census described him as aged twenty-seven and his profession as a farmer. Like his brother, this Brown was a bachelor, only a couple of years different in age, and from Indiana.

William was born December 1, 1842, in Madison, Jefferson County, Indiana. After moving to Illinois with the rest of the family, he was mustered into Company C, 8th Illinois Infantry on July 25, 1861, and was discharged for disability on June 30, 1862.

After moving to Montgomery County with his brother, George, he spent the remainder of his life in the area. Although William may not have been as active in the formation of Montgomery County and the city of Independence as George had, he was one of many signatories, along with George and several other citizens of the county, to send a letter to Governor James M. Harvey concerning several electoral irregularities during the formation of Montgomery County (Brown *et al.*, 1869, p. 50).

William Perry died at his parents' home on October 13, 1881, of consumption and was buried in Mount Hope Cemetery in Independence. He never married.

As with George, it's not possible to ascertain exactly where William Jr. was located at the time of the 1870 census. But he and George were conceivably only a couple of miles from the Ingallses. As such, he lived close enough to be a possibility as our Christmas Mr. Edwards, at least. After all, William was also a bachelor, though, like George, his home wasn't on the way to Independence. Another point . . . he had a disability serious enough to cause his discharge from the service. So, while he was able to farm, at least in some way, he didn't appear to be as active and mobile as George, or as likely to swim across an icy winter creek.

So, just as we discounted George as a potential full Mr. Edwards, William was likewise excluded. And it's very improbable he was the Mr. Brown who brought the Christmas presents, as well.

L. Brown

According to *The 1881 Atlas*, L. Brown owned eighty acres of land in Rutland Township in the western half of the southwest quarter of section 30. His (or her . . . widows and female heads of households were allowed to file claims and buy land) residence was on the western side of Illinois Creek, about four to five miles from the Ingalls family. Unfortunately, little else is known about L. Brown. There are no land patents recorded under that name in Montgomery County and we couldn't find him/her in the 1870, 1875, or 1880 censuses. Nor was that name listed as one of the patrons in *The 1881 Atlas*.

Even assuming L. Brown was male, and knowing he lived just over four miles from the Ingallses on the other side of a creek, this particular person seemed unlikely to be either Laura's "Mr. Brown from across the creek," or our full Mr. Edwards. He's not on the way to Independence, his land is a little far away to be considered a neighbor, and, as women could homestead or purchase land, for all we know, "he" wasn't even a "he!"

Other Browns Living in Independence, or Independence Township

There were several other Browns listed in the 1870 federal census and other sources. Reviewing the occupations of their neighbors, land patents granted to neighbors, and *The 1881 Atlas*, most of these Browns were living either in the city of Independence or on the eastern edges of Independence Township, toward Liberty and Drum Creek Townships, and thus were highly unlikely to be Laura's Mr. Brown due to distance.

Though some of them were bachelors, none of them were from Tennessee, wild or not, and, of course, none of them were neighbors. Additionally, a couple of them simply arrived in the area too late. These include Josiah Johnson Brown, a rather remarkable man whose life warrants its own full biography; his brother, David B. Brown; William M. Browne of Rutland Twp.; David B. Brown, a young lawyer who died just a couple of weeks after Carrie Ingalls was born; Andrew John Brown of Fawn Creek Twp.; and N. Brown, a builder from Bavaria.

There was another person lurking amongst these unlikely candidates, however, that we *did* examine more closely—and for a pretty good reason. Remember C.M. Thompson? The bachelor carpenter who lived in Independence but may also have been the same as Charles M. Thompson who settled on land near the Ingallses . . . and seemed to be a solid match for Laura's Mr. Thompson who helped build the family cabin? His roommate in Independence, who likely stayed with Charles on his land near the Ingallses, was another Fred Brown.

Fred Brown of Independence

Listed on the 1870 census as living with C.M. Thompson, Fred Brown, twenty-three, was described as a bachelor and carpenter from Illinois. In Independence, Fred was living in the same household as C.M., who was also a carpenter from Illinois, as well as a third carpenter, David Ellis, from Ohio. Given that Fred and C.M. were both from Illinois, both carpenters, both close in age, and were living together in Independence, it's reasonable to assume these two men knew each other well . . . possibly even coming out from Illinois together.

And if our C.M. was, in fact, Charles M., who had a new farm near the Ingallses, Fred could easily have spent time at C.M.'s place, helping him develop his farm and home. Charles Ingalls had promised to trade work with Mr. Edwards (called Mr. Thompson by Laura in early drafts of *LHOTP*), so it's easy to see how Fred Brown might have come into acquaintance with the Ingallses. They might all have worked on C.M.'s cabin together, and maybe even the Ingallses'.

While it was all but impossible Fred was the full Mr. Edwards, he couldn't be completely written off as at least partially connected, via the Christmas story, either. There were too many potential ties. The fact that Laura's early *LHOTP* manuscripts stated Mr. Thompson helped build the house, and *Pioneer Girl* stated Mr. Brown brought the gifts, put these names closely together. As such, these two carpenter friends could have been the two mentioned by Laura. If Fred knew the Ingallses through his friend, Charles M., possibly spending time working together, he might have decided to do something heroic for the Ingalls children and fetch the Christmas gifts. He lived in Independence, and was a bachelor, so would have been free to do something of this nature. And, though it's a bit of a stretch, the fact that he could have been good friends with the Ingallses' neighbor, Charles M. Thompson, maybe even spending time with him and Pa building Charles' cabin, brought it into the realm of possibility.

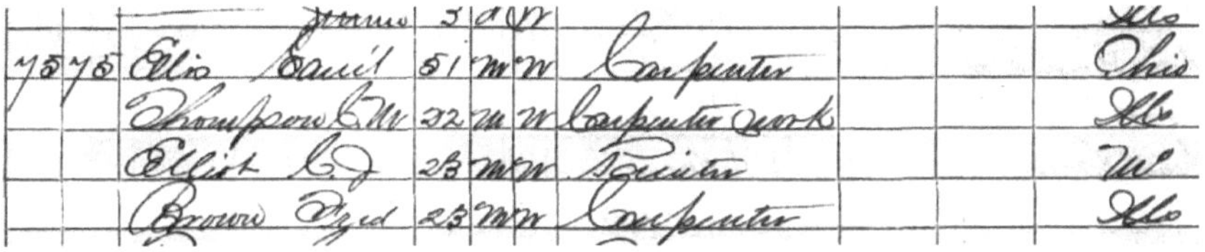

75	75	Ellis Daniel	51	M	W	Carpenter	Ohio
		Thompson C.M.	32	M	W	Carpenter work	Ills
		Elliot C.J.	23	M	W	Painter	Me
		Brown Fred	23	M	W	Carpenter	Ills

Figure 17 - C.M. Thompson and Fred Brown in the 1870 census in Independence

Conclusion

If Laura did, indeed, use the correct name of Mr. Brown in her early drafts to describe the man who brought their Christmas presents from Independence, crossing a dangerous creek to do so, and then spending the day with the Ingallses, we had a few suspects we couldn't exclude. John Brown, of Caney Township, and George A. Brown, of Fawn Creek Township, were two who remained on the "possible" list. John was a stronger contender than George, but neither seemed to fit the emotional side of this clue. Would either of them have had a reason to be in close enough relationship with the Ingalls to take a risk in crossing a raging winter creek with Christmas gifts? Or close enough to spend an entire holiday with the Ingalls family? We could find no compelling reason they might have made that kind of intimate connection.

Fred Brown of Independence, a bit of a wildcard for our Christmas Mr. Brown, also made that short list of candidates, however. While we needed to make a slight leap for our case to hold together, that being the assumption Fred's Independence roommate, C.M. Thompson, and Charles M. Thompson were one and the same, it all fell together beautifully if those two names actually did represent the same man.

Fred could easily have met and formed a relationship with Pa while staying or working with Charles M., who lived close enough to the Ingallses to be considered a neighbor . . . and who lived across a creek from the family. And as Fred's primary residence was in Independence, he could easily have brought the Ingallses' gifts, either of his own volition or after being asked by his friend, Charles M. Thompson to do so for his neighbor.

His bachelor status would have meant he was free to spend the day with the Ingallses, too. And, of course, his name was Mr. Brown. Laura's assertion that a Mr. Thompson helped Pa build the house and a Mr. Brown brought the Christmas presents linked those two names in our minds. And here, with Fred and Charles, a Mr. Brown and a Mr. Thompson, being closely connected, it just felt logical.

Because he seemed the likeliest of all the Browns to have had a firm reason to be in close relationship with the Ingallses that it was plausible he would perform this kind, and risky, favor . . . and because he had a roommate named Thompson . . . and because he checked so many other boxes, we think Fred Brown was the likeliest hero of the Ingallses' 1870 Christmas.

– 9 –
Tennesseans and Bachelors

IN LAURA'S RECOLLECTIONS of Mr. Edwards, she described him as a bachelor from Tennessee. There were many bachelors living near the Ingallses, according to the 1870 census. And some Tennesseans. Two of their neighbors were both Tennesseans *and* bachelors. So that was a very good place to start on the next leg of our hunt.

William F. Johns of Independence Township

The 1870 Census listed William as living in Independence Twp., working a farmer, and having been born in Tennessee. He was described as thirty years old, though other documents informed us he was actually thirty-five at this time. The census also made it clear that, although he was in Independence *Township,* he was not in the *city* of Independence. And when he married Columbia A. Jackson in Independence on August 27, 1873, their marriage license described him as "of Independence" and aged thirty-seven. Columbia was "of same place" and aged twenty-four.

Whether, like the census, the marriage license differentiated between "Township" and "City" is uncertain, but by the time the 1875 Kansas state census came around, William and Columbia were definitely living in the *city* of Independence and he had become a merchant. By June of 1880, they had returned to Columbia's former hometown of Spring Hill, Johnson County, Kansas, where he was a dry goods merchant and where his parents-in-law had come to live with them. William and Columbia remained in Spring Hill until their deaths in 1909 and 1937, respectively.

Could William, this once Tennessee-bachelor-farmer turned Kansan-married-merchant be Laura's "wildcat?" We searched for additional clues to find out.

At the time the Ingalls family and Mr. Johns were all living in Montgomery County, William had not yet married Columbia, so the bachelor part was satisfied. We know William retained his bachelor status until 1873 and, in the 1870 census, he was dwelling in Independence Township, which neighbors Rutland Township, so he could also have been inside our prime search area.

The 1880 and 1900 federal censuses gave us a little bit more information. Not only was William a Tennessee native, but both his father and mother were also born there, so he was Tennessean to the core. Could he ever have been considered a neighbor to the Ingalls family, though? Or even have known Charles Ingalls? We needed to establish a more precise location for Mr. Johns to discover the answer to that question.

Referring again to the *BLM GLO Database*, and the neighbors listed in the census, we determined that William was located in the northeast corner of Independence Township, close to Drum Creek and Liberty Townships, about nine and a half miles away from the Ingallses' corner of Rutland Township.

But, digging deeper into land records, we discovered a patent for 160 acres was issued in the name of William F. Johns, dated September of 1873. The land in question was the NW1/4 of section 23 in T34S-R14E, which was part of Caney Township, the Township just south of Rutland and kitty-corner to Independence Twp. This was about three and a quarter miles south of the Ingallses' little house, so a little far from them to be a "neighbor," but not completely out of the running, either.

To complicate matters, there happened to be another W.F. Johns enumerated nearby in the 1870 census. This one was in the city of Independence, aged thirty-two, a carpenter and a bachelor . . . but he was born in Missouri. So, was our "Tennessee William" the one who received the patent? And even if he was, would it impact our conclusion?

It seemed unlikely that someone located in Independence Twp., outside of the city, would also be settling land in Caney Twp. But another family listed close to William in the census did just that. Henry B. McHugh, listed just four households before William, settled on land in S18-T34S-R14E at about the same time—the claims for both quarter-sections being filed in September of 1871—and almost two years before William and Columbia's wedding.

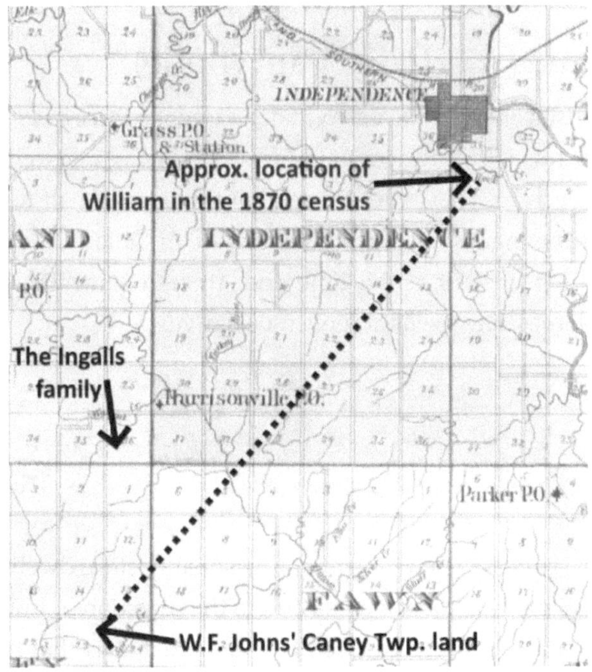

Figure 18 - Map showing the general location of W.F. Johns in Independence and Caney Twps. and the location of the Ingalls family

So, even though it was feasible our William could be the one with the Caney Twp. land, there was a lack of conclusive (or even mildly persuasive) evidence either way. And, because both candidates were relatively close to each other (either in, or in the vicinity of Independence) we determined it could have been either one of them. So, for the purpose of our quest, we evaluated them together.

As per the census, they were both on the far side of Onion Creek, between the Creek and the Verdigris River, but a long way away from the Ingallses. Although the Caney Twp. land was closer, it was also too far away. And, even when looking at the direct line of travel between the two Townships, although it went relatively close to the Ingalls family, it seemed unlikely to be conducive to a relationship developing between either Mr. Johns and Pa. So, neither of these bachelors really fit the bill, even if one was from Tennessee. They were both just too remote and distanced from Pa to be our "Tennessee Wildcat."

James Sands (& Henry VanWinkle)

The 1870 census showed H. VanWinkle, a twenty-three-year-old farmer, and James Sands, a twenty-year-old farmer, residing in dwelling #122 in Independence Twp. They were living about two and a half to three miles northeast of the Ingalls family, on the far side of Onion Creek. Both men seemed to be bachelors at the time and, though VanWinkle was from Wisconsin, James Sands was a Tennessee native.

122	110	VanWinkle Ho.	23	m	w	Farmer		400	Wis
		Sands James	20	m	w	Farmer		200	Tenn

Figure 19 - H. VanWinkle and James Sands in the 1870 census in Independence Twp.

With that Tennessee pedigree and a reasonably close dwelling, as well as residing on the far side of a creek and in the direction of Independence, James seemed a promising suspect. It was a great start that he was from the right state and not too far away from the Ingallses. But was he there at the right time?

The *BLM GLO Database* indicated that J. N. Sands preempted eighty acres in the SE quarter of section 35 of Rutland Twp., with his patent being issued in October of 1873. The original tract book from the BLM indicated this land was actually sold October 3, 1872, and a small handwritten note beneath the entry for J. N. Sands gave his name as *James N. Sands.* This land adjoined section 36, right next to where the Ingalls family lived. But it was purchased too late to have put James in contention for any part of our Mr. Edwards.

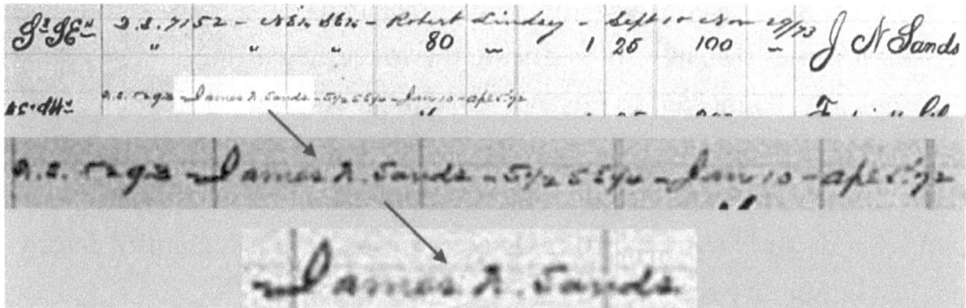

Figure 20 - Entry for J. N. Sands in the BLM General Land Office's tract book

We also found an interesting little side note in our research. Payment records for the sale of school lands in Montgomery County indicated the Sands and VanWinkle families ended up settling on the very quarter section where the Ingalles had been living. The western half of the southwest quarter of section 36 of Rutland Twp. was purchased by James Sands' older brother, *Joseph* (who also had an expired claim in section 35), and the eastern half was purchased by Henry VanWinkle.

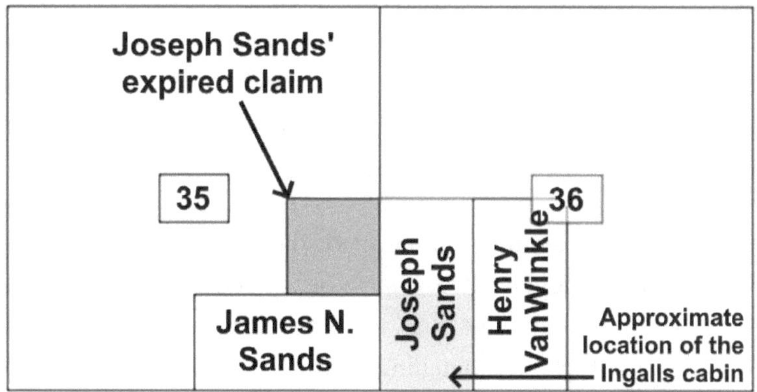

Figure 21 - Location of James Sands', Joseph Sands', and Henry VanWinkle's land in sections 35 & 36 of Rutland Twp.

James Nathaniel and Joseph Payne Sands were two of the children of Benjamin Sands and Rosanna Henderson. The family came from Tennessee, where both James and Joseph were born, before moving to Washington County, Iowa, where Benjamin preempted 160 acres of unimproved land. Though most of the family stayed in that vicinity for most of their lives, and Joseph was found in Iowa in both the 1870 and 1880 censuses, James was in Kansas during the 1870 census.

Joseph was connected to Henry VanWinkle, James' roommate, beyond purchasing adjoining land, because Joseph married Henry's younger sister, Lucinda Belle on August 24, 1868, in Washington County, Iowa. So, James Sands and Henry VanWinkle were from the same extended family, not just temporary roommates.

VanWinkle's purchase in section 36 was dated December 27, 1871. Though that's the same year the Ingallses left Kansas, we already know that, in order to be able to purchase land, VanWinkle had to settle on it prior to purchase. So, it was possible he could have been there when the Ingallses were. And if he was there, James, our Tennessean, would have been close by.

This didn't make James any more viable as our Mr. Edwards, but it was interesting because Laura had written about two sets of bachelors. In the earliest version of *LHOTP*, one pair was named "John Turner & Jones" and the other pair were "Dick & Tom" (Wilder, no date b, pp. 9–12). In a later manuscript, they were "Sam Turner & Bill Jones" and "Tom & John" (Wilder, no date d, pp. 58–61). Perhaps Sands and VanWinkle were Laura's "Dick/John and Tom." Or, perhaps, they were her "John/Sam Turner and Bill Jones."

James Sands and William F. Johns were the only Tennessee bachelors listed in Rutland, Independence, Caney, or Fawn Creek Townships in the 1870 census . . . and neither of them were close enough, likely there at the correct time, or sufficiently matching Laura's various descriptors to be in the running for our Mr. Edwards.

But there were other bachelors who lived within two to three miles of the Ingallses besides VanWinkle and the Tennesseans. And it was time to see what we could find out about them.

John L. Rowles

John L. Rowles was born in Virginia or Maryland in October of 1847 and farmed 160 acres in the eastern half of section 34 of Rutland Township, which he entered and settled on in October of 1869 and purchased on September 9, 1871. Rowles' parcel was just over a mile away from the Ingallses' property and was next to land owned by Dr. Tann, also in section 34. Tann and Rowles had something more in common than proximity, too—they were both of African descent.

So, though he was unmarried, it is very unlikely he is Laura's "Mr. Edwards." Laura mentioned only one African American man in *LHOTP*, whom she wrote as Dr. Tan. She described him as the "first black man" she had ever seen, so it is unlikely she wouldn't have noted John Rowles' ethnicity if he had any part to play in Mr. Edwards.

Washington Fain Reser

Unlike other bachelors, Civil War veteran Washington F. Reser did not appear in the 1870 census in Rutland Twp. But land records revealed his presence close to the Ingalls family by the fall of 1870 at the very latest.

His parcel comprised 158.84 acres and straddled the southern edge of Rutland Twp., as well as the northern edge of Caney Twp., the northeastern corner of which was about a half-mile away from the Ingalls family.

The tract book entry for this land indicated it was improved and settled on October 11, 1870, the claim was filed June 26, 1871, and the date of sale was November 10, 1871. The date of settlement was almost exactly one month after the Osage Indians formally agreed to leave the Diminished Reserve and before they had agreed to its being surveyed. Because this land wasn't available for settlement prior to the Osage's agreement,

Washington could have been living on the land prior to October of 1870, but unable to legally register his presence until the law allowed him to do so.

So, Washington could easily have been in the area around the time the Ingallses arrived, and he most certainly was by the time the Christmas story happened in 1870. The problem with him as a candidate for Mr. Edwards was that he was living too close, in the wrong direction, not across a creek, not beyond woods, and wasn't from Tennessee, though he did have grandparents from that state.

Another point against him as a suspect was that Washington returned to Hickory County, Missouri, where his widowed mother lived, within a few years. He remained in that area for the rest of his life, passing away at the grand old age of 92. He became a well-respected citizen of the county, where he and his wife produced twelve children. Of those who survived to adulthood, four became either doctors or dentists. Washington himself served as postmaster for several years, ran a general store (which he passed on to his son, Winer D. Reser), and continued to farm. Hardly the credentials of a wildcat from anywhere, let alone Tennessee.

Figure 22 - The Washington Reser Store at Preston, Hickory County, MO, 1890

Sets of Bachelors

In *LHOTP*, Laura described one of her sets of bachelors:

> He [Pa] had found some more neighbors. . . . two bachelors were living in one house. They had taken two farms, and built the house on the line between them. One man's bunk was against one wall of the house, and the other man's bunk was against the other wall. So each man slept on his own farm, although they were in the same house and the house was only eight feet wide. They cooked and ate together in the middle of the house (*LHOTP* ch. 7 "The Wolf-Pack").

This passage appeared to describe the situation of Henry VanWinkle and James Sands, whom we opened this chapter with. But in early *LHOTP* manuscripts, Laura mentioned TWO sets of bachelors . . . the ones who shared the house built on the line between their adjoining properties, and one other. We turned our eyes to the other possible set.

Marcelous "Adelbert" Streeter & Daniel Everett.

M.A. Streeter, aged twenty-three, and D. Everitt [*sic*], aged thirty-four, appeared in households 19 & 20 in Caney Township in the 1870 census. But the connection between these families went back to at least the 1840s, when the Streeters and Everetts preempted land in neighboring sections of Richmond Township, McHenry County, Illinois, and appeared next to each other in the 1850 federal census. By 1851, the two families moved together to Otto, Kankakee County, Illinois and appeared next to each other again in the 1860 census. These two families weren't just neighbors and close friends, however. They also became connected by marriage—Adelbert's mother was an Everett.

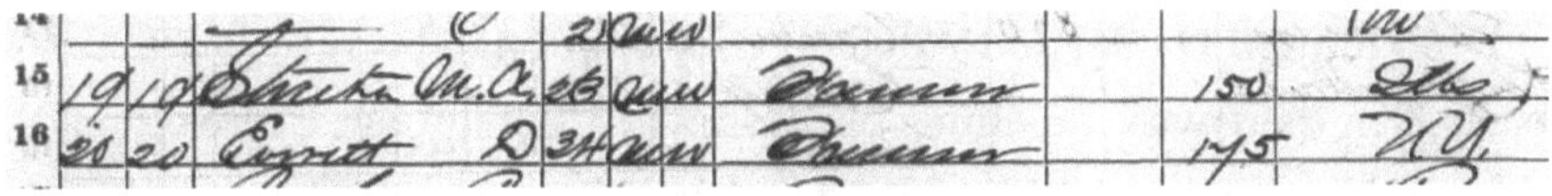

15	19	19	Streeter M.A.	23	m	w	Farmer		150	Ills
16	20	20	Everett D	34	m	w	Farmer		175	N.Y.

Figure 23 - M. A. Streeter & D. Everett in the 1870 census in Caney Twp.

These families lived together and moved together for decades, but, after the Civil War, Adelbert and Daniel, like so many veterans, left their family homes and relocated to Caney Twp., Montgomery County, Kansas.

Adelbert entered 160.66 acres in NW1/4 of section 1 and he indicated his date of settlement and improvement was March 15, 1870. His declaratory statement was filed July 6, 1871. The final date of sale was July 11, 1871, and the final patent was issued in March of 1873.

Even though Adelbert and Daniel appeared next to each other in the 1870 census, their land wasn't adjoining. Daniel entered the NW1/4 of section 11 of the same township with a stated date of settlement and improvement of May 10, 1870. His declaratory statement was filed July 10, 1871, and the date of sale was October 11, 1871, with the patent being issued in July of 1873. Daniel's land was about one and a half to two miles southeast of the Ingalls family—adjacent to, and directly south of, the land of John Brown of Caney Township, who we discussed earlier.

In Zochert's biography, he wrote:

> Yet in the first draft of her book, and in some notes about her life made before the Little House books were written . . . [she] mentions two bachelors, John Turner and Mr. Jones; two other bachelors living up the creek, Dick and Tom.

Though neither set of the bachelors we found matches the names Laura provided (John Turner and Mr. Jones/Dick and Tom), these were the two sets most likely to be known to and interacted with the Ingallses. Perhaps Laura just made up names for people she could barely remember. "Dick and Tom" were part of a popular phrase, "Tom, Dick, and Harry," at the time. It was a way of "naming" just any person in general. Or perhaps she just remembered incorrectly. There were no local pairs of bachelors with the exact names Laura noted when the Ingalls family lived in Kansas.

Even though Daniel and Adelbert may well have been two of Laura's bachelors, there was something else noteworthy about Mr. Everett; he was the only candidate for Mr. Edwards whose last name also began with the letter "E." "Everett" was about as similar to "Edwards" as "Nellie Owens" was to "Nellie Oleson." So, could he have been Mr. Edwards, if only in part? If Mr. Edwards was a composite character, like the three women who made up the composite character of Nellie, it was a possibility.

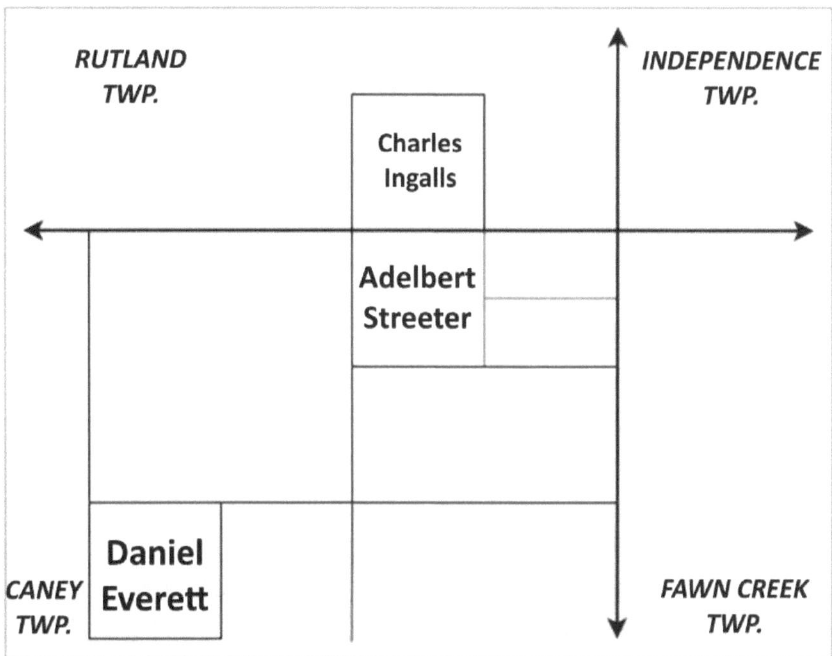

Figure 24 - Location of Daniel Everett, Adelbert Streeter, and Charles Ingalls in Montgomery County, Kansas

Another thing to consider, Laura mentioned an "Edwards and Stover" in earlier manuscripts of *LHOTP*. Perhaps this "Edwards and Stover" were actually Everett and Streeter. Daniel Everett was thirty-four at the time of the census, by far the oldest bachelor living near the Ingallses, and considered relatively old to even be a bachelor in 1870. And this fit, as Laura referred to Mr. Edwards as an "old batchelor" [*sic*] in an early manuscript (Wilder, no date a, p. 44).

Trying to establish a connection based only on an age and a last name starting with the letter "E" is a pretty big stretch, however. Our Mr. Edwards came with a great number of very specific descriptors, most of which Daniel didn't match.

For example, Daniel settled his land in May of 1870, so he couldn't have been the person that helped Pa build the little house. He also didn't hail from Tennessee, nor was there a creek to cross between the Everett and Ingalls properties, and there were no obvious woods between them. We also know Daniel remained in Caney Township until at least July 1871, when he filed his Declaratory Statement, so he didn't leave when the Ingalls did in the spring of 1871, which Laura said Mr. Edwards did.

But what about those Christmas presents? Could Daniel Everett have been the man who kindly brought them from Independence?

Daniel certainly was close enough to the Ingallses to have known them. Traveling as the crow flies, Daniel would have had to pass over a corner of section 36 of Rutland Township, very close to the Ingalls family, and would have had to pass their property to get home when traveling from Independence. Additionally, he would have had to traverse Onion Creek on his way to and from town. But that clue only fits if we adopt the alternative reading of the Christmas story, in which Laura may have ordered the details wrong and placed "Mr. Edwards" across a creek from the Ingallses when he was actually on the same side of the creek. If she did get that information muddled, Daniel could have, indeed, crossed a creek after fetching presents from Independence, but it wouldn't have been a creek between their properties.

Daniel only remained a candidate for the Christmas "Mr. Edwards" if we believe Laura made a mistake regarding his home's location. But she was pretty adamant about the point. In chapter 17: "Pa Goes to Town":

> On his way to town [Independence] that morning, Pa had stopped at Mr Edwards' house and asked him to come over every day to see that everything was all right.

Do you see the problem? Pa stopped at Mr. Edward's house *on the way to Independence*. So, Mr. Edwards almost certainly lived between the Ingallses' house and Independence. Daniel Everett, on the other hand, lived in the opposite direction.

Thus, though Daniel Everett met some of the "Mr. Edwards" criteria, it's unlikely he was Laura's "Mr. Edwards." He could have been an outside possibility for the person who brought the Christmas presents if Mr. Edwards was a composite character, but even that didn't appear likely.

There were other candidates, all Tennessee natives, dotting the countryside around the Ingalls land, but none of them were bachelors at the time of the 1870 census, so we had to discount them on that point alone. If nothing else, Laura was clear that Mr. Edwards wasn't married!

Some of those Tennessee men included: Samuel D. Best, who was married with eight children by the time his family moved to Montgomery County in 1869–1870, David H. Mikel, who was living with his wife and two children by the time of the 1870 census, and G.W. Hunt, who, with his wife and children, had moved to the area by 1870 at the latest. The Hunts, however, are worth a closer look at for another reason.

G. W. Hunt

George W. Hunt was born in April of 1838 in Blount County, on the eastern border of Tennessee by the Great Smoky Mountains. On Feb 17, 1857, he married Sarah Alexander, another Tennessee native, and two and a half years his senior, in Blount County.

For a period after their marriage, they remained in Blount County, residing next door to George's father and stepmother. During this period, George and Sarah had three children.

The oldest, Nancy Jane, was born in 1858 but died at the age of two, in December of 1860. Almost exactly one year earlier, Nancy's brother, Columbus B. Hunt, was born. The family then moved to Iowa, where at least three more children, possibly four, were born. We know for certain that, by the time the family was listed in the 1870 census, there were four more children in the family, one of which was born in the spring of 1870. William Henry was born in 1866, "F. A," (a boy, full name unknown) was born c.1868, and L. A. (possibly Lydia A.) was born c.1869, all in Iowa. The baby of the family, Martha M., was probably born in April of 1870.

Several Hunt family researchers indicate that George died in October of 1870, though they disagree on where. One thing that is certain is the family arrived in Montgomery County by the spring of 1870 at the latest.

The 1870 census indicates the Hunts were living on a 160-acre quarter section next to Henry VanWinkle and James Sands at that time. Looking more closely at the census, the location of their neighbors, and the *BLM GLO Database*, we could discern the Hunt family's land was almost certainly spanning sections 19 and 30 of Independence Township. A land patent for the S1/2 SE1/4 of section 19 and the N1/2 of the NE1/4 of section 30 was granted to Sarah E. Hunt, who was almost certainly G. W. Hunt's wife. The fact the patent was issued to Sarah supported the belief that George had indeed died in 1870.

It also placed the Hunts roughly two and a half miles away from the Ingallses and on the far side of Onion Creek (about a half-mile west from the western edge of the present-day Independence Municipal Airport).

Given the size of their family, their arrival from Iowa, and their proximity to James Sands and Henry VanWinkle, it's possible the Hunts were the family that Laura wrote about in chapter 7 of *LHOTP*, "The Wolf Pack":

> When he came to [the covered wagon], he found a man and his wife and five children. They had come from Iowa . . . the bad night air so near the creek had given them fever 'n' ague. The man and his wife . . . were too sick to stand up . . . so Pa did what he could for them, and then he rode back to tell the bachelors about them. One of them rode right away to fetch that family up on the High Prairie, where they would soon get well in the good air.

It's also possible G.W. was the married man who died digging his well, which Laura described in an early *LHOTP* manuscript (Wilder, no date c, p. 75). And we know he died before his land patent was granted because it was issued in the name of his widow, Sarah Hunt (U.S. Gen. Land Off., 1874).

Sarah Hunt, James Sands, and Henry VanWinkle in Iowa

In the 1885 Iowa state census, Sarah was listed along with her son, William, in Oregon Twp., Washington County, IA (where they lived until at least 1905). This happened to be the same Township where the Sands and VanWinkles also lived. James N. Sands lived the rest of his life there after leaving Kansas and two of his brothers also lived close to the Hunts. Perhaps the families had already known each other before they headed to Kansas, or maybe it was a lifelong friendship forged on the Kansas prairie.

– 10 –

Other Neighbors

THERE WERE A FEW other close neighbors to the Ingalls family, as shown in the 1870 census, the *BLM GLO Database*, etc. Some of these neighbors arrived in the area after the Ingalls family but, if Mr. Edwards did turn out to be a composite character of good neighbors, one or more of these men might have had a part to play . . . even if it was a later portion of the *LHOTP* timeline, such as the Christmas story or when the Ingallses left Kansas.

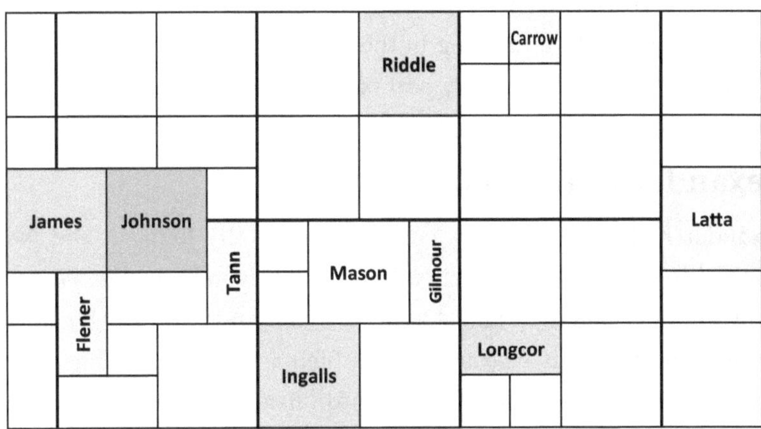

Figure 25 - Map showing the location of several neighbors of the Ingalls family

Bennet and George Tann

Bennet Tann, aged 68, his wife, Mary, 56, and son George, 34, were listed immediately before the Ingalls family in the 1870 census. Their household also included a domestic servant by the name of Mary Berry. The Tann family came to Kansas from Lycoming County, Pennsylvania, where Bennet was a free black man as early as 1830, over thirty years before the American Civil War.

George was listed as a physician in the census and Laura wrote about him in *LHOTP*, chapter 15, "Fever 'n' Ague":

> Then the doctor came. And he was the black man. Laura had never seen a black man before and she could not take her eyes of Dr Tan [*sic*]. He was so very black. She would have been afraid of him if she had not liked him so much.

Dr. Tann eventually helped cure the Ingalls family and several other settlers of "fever 'n' ague" (malaria) and went on to become a celebrated physician in the area. He died in 1909 and is buried in Mount Hope Cemetery, Independence. His father, Bennet, died in February of 1881, having resided in Rutland Township until his death.

Laura correctly named Dr. Tann (though with the slight misspelling, "Tan") in *LHOTP*, and assigned him a very specific story that matched exactly what we learned about him. But he didn't match any of our criteria other than proximity and being in the area at the correct time, so it was certain he did not comprise any part of Mr. Edwards.

Alexander K. Johnson

Alexander K. Johnson was the son of Joseph Kelly Johnson and Nancy Irwin Caldwell, and was born circa 1834, probably in Partridge, Woodford County, Illinois, where he had at least one older and five younger siblings. The 1850 census listed Alexander with his parents and siblings, though there was also another Alexander Johnson listed with other members of the Caldwell family in Tazewell County, IL, in the same census. So, our

Alexander may have been listed twice, once with his immediate family and once with his extended family on his mother's side.

Alexander married Sarah Ann Parkhill in Tazewell County in September of 1856. Sometime between 1865–1870, Alexander and Sarah relocated to Rutland Twp. with four of their eventual six children, where they farmed on 160 acres spanning sections 26 and 35. The Johnson property adjoined Bennet Tann's land and was less than three-quarters of a mile from the Ingalls family. Walnut Creek also ran west to east across the southernmost quarter of their property.

Over the next several decades, the Johnsons toggled between Caney Township and Indian Territory (present day Oklahoma), near Bartlesville and a neighboring town, Dewey. Interestingly, Dr. George Tann, their Rutland Twp. neighbor, did as well. Sarah eventually died in Caney Twp. in 1911. Three years later, Alexander also died, though he had moved back to Dewey by this time. He was buried in Sunnyside Cemetery in Caney, where some of his children are also buried.

> The funeral of A. K. Johnson, 80 years old, who died Wednesday at his home in Dewey, Okla., was held yesterday. The body was taken to Caney and given burial. He was one of the early settlers of that community. (*The Coffeyville Daily Journal*, 1914, p. 4)

So, might Alexander have been a part of "Mr. Edwards?" The Johnson's home appeared to have been less than a mile away to the northwest from where Pa likely built the family cabin. Historic maps indicated this was also on the far side of a small creek—which *The 1881 Atlas* suggested was a tributary of Walnut Creek (U.S. Geol. Survey, 1886, 1894, 1905, 1959; U.S. Dept. of Agric., 1941).

However, he wasn't a bachelor and wasn't from Tennessee. He also stayed in the area after the Ingalls family returned to Wisconsin, so he didn't hit the mark on any of those descriptors.

We're also not exactly sure when the Johnsons arrived in Rutland Twp., but the agricultural schedule of the 1870 census indicated he had improved fifteen acres of his land by June of 1870, and his farm was one of the most valuable in the area, so it's likely they arrived by 1869 or very early 1870. The Johnsons would have had to cross a small creek to reach the Ingalls property and to reach Independence, but they weren't a long way away. However, it's possible the Johnsons were the Robertsons Laura wrote about in *Pioneer Girl.*

In *Pioneer Girl,* Laura described how Pa heard a woman calling for help "down the creek toward Robertson's" and went to their home to investigate (Wilder, 2014, p. 11). The Johnson's home was one of the closest homes to the Ingallses at this time that housed a married couple. It was located next to Walnut Creek and was one of the only reasonably located homes Pa could have hurried to and looked around, or even heard, from that distance.

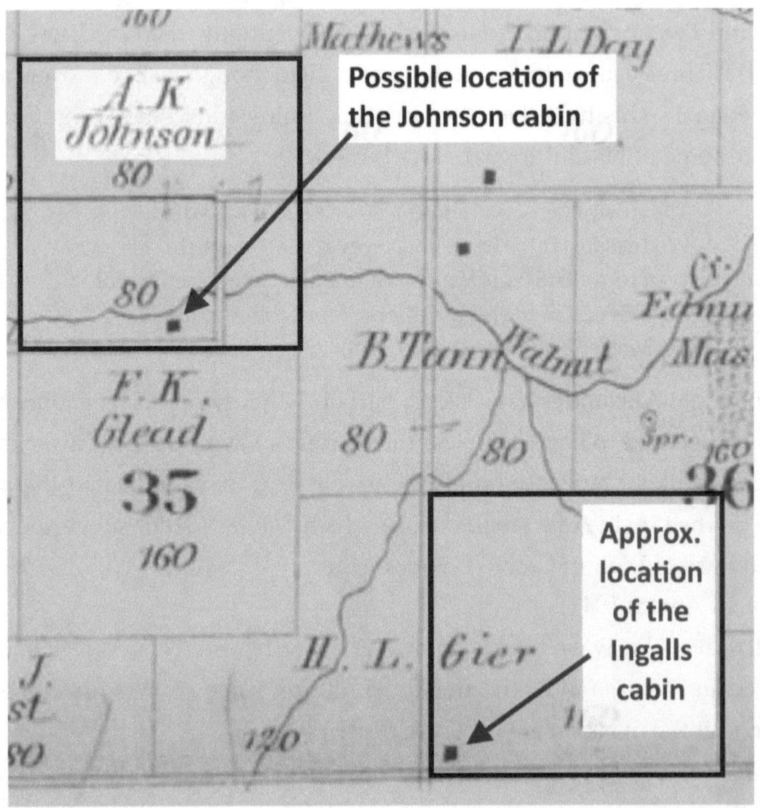

Figure 26 - Locations of the Ingalls, Johnson, and Tann families (derived from The 1881 Atlas)

Laura also recounted the day Carrie was born and Laura had returned home from her time with Pa and Mary at the Indian camp, "the black Dr. was there and Mrs Robertson . . ." (Wilder, 2014, p. 14). This was significant because the Johnson's land adjoined Bennet Tann's property, where Dr. Tann was also residing at the time, and their homes were only about a half-mile apart. And, of course, there is a similarity between the names "Johnson" and "Robertson." Thus, it was far more likely that Alexander Johnson was Laura's "Mr. Robertson" (referred to as "Mr. Scott" in *LHOTP*) than "Mr. Edwards."

George Newton Longcor

About a mile to the east of the Ingalls land was the home of George Newton Longcor and his wife, Mary Jane Gilmour (aka "Gilmore"). Though George appeared in the Rutland Twp. census, his land was just over the border, in section 31 of Independence Twp., where he was erroneously enumerated as G. N. Lunker.

George was one of the best documented of all the Ingallses' neighbors as a result of his tragic life story—a story that began with his birth in 1842 in Indiana. The first part of this dramatic tale slightly detours from our hunt, but we thought it more than worthy of inclusion here because of its historical significance, so we hope you will indulge us.

George was the son of Anthony "Doc" Longcor & Mary "Polly" Adaline Hughes and was the second oldest of twelve siblings: nine girls and three boys.

George first appeared in the 1850 census, when his family was living in Honey Creek, Adams County, Iowa, on land neighboring that of his uncles: Salem, Washington, and George Longcor. Ten years later, the family was living in Belfast, Van Buren, Lee County, Iowa and his father had changed professions—from farmer to silversmith.

At the age of nineteen, George enlisted in the Union army on June 15, 1861, and was mustered into service February 1, 1862 in Canton, Missouri, where he became a Private in Company G of the 21st Regiment, Missouri infantry. He was just over five feet five inches tall, with auburn hair, hazel eyes, a light complexion, and worked as a blacksmith (Allen, 1863).

Three years after the end of the Civil War, in 1868, George married Mary Jane. The following year, their son Robert A. Longcor was born in Adair County, Missouri, but he died of "lung fever" in May of 1870, after the Longcors, along with Mary Jane's parents and siblings, had relocated to Montgomery County. George was eventually issued a patent for 79.01 acres in S31-T33S-R15E, directly adjoining section 36 of Rutland Twp., where the Ingalls family was residing. In fact, in the 1870 census, George was listed directly after the newly-born Caroline "Carrie" Ingalls.

Tragedy for the Longcors continued into 1871. The year began well, with the birth of their daughter, Mary Ann Longcor, on January 5th. But just five days later, Mary Jane died, probably as a result of complications during labor.

Around this time, Mary Jane's parents decided to join her uncle, John Wilson Gilmour, in Oregon. This left George alone with his newborn daughter.

George, like his in-laws, eventually decided to move closer to family and return to Iowa—a decision that was to cost him his life. In November of 1872, George and his infant daughter were murdered by the infamous "Bloody Benders" in Labette County, KS, while en route to Iowa. The evidence indicated the young Mary Ann was buried alive with her murdered father. After their bodies were found, they were taken back to be buried next to Mary Jane and Robert, on either the Longcor or Gilmour farm, though no trace of their graves exists today (*The Border Sentinel*, 1873, p. 2; Nobel, 2013; Cappello, 2019).

The Ingalls Family and the Benders

Laura described a semi-fictionalized version of these events in quite detail in the "Brandt Revised" and "Bye" drafts of her "Pioneer Girl" manuscript, probably at the prompting of Rose Wilder Lane. She also spoke about the Benders in a speech she gave at the Detroit Book Fair (Oct. 16, 1937), which contained details that were clearly not factual, such as the location of the Bender home. This is discussed in detail in *Pioneer Girl Perspectives* (Koupal).

George Longcor had one of the most remarkable and heartrending stories of any of the Ingallses' neighbors, but could he have been any part of Mr. Edwards?

It was probable Pa Ingalls knew George Longcor as one of their closest neighbors, even if the rest of the Ingalls family never met him. Of course, he wasn't a bachelor or from Tennessee. We also don't know for sure when George arrived in Montgomery County, but we do know it was sometime between the birth and death of his son Robert, so it was certainly within a few months of the Ingalls family's arrival, if not sooner. There was no creek between the Ingalls property and the Longcor farm, but there was a creek between George's land and Independence. Pa would also have passed close to Longcor's land when traveling to and from Independence. Thus, if Mr. Edwards was a composite character, it is certainly possible that George was a part of that composite. It's unlikely that he's the Mr. Brown who brought the Christmas presents, as he had his own family to be with. He could have traded cabin-building work with Pa, though that's unlikely given he had several in-laws living nearby, too. The likeliest portion of Mr. Edwards' character he contributed to, if any at all, would have been to have kept an eye on the family when Pa went to town.

Robert B. Gilmour

Robert Bronaugh Gilmour, who was George Longcor's father-in-law, was born November 1, 1819, in Christian County, Kentucky, the son of George Gilmour and Polly Terrell Hickman. He was the sixth of George and Polly's nine children.

Robert's mother died on March 17, 1829, when he was still just nine years old and his father, George, died on October 31, 1835, when he was fifteen.

In 1848, Robert married Mary Ann Carter in Illinois and, in the 1850 census, they were living with Robert's older brother, James Gilmour, in Hancock County, IL. Robert and Mary's first child, Elizabeth, also appeared in that census, aged one.

Sometime between 1855–1858, the family moved to Missouri, where they were farming in Benton Twp., Adair County, and had four additional children: Mary Jane (who married George Longcor), Frances, George, and Isabelle. These children were all born in Illinois except Isabelle, who was born in Missouri.

By 1870, they had moved to Rutland Twp., where they were residing close to their daughter, Mary Jane, and her husband, George Longcor. The Gilmours weren't in Kansas very long before Robert decided to join his brother, John Wilson Gilmour, in Oregon's Willamette Valley, settling in Linn County. However, school land payment records told us Robert also purchased eighty acres (E1/2 NE1/4 section 36 of Rutland Twp.) in January of 1872 and was still making payments on it in 1881 (Montgomery Co., KS, Clerk's Off., 1881). Curiously, Robert was listed as Robert *E.* Gilmore in the payment records. This parcel was directly adjacent to land settled by Edmund Mason (whom we discuss in the next section), to the east, and in the diagonally opposite corner of the section to the Ingalls family (see Figure 25 on p. 105).

Robert died in Linn County, Oregon, in 1882, where he is buried in Sand Ridge Cemetery, Lebanon.

Figure 27 - Grave of Robert B. Gilmour in Linn County, Oregon

Joseph L. James

Joseph Lee James was a first cousin once removed, to Margaret James, who married James Flener, who we meet a little further down. They both arrived in 1870 and their land adjoined; in the 1880 census, they were on the same page.

Joseph L. James was born in Ohio County, Kentucky, on the 7th of March, 1827, to Samuel James and Sally Borah. The family was of English descent via his grandfather, John James, who had immigrated to Virginia, where he was prominently involved with the tobacco business. He was an inspector of tobacco at Richmond for a number of years.

Joseph L. James was raised in the "Blue Grass State" and, on December 25, 1850, married Martha A. Shelton. Martha was a daughter of Ralph Shelton, of Butler County, Kentucky.

Mr. James lived in Kentucky until the year 1870, when, on July 5, he arrived in Montgomery County. His preemption consisted of one hundred and sixty acres located about one to one-and-a-half miles to the northwest of the Ingalls property. In June of 1907, Joseph recounted his arrival in the area at the office of *The Times* in Independence:

> He brought with him a family of thirteen, including his wife, their ten children and his mother-in-law. When he took his claim in the neighborhood of the present town of Wayside, there were a few other settlers in that vicinity but he was the first one who brought his family with him. (*The Times*, 1907, p. 5)

Joseph died July 2, 1916, at the age of eighty-nine in Independence, at the home of his son, H.K. James, and is buried in Harrisonville cemetery, close to the eastern edge of section 36 of Rutland Twp. Ten years prior to his death, there had been reports in the local newspapers concerning a serious family dispute over oil rights on the James land, with accusations of assaults between his sons as well as rumors of either one of his sons or a nephew assaulting Joseph himself (*The Evening Star*, 1906b, p. 1; *The Times*, 1906, p. 4).

James A. Flener

James A. Flener was born in Ohio County, Kentucky, on the 13th of February, 1846. Harrison Flener, his father, was a native of the same county, as was his mother, Mary A. Smith.

When the Civil War broke out, James enrolled, at only fifteen years old, as a member of Company "H," Seventeenth Kentucky Infantry. He served from August of 1861 to February of 1865. After receiving his discharge, James returned home and remained on the family farm until his marriage, in October of 1868, to Margaret, daughter of Mosby and Betsy James.

In 1870, James and Margaret relocated to Rutland Township, Montgomery County, and took up a claim, residing just over a half-mile from the Ingalls family. Margaret died on January 6, 1875, but James continued to live on his original claim until the year 1883, when he sold it and purchased a farm of one hundred and twenty acres, one mile north of the town of Caney, on Cheyenne Creek.

Samuel Riddle

Samuel Riddle and family lived about one and a quarter miles NNE of the Ingallses' land, and directly west of land belonging to Edmund Mason (the subject of our next section) in Independence Twp. The Riddles were some of the Ingalls family's closest neighbors.

Samuel was born to Samuel and Nancy Riddle, both Virginia natives, on October 21, 1833, in Muskingham County, Ohio. By 1850, the family was living in Walnut, Gallia, Ohio, where both Samuel Sr. and Samuel Jr. were working as laborers. It was also in Gallia County where Samuel Jr. was married to Minerva Ellen Zinn on May 22, 1857. Minerva was ten years Samuel's junior, aged about sixteen when they were married.

The family stayed in Walnut until at least 1863 but, by 1867, they were living in Iowa. The stay in Iowa didn't last long, however, and by December of 1869 the family was living in NE1/4 S25-T33S-R14E, Rutland Twp. Samuel filed his declaratory statement August 17, 1871, and claimed his date of settlement was December 26, 1869. By this time, they had three children: Artemisia, Samuel, and Jesse.

By 1870, Samuel was working a 160-acre quarter section with twenty-five acres of improved land, eight acres of woodland, one hundred and twenty-seven unimproved acres, and had two horses. He purchased the land on November 15, 1871, and received the patent on July 15, 1873 (Bur. of Land Mgmt., no date, p. 45).

Like several of the Ingallses' neighbors, the Riddles moved south to Oklahoma (Indian Territory), where Samuel died about a month before his fifty-first birthday.

Although Samuel was one of the Ingallses' closest neighbors, and he was also one of the areas earliest settlers, he is unlikely to have been Mr. Edwards. While he, along with all the other suspects we've noted, could have helped Pa build his cabin, it isn't likely. His name wasn't a match for Laura's early use of "Thompson" as the person who helped Pa, and he certainly wasn't a bachelor. With a family of his own to house and provide for, it's unlikely he would have prioritized building Pa's cabin, let alone spend an evening with them enjoying a night of "home life."

Oliver Carrow

Roughly two miles northeast of the Ingallses' home, in the direction of Independence, was the land of Oliver Carrow. In fact, his Independence Township homestead neighbored a very interesting piece of land we mention in the next section.

Oliver was born in July of 1830, in French (Lower) Canada. His parents are unknown but his original last name may have been "Carreau." Nothing is really known about Oliver until he appeared in the 1860 U.S. Federal census, when he was working as a laborer in Chippewa Falls, Wisconsin. Eight years later, on July 14, 1868, he married Rachel McCune (aka Gretchen McCuen) in Washington County, Iowa. Roughly a year later, their first child, Elizabeth, was born, also in Iowa.

Shortly after Elizabeth's birth, the Carrow family relocated to Independence Township. Records indicate they arrived by November

1869, so they were among the earliest settlers in the vicinity of the Ingalls family. The Carrow family also appeared in Independence Township in the 1870 census, where Oliver was listed as farming. This census revealed he couldn't read or write.

It appeared the Carrows had left Kansas by the spring of 1871 as their second child, Samuel Oliver Carrow, was born on March 20, 1871, in Wayland, Henry County, Iowa. However, Oliver's land in Independence Township was formally purchased on July 12, 1871, with the patent issued on March 15, 1873. Oliver and Rachel eventually sold this land to Jacob Russum.

The Carrows remained in Henry County, Iowa, for a few years and their second son, John, was born there on January 24, 1874. Their second daughter, Elmira, was born c. 1875 and was also probably born in Iowa, though some records indicate Kansas.

With the exception of a perfectly located property, across a creek, beyond woods, about two miles away, and on the way to Independence, nothing else really matched. Like our previous candidate, Oliver had a family to provide food and shelter for, and his name certainly wasn't "Thompson." So, likely, he wasn't any part of our Mr. Edwards, either.

John Stephens Latta

John Latta's land was also about two miles away from the Ingallses, close to Harrisonville. In fact, John Latta was listed immediately before Oliver Carrow in the 1870 census.

John was the son of Ephraim Latta and Eliza Armstrong and was born on August 8, 1838, in Pennsylvania. He, along with his wife, Charlotte, and daughter, Laura, arrived in Montgomery Kansas in 1870 (Edwards, 1881, p. 11). Their second child, John Jr., was just two months old at the time of the 1870 census and was born in Kansas, whereas Laura was born on January 12, 1869, in Jefferson County, Iowa.

The Lattas remained in Kansas until 1884, during which time they produced five more children: Claude, Maude, Martha, Gilbert Hugh (or possibly Hugh Gilbert), and Robert Alexander. When they sold their land, they announced in local newspapers they were planning to relocate to Texas, but it appears they spent a few years in Indian Territory before ending up in Louisiana, which is where John died in April of 1894.

Just like our previous neighbors, John's only possible link to our Mr. Edwards is through the location of his property. And, while a good match for that, it wasn't enough to put him in any real contention for our Tennessee Wildcat.

– 11 –

Edmund Mason

IF YOU'VE SPENT any time wondering about the true identity of Mr. Edwards, or you've explored any of the many *Little House*-related groups on social media, or even visited some *Little House* locations, you almost certainly have come across the name "Edmund Mason." Though there have been many theories as to who the real Mr. Edwards is, Edmund Mason is the name that has appeared again and again as the likeliest of candidates. Some have even claimed he was Mr. Edwards, in full. So, of course, Mason warranted particular attention.

Why had his name been connected so frequently with Mr. Edwards? There were a few reasons: he was enumerated close to the Ingalls family in the 1870 census of Montgomery County, KS; his first name was "Edmund"—which is somewhat similar to "Edwards"; he was, at times, referred to as both "Edmund" and "Edward"; and he was a bachelor at the time the Ingallses lived in their little house on the prairie.

As a result, many people have declared, in *Little House* forums and groups, and in other *Little House* arenas, that Edmund *was* "Mr. Edwards." And that, a handful of people seemed to have decided, was the end of it.

However, the provided proof that Edmund Mason was, in fact, our Mr. Edwards had been rather thin, and largely hinged on circumstantial evidence, such as his proximity to the Ingallses at the correct time and the Edmund/Edwards name similarity. That wouldn't remotely be enough to close the case in court. If proximity was the best criterion, for example, we had already established far better options.

Regardless of what others believed, however, our goal was to uncover the truth, no matter what it might be. So, we did what any good researcher would do; we ignored previously held theories and postulations and measured Mr. Mason, in the most unbiased manner possible, against all the clues and information we had assembled and ascertained.

Because he had been proclaimed "Mr. Edwards" by some, however, we wanted to give an especially thorough examination of his life and candidacy as Laura's "Mr. Edwards." We soon discovered that whether he was, in whole or part, our man, he certainly was interesting.

Figure 28 - Portrait of Edmund Mason

Early Life

Edmund was born to Thomas and Joanna Mason at Colmans Farm in the English village of Lifton, just eight years into the reign of the young Queen Victoria. Lifton, located in southwest England, in the county of Devon, was a "considerable village, pleasantly situated in the valley of the river Lyd, about a mile from its confluence with the Tamar . . . on the mail road" (White, 1850, pp. 803–804). With about 780 inhabitants, it was home to five inns and taverns, five carpenters, four shopkeepers, three blacksmiths, two shoemakers, two saddlers, two lime merchants, and over thirty farmers, one of whom was Edmund's father, Thomas.

Figure 29 - Colmans farm, Lifton in July 2023

When Edmund was born, civil registration of all births had been mandatory in England for eight years, following the *Birth, Marriage and Death Registration Act* of 1836, which came into effect in July of 1837. Accordingly, Edmund's parents registered his birth in the Tavistock district on September 22, 1845 (FreeBMD, no date). As a result, his actual birth certificate can still be obtained.

Though some biographies and other records, including his obituary, state Edmund was born on September 14, 1846, or thereabouts, that error can be explained. Most of those contemporary writings and records drew the date from Mason's tombstone. So, if that gravestone was incorrect, they all were. And it was incorrect because we know this for a fact: official English records confirm he wasn't born in 1846 at all. His legal birth certificate confirms he was born a year earlier, on Tuesday, September 2, 1845 (Gen. Register Off., 1845).

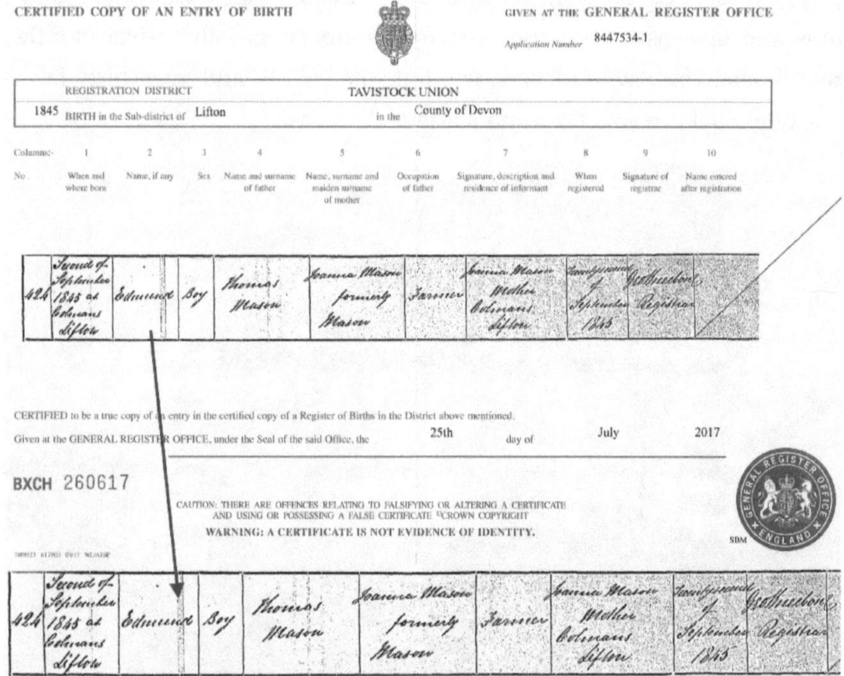

CERTIFIED COPY OF AN ENTRY OF BIRTH

GIVEN AT THE GENERAL REGISTER OFFICE

Application Number 8447534-1

REGISTRATION DISTRICT TAVISTOCK UNION

1845 BIRTH in the Sub-district of Lifton in the County of Devon

Columns:- No.	1 When and where born	2 Name, if any	3 Sex	4 Name and surname of father	5 Name, surname and maiden surname of mother	6 Occupation of father	7 Signature, description and residence of informant	8 When registered	9 Signature of registrar	10 Name entered after registration
424	Second of September 1845 at Colmans Lifton	Edmund	Boy	Thomas Mason	Joanna Mason formerly Mason	Farmer	Joanna Mason Mother Colmans Lifton	Twentysecond of September 1845	[illegible] Registrar	

CERTIFIED to be a true copy of an entry in the certified copy of a Register of Births in the District above mentioned.

Given at the GENERAL REGISTER OFFICE, under the Seal of the said Office, the 25th day of July 2017

BXCH 260617

CAUTION: THERE ARE OFFENCES RELATING TO FALSIFYING OR ALTERING A CERTIFICATE AND USING OR POSSESSING A FALSE CERTIFICATE ©CROWN COPYRIGHT

WARNING: A CERTIFICATE IS NOT EVIDENCE OF IDENTITY.

SDM

424 Second of September 1845 at Colmans Lifton | Edmund | Boy | Thomas Mason | Joanna Mason formerly Mason | Farmer | Joanna Mason Mother Colmans Lifton | Twentysecond of September 1845 | [illegible] Registrar

Figure 30 - Official birth certificate of Edmund Mason

Figure 31 - Edmund Mason's gravestone with incorrect birth date

This date was substantiated in additional sources, and via considerable corroborating evidence, but it somehow remains a point of contention in *Little House* circles. Folks are stuck on the fact that Edmund Mason's gravestone listed a different date of birth. To many, this is inconceivable. How could such an error happen on a gravestone, of all things? But just like a popular *Little House* forum recently explored, the error was more common than you'd think. In that particular discussion, however, it was Willie Owens, the brother of Nellie Owens (one of the three women who made the composite character of Nellie Oleson) whose birth date and gravestone date were significantly different. Simple human error, lack of records, non-communication with loved ones, frequent lack of celebrating birthdays, and other reasons were in play. But the facts of Mason's birth are confirmed by legal documentation: he was born on September 2, 1845.

As was the norm in England at the time, shortly after his birth, Edmund was baptized. Although Lifton contained Baptist, Wesleyan, and "Bible Christian" chapels, as well as St. Mary's parish church, which was Anglican, Edmund wasn't baptized in that village. Thomas and Joanna had him christened four to five miles away, just over the county border, in Launceston, Cornwall, on September 19, 1845 ('Christening Record for Edmund Mason', 1845). His baptismal record indicated the family's place of residence was then in Launceston, as well, which is interesting. Born in Lifton on September 2nd but living in Launceston a mere two weeks later? Curious. But we did learn this: the record of his baptism solidified that Edmund wasn't born in 1846 as previously believed.

In both his civil birth registration and his baptismal record, his name is recorded as *Edmund* rather than *Edward* Mason. But to add to the confusion, there *was* an Edward Mason who *was* born in 1846, also in Lifton, and whose birth was also registered in the Jul-Sep quarter. Edward, however, was the son of John and Ann Mason, and he was Edmund's double first cousin. Edward Mason, therefore, was definitely not our Edmund Mason.

Edmund's father and Edward's father were brothers, and their mothers were sisters. To further complicate things, these sisters, Joanna and Ann, who married the Mason brothers, also had the maiden name of Mason.

Though they were almost certainly related in some way by blood to the men they married, their exact relationship, if any, was a little murky.

Edmund was the seventh of nine children born to Thomas and Joanna and the middle of five sons. His father worked as a farmer and appeared to have been reasonably successful—the size of his farm increased by twenty acres between 1851 and 1861 and the family always had at least one servant living with them (The Nat'l Archives (UK), 1851, 1861). Thomas, however, did not own his farm. He rented it, as did the vast majority of farmers in the village (White, 1850, p. 804).

While Thomas' sons were too young to work, he employed agricultural laborers to help on the farm. But as the boys grew older, they were able to take on the work instead. The family was shaken, however, when Thomas died on March 22, 1866, at the age of 56. His father had died just as Edmund was approaching his twenty-first birthday.

At Thomas' death, Edmund and his younger brother, Thomas Henry, both stood to inherit a total of £50. Under the terms of his will, they would both receive £30 six months after Thomas' death, and the remaining £20 eighteen months later. Their older brother, John, who was already in America by this time, inherited only "if he should live to return[,] the sum of twenty pounds" (Mason, 1866).

Less than a year after his father's death, and having reached adulthood, Edmund left his home in rural southwest England in 1867 and headed to Canada with his initial £30 inheritance, worth about $3,200 in 2020, in his pocket. This same year, in the big woods of Wisconsin, Charles and Caroline Ingalls were celebrating the birth of their second daughter, Laura.

The time between his arrival in Canada and when he arrived in Montgomery County was a little vague. Whether Canada was a destination, or just the first port in his journey to join his brother John in America wasn't clear, but at some point, Mason arrived in the U.S.

His great-granddaughter, Joy Mason Allen, in correspondence with fellow Mason family member, Sharon Easley (née Mason), claimed Edmund stayed in Canada only a short time and may have worked as a scout or teamster alongside John at or near Fort Scott, Kansas, (about ninety miles northeast of Independence) (Easley, 2016–2017). However, we have been unable to find any records substantiating this claim.

The 1885 Kansas state census indicated that Edmund arrived in Kansas from "Cherokee Nation." This referred to what is now the northeast corner of Oklahoma, previously Indian Territory, the boundary of which was just a few miles south of Rutland Township but borders on Montgomery County. However, it was clear that, just a couple of years after setting sail from England, Edmund arrived in Montgomery County in 1869, following in the footsteps of his brother, John.

John, who was more than ten years Edmund's senior, had left the family farm in England at the age of twenty-one (in 1855 or 1856) and relocated to Leavenworth, Kansas, where he worked as a teamster for the U.S. government and was a scout and messenger for cavalry leader "Phil" Sheridan "during the [civil] war and immediately after" (Duncan, 1903, p. 760).

General Philip Sheridan

In September 1867, Sheridan was assigned by the general in chief to the command of the Department of the Missouri, with his new headquarters at Fort Leavenworth, Kansas, about 190 miles NNE of where Independence would be founded. This post was considered the most important in "the frontier West." The department was responsible for Indian Territory, Kansas, Colorado, Nebraska, & Wyoming Territory. (Burr and Hinton, 1889, p. 343).

Eventually, in July of 1869, John settled in Rutland Township, Montgomery County, where he claimed the land (spanning parts of sections 13 and 24) on which he farmed until his death.

Brothers Thomas Henry and James followed suit by emigrating to the U.S., and both lived in the same area of Montgomery County as their brothers for a while. Thomas Henry was living with John on June 1, 1870, the date of the 1870 federal census. But, eventually, he purchased his own land along the southern edge of section 24, just a half-mile south of John's land and one mile north of Edmund's.

James, on the other hand, arrived in 1872. He was listed as living with one of John's neighbors, Henry Sang, on the 1875 state census, in household #133. At this time, he was twenty-two, single, had a real estate value of $700, and was noted as having arrived in Kansas from England. By 1880, he was living with Edmund. But in *The 1881 Atlas*, he's noted as owning 145 acres of land, bordering on H. Sang's land in section 24, between John and Edmund.

James & Thomas Henry Mason

James Mason is buried in Harrisonville Cemetery, not far from the various Mason claims. He died on February 15, 1900, when he was forty-seven years old. Edmund and his older brother, John, are also buried there. James was reported to have died at Edmund's home. Thomas Henry died early 1873, possibly after relocating to Cherokee County, which is in the very southwest portion of Kansas. James may have inherited or purchased his land after his brother's death, which is why young James would have already acquired land worth so much in such a short time.

Why did we care so much about Edmund's brothers, their comings and goings, and their homesteads? Beyond giving us a little more insight into Mason's life, all this information had a rather important impact on our hunt. During the time period chronicled in *LHOTP*, it appeared that three of the four Mason brothers were living within less than two miles of each other.

So, Edmund may have been a bachelor during this time, but he was certainly not alone.

After Edmund arrived in Montgomery County in 1869, he settled at some point on land in the same section as the Ingallses. We'll address this more thoroughly later but wanted to briefly discuss it now because the proximity of that piece of property had been what many people cited as "proof" that Mason *was* "Mr. Edwards." After all, Mason's land was in section 36, thus it was close to the Ingallses'. However (and it's a HUGE "however!") *that* parcel of land lacked two important features: it wasn't two miles away, and there wasn't a creek to cross between it and the Ingallses' cabin.

The exact location of Mason's parcel was just inside the northern edge of section 36, which was, as we've already stated, a section reserved for school use. His biography corroborated this fact as it had been "... purchased of the state school fund and was without improvements" (Duncan, 1903, p. 507). The land was less than a mile from where Charles and Caroline Ingalls would settle shortly after, in the southwest quarter of section 36.

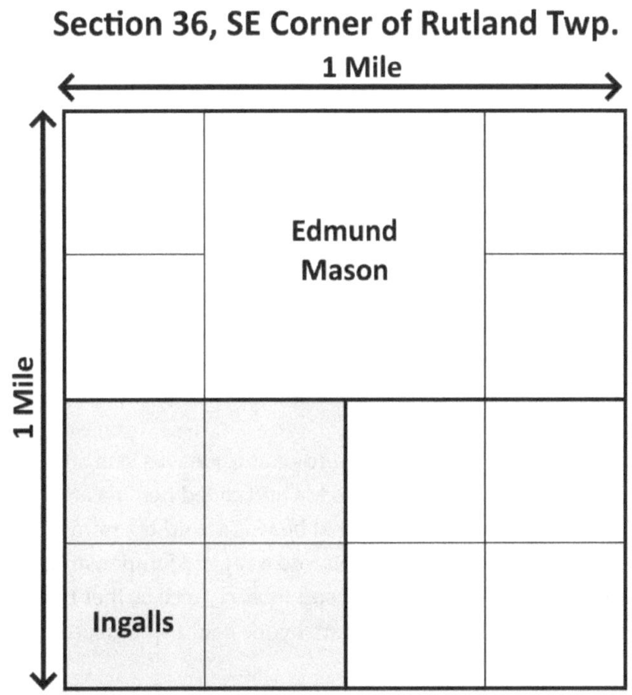

Figure 32 - Section 36 of Rutland Twp., showing the location of Edmund Mason's land and approximate location of the Ingalls family.

But how could this parcel be the one Laura so clearly described in *LHOTP*? The one that was two miles away and across a creek? It just didn't seem to fit. We puzzled over it before pushing on to other clues to see if we could piece it all together.

Did Edmund Mason Match Laura's Description of Mr. Edwards?

With Edmund Mason's birth, emigration, and eventual settlement in Montgomery County verified, we returned to Laura's early drafts and descriptions for clues to either confirm or preclude Mason as a possible "Mr. Edwards" candidate.

In *LHOTP*, the first encounter with Mr. Edwards that Laura wrote about was when he helped Pa build the family cabin. She described the encounter in chapter 5, "The House on the Prairie":

> They had a neighbor, only two miles away on the other side of the creek. Pa had met him in the woods. They were going to trade work and that would make it easier for everyone.
>
> 'He's a bachelor,' said Pa, 'and he says he can get along without a house better than you and the girls can. So he's going to help me first. Then as soon as he gets his logs ready, I'll go over and help him.'
>
> ....
>
> Early next morning Mr Edwards came. He was lean and tall and brown. He bowed to Ma and called her 'Ma'am' politely. But he told Laura that he was a wild-cat from Tennessee. He wore tall boots and a ragged jumper, and a coon-skin cap, and he could spit tobacco juice farther than Laura had ever imagined that anyone could spit tobacco juice.
>
> ....
>
> Mr. Edwards said he must go. It was a long way back to his camp on the other side of the woods and the creek. . . . He said a bachelor got mighty lonesome, and he surely had enjoyed this evening of home life.

Was Edmund Mason's physical appearance congruent with Laura's description? We don't have the luxury of photos of most of our suspects, but we do have one of Edmund Mason. Take a look at this portrait of Edmund and his older brother, John:

Figure 33 - Portrait of John and Edmund Mason, undated

When you compare Edmund to John, he does look like he might have been lean and tall. Despite being English, an ethnic group known for pale skin, as a farmer, it's more than possible he was brown and tanned from working outdoors. However, it's unlikely the son of a reasonably affluent farmer from Devon would have "bowed to Ma and called her 'Ma'am,'" That's far more southern (. . . perhaps even Tennessean!) vernacular than English. The term "ma'am," would have been reserved for the Queen and it's unlikely an Englishman would have used it with a non-royal person.

Considering more of Laura's description, it was even more unlikely that an Englishman would have the habit of spitting tobacco juice—chewing tobacco was practically unheard of in England. The most common "alternative" use of tobacco in the mid to late 1800's was in the form of "snuff" (Wing, 2014). Snuff, at least in England, was a powdered form of tobacco you sniffed into your nose. Therefore, spitting tobacco juice was, and remains, a highly unlikely habit for an English son of a fairly well-off farmer to have acquired or practiced.

Similarly, coon-skin caps, along with ragged jumpers, were an unlikely fashion choice for an Englishman of moderate means. Not completely out of the question, of course, but improbable. Especially given the photo we have of Edmund displays a rather refined fashion sense and careful grooming.

So, while Mason could have been tall, thin, and possibly tan, the rest of the descriptors just don't make logical sense. If you add it all together, our "wild-cat from Tennessee" doesn't sound, or look, a lot like this son of a successful Devonshire farmer. Especially if you add in the "corn shuck" beds Mr. Edwards reportedly slept on. Corn was grown far more widely in America than England, and Mason likely grew up sleeping on the typical mattresses stuffed with hay, wool, or horsehair, or even on woven reed mats. These mattresses would have been suspended on a wooden bedframe by straps of either rope or wool.

Before we completely discounted Mason on purely physical considerations, however, we examined Laura's clues further, beginning with his name.

What's in a Name?

One argument in favor of Mason as Mr. Edwards had always been a point of contention for us. It never really seemed logical. When we'd heard people declare Mason *was* Mr. Edwards based on the two men having similar sounding names, it had always seemed like a huge and unreasonable leap. But folks drawing heavily on the Edmund/Edwards name connection seemed to believe the similarity between the two was some sort of obvious proof.

So, quelling our own gut reactions to the presumption of similar sounding names having some sort of import, we asked ourselves a simple question: Was there any way to confirm or discredit the belief that the names Edmund and Mr. Edwards were connected and meant something significant in our quest?

Edmund Mason, though clearly not "Mr. Edwards," *was* frequently referred to as "Ed," "Edward," and even "Edwin." There had been articles published in local newspapers which referred to him as both "Edward" and "Edmund" Mason—sometimes within the same piece! (e.g. *Independence Daily Reporter*, 1906, p. 1). In fact, he was listed as "Edward" in both the 1861 English census as well as the 1900 Federal census of Montgomery County. Also, Mason was frequently known as just "Ed," and is listed as such in the 1870 Federal census. So, it was possible that Laura remembered him being called "Ed" or "Edward" and simply assigned that name to the character in her book.

But there was an issue. A rather large and significant one. One of the problems that arose when we concerned ourselves with the interchangeability of Edmund and Edward, was that it's unlikely Pa would have ever called Mason by his first name at all.

In chapter 9, "Fresh Water to Drink," Pa and Mr. Scott are digging the well. Mr. Scott thinks worrying about gas in the well is foolishness, so he begins digging without checking first. Pa comes out of the cabin and finds Mr. Scott passed out at the bottom of the well.

> The windlass began to creak and Pa began to whistle. Laura and Mary were washing the dishes and Ma was making the big bed, when Pa's whistling stopped. They heard him say, 'Scott!' He shouted, 'Scott! Scott!' Then he called: 'Caroline! Come quick!'

Later, in chapter 19, "Mr. Edwards Meets Santa Claus," we see another example.

> The door-latch rattled and someone said, 'Ingalls! Ingalls!' Pa was stirring up the fire, and when he opened the door Laura saw that it was morning. The outdoors was grey.
>
> 'Great fish-hooks, Edwards! Come in, man! What's happened?' Pa exclaimed.

When Laura depicted Pa speaking about, or to, another male, Pa was always using the man's last name. Mr. Scott and Mr. Edwards were always "Scott" or "Edwards," even when they'd clearly become friends. Likewise, Mr. Edwards and Mr. Scott called Pa "Ingalls" instead of "Charles." The earliest of Laura's drafts, as well as all the published *Little House* books, exemplified this period practice of males referring to each other *only* by their last names.

So, while it's understandable that people see a connection between the similarly-sounding names of Edmund and Edwards, it's actually *very* unlikely to have meaning in this instance. Men called each other by their *last* names at that time and in that place, so Laura might never have even heard Mason's first name . . . and even if she had, she would have heard "Mason" the vast majority of the time. So, to her, he would have been "Mr. Mason" not "Edward" or "Mr. Edward." And there's no way around it, "Mason" sounded nothing like "Edwards." So, the name argument held absolutely no weight.

Trading Work with Pa

Although there's fuzziness regarding exactly when the Ingalls family arrived in Montgomery County, it was definitely sometime in autumn of 1869. As we've noted, Pa was still in Missouri in late August, and he would have needed their cabin built before winter arrived in Kansas. If the Ingalls family had left Chariton County, Missouri, even at the very end of August, they still had about a three-hundred-mile trip down to Rutland Township. At our twelve miles per day average for teams pulling loaded wagons, that meant about a twenty-five day trip with no stops or days off to rest. The likeliest scenario, even if Pa did head out immediately after signing those legal documents in Missouri at the end of August, was that the family arrived as early as the first part of October.

This would have been close to the time Edmund Mason arrived as well, though the exact date isn't clear. If Mason did arrive at the same time, however, as another newcomer to the area, it was certainly reasonable to believe Pa and Edmund Mason could have helped each other build their respective cabins.

But that possible collaboration brought us to consider another clue Laura left us. Pa needed help because Ma became injured and likely couldn't have helped with the heavy tops of the log walls anyway. And if Mr.

Edwards was the bachelor (and, therefore, alone) Laura insisted he was, it made sense he could have used Pa's assistance, as well.

Yet, why would Edmund Mason need to trade work with Pa if at least one of his brothers, John, was living nearby? It's even possible that another brother, Thomas Henry, was also in the area by this time (he appeared with John in the 1870 census). If two, or three, brothers were living near each other, surely they would have helped each other build their homes rather than relying on the help of a stranger, right? Lifting heavy logs was too much for Ma when the walls got too high, so, naturally Pa would have welcomed assistance. But Mason would have already had plenty in the form of his brother(s), so had no need to "trade work."

On the other hand, Mason had only left England in 1867 and hadn't been in the U.S. very long (in North America less than two years), so he likely wouldn't have been familiar with the process of building log structures. He hadn't settled anywhere long enough to have built himself one by that point. Additionally, he was raised on a farm, not in a family of carpenters. And no English dwellings were made using this method of construction. For similar reasons, it's unlikely that John or Thomas Henry had any more cabin-building knowledge than Edmund, though John's longer time in the U.S. certainly could have meant he'd learned log construction methods along the way. Even so, though Mason might not have been much expert help to Pa, it was reasonable for Edmund to have wanted the help of an experienced carpenter and pioneering cabin builder such as Pa.

Because Pa was a very capable carpenter, he probably only needed an extra pair of hands and a little muscle from someone who could work hard and follow directions. Edmund Mason, at twenty-four years old, was nearly ten years Pa's junior, so it's feasible Pa was happy to trade his experience and practical knowledge for Edmund's youth and physical strength. From Edmund's perspective, not only would he have had someone to help him build his own cabin, but Pa would also have been in a position to teach him the valuable skills of how to do it.

Still, the likelier scenario was that Pa, who would have been in a hurry to get a roof and walls up to protect his family from weather and other dangers, would have opted for someone more experienced to give him a hand. And Edmund Mason would have likely enlisted the help of his brothers rather than a stranger when he built his own home. We can't forget that there were a lot more "neighbors" around than Laura had led us to believe, too. So, Pa had a lot of options of who to ask for help.

And, of course, all this assumed Edmund Mason was actually living on his section 36 parcel at the right time to help build the Ingallses' cabin. And that assumption was not as clear cut as we first believed.

Living Two Miles Away on the Other Side of the Woods and Creek

The location clue Laura left us was important. When Edmund Mason and the Ingallses lived in the same section 36, in the southeasternmost section of Rutland Township, they were in very close proximity. The furthest away Mason could have lived was less than one and a half miles away from the Ingallses' (furthest corner to furthest corner of their lands). However, later maps of Rutland Township indicated Edmund Mason's residence was probably less than a mile from the location of the Ingalls cabin.

Laura wrote that Mr. Edwards said it was "a long way back to his camp." And she also wrote he lived two miles across a creek and beyond woods. A child her age would have had no way of determining distances, even if she remembered overhearing or seeing them when she was two, which was her age at the time the cabin was being built. So, she probably heard those statements of distance and location from her parents when she was much older. Obviously, adults would have been far more accurate about such things and, therefore, more reliable. It was logical to assume, then, the location of Mr. Edwards' land, two miles across a creek and beyond woods, was fairly accurate. Mason's section 36 parcel, therefore, was too close.

Other researchers had discovered several of Laura's other estimations of distances regarding the area weren't always accurate. For example, in *LHOTP,* she described Independence as being forty miles away, whereas, in reality, it was only about ten miles. This mistake was largely due to her initial misbelief that the little house was in Indian Territory, which was, indeed, roughly forty miles away in Oklahoma (*see* Foreman, 1933, pp. 8–11; McFarland, 1933, p. 22).

However, assuming in this instance that Laura's estimate (of how far Mr. Edwards' house was from her own) was somewhat accurate, based on later conversations with adults who would have been more accurate about such things, Mason's home could have been in any part of an area including, at least in part, sections 22-27 & 34-36 of Rutland Twp, sections 1-3 & 10-12 of Caney Twp. (due south of Rutland Twp.), sections 19-20 & 29-32 of Independence Twp. (due east of Rutland), and sections 5-8 of Fawn Creek Twp. (southeast of Rutland). In a minute, we'll discuss why the Independence Township area came into sharp focus.

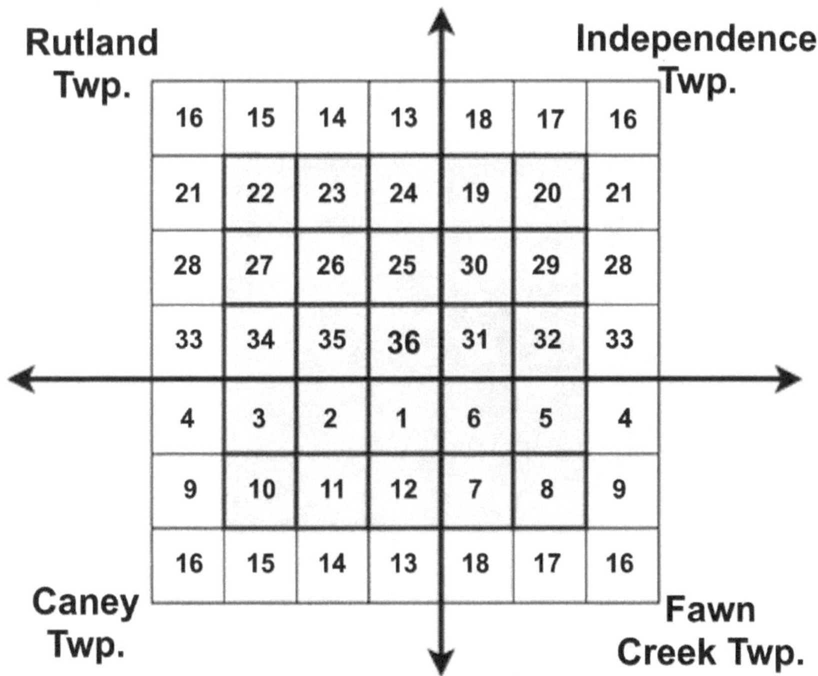

Figure 34 - Townships and Sections (shaded) within two miles of the Ingallses' cabin in section 36

Two creeks (Walnut Creek and another small tributary of Onion Creek) ran through Mason's section 36 land (though the original survey from 1871 showed just one). And whether he lived on the "other side" of either of these waterways was another matter. Later atlases of Montgomery County show his dwelling as being on the Ingallses' side of the creeks, but, of course, he hadn't yet built his house when he first secured the land. So, it's plausible he could have started with a shanty or a camp in one location and built a proper home later in another, like the Ingallses did when they arrived at Plum Creek. They lived first in the dugout for a year and then built their frame house later in another location on their property.

According to *The 1881 Atlas,* there was a third creek that passed into the area of the Ingalls land (the SW quarter of section 36) but it didn't need to be crossed when heading to Mason's, and was a very small creek anyway. The largest creek in the area was Onion Creek, which both Mason and the Ingallses would have needed to cross to reach Independence. However, it wasn't between the Ingallses' land and Ed Mason's.

Figure 35 - Walnut Creek flowing through Edmund Mason's land in section 36, Rutland Twp.

Also, full "woods" at the time were located in close proximity to rivers and creeks, so if there were no significant creeks between their properties, it's unlikely there were any real woods, either. Laura confirmed this herself in "The House on the Prairie" chapter:

> All around them there was nothing but grassy prairie spreading to the edge of the sky.
>
> Quite near them, to the north, the creek bottoms lay below the prairie. Some darker green tree-tops showed, and beyond them bits of the rim of earthen bluffs held up the prairie's grasses. Far away to the east, a broken line of different greens lay on the prairie, and Pa said that was the river.
>
> 'That's the Verdigris River,' he said, pointing it out to Ma.

Laura then mentioned, twice, how Pa gathered the logs for their cabin from the creek bottoms. Comparing historic maps with current maps and aerial photography showing the locations of the various creeks in the area and the Verdigris River, Laura was almost certainly describing Onion Creek as the source of those logs, which lay beyond Edmund Mason's land. A local newspaper article of the period described Onion Creek as having "[a] belt of heavy timber which lines the Creek throughout almost its whole extent" (*South Kansas Tribune*, 1871e, p. 1). Furthermore, "[w]hen the first settlers arrived, they took note of stands of timber along the Verdigris and Elk Rivers, on Onion . . . and Clear Creeks. In some places, the forest trees were of enormous growth. Many . . . were made into . . . lumber, with some being three to four feet in diameter" (Harper, 1988, p. 22,24). Onion Creek and the Verdigris River would have been the two most prominent waterways visible from the little house.

However, a reasonably large tributary of Onion Creek, called Walnut Creek, ran diagonally from southwest to northeast through the north-western quarter of section 36, and across part of Edmund Mason's land. This creek was also lined with trees (not exactly a "wood," but there were trees) and was only about one half to three fourths of a mile away to the north of the little house site, so this could possibly have been the creek Laura was referring to. While it's true that later maps of the area depict Edmund Mason's home on the Ingallses' side of this creek, we can't discount that he could have had a first home/shanty on the other side of it. It does seem odd that Laura would have described some trees along a small creek as "woods," though. And, you didn't have to cross Walnut Creek to get to Mason's land unless you wanted to.

Thus, Edmund Mason's section 36 property just didn't match Laura's description of Mr. Edward's location. It was too close, the creeks didn't correspond with Laura's description, and there didn't seem to be a stand of trees large enough to be called a "wood" between Mason and the Ingallses. If we added all those issues to the others we'd already noted, it was easy to completely cross him off our list as at least a "full" Mr. Edwards.

But . . .

Even though the section 36 location of his farm was well established in various documents, and most researchers had presumed that's where he was living when the Ingallses arrived, we came upon some information that made us ask an entirely different question: What if that "too close and not really geographically congruent with Laura's description" property wasn't where he was actually living at the time? What if he settled on section 36 or purchased that land *after* the Ingalls family had left Kansas or, at least, sometime well after their arrival?

Or, more to our eventual discoveries, what if Mason claimed *two* pieces of land at the same time?

A nugget of information we found begged those questions to be answered and, frankly, threw a mind-blowing twist into our investigation.

On the *BLM GLO Database* web site, we found the only *federal* land patent issued to Edmund Mason (there is a *state* patent for his section 36 parcel, however). This federal patent, issued in October of 1873, was for 37.78 acres and was comprised of the northwest quarter of the northwest quarter, section 30, township 33 south, range 15 east of the 6th Principal Meridian. The land, being clearly laid out in the northwest (top left) corner of section 30 on the original survey plat map (see Figure 36 on page 139), was in a particularly interesting position relating to the Ingallses, as well as Independence, which we'll get to in a moment.

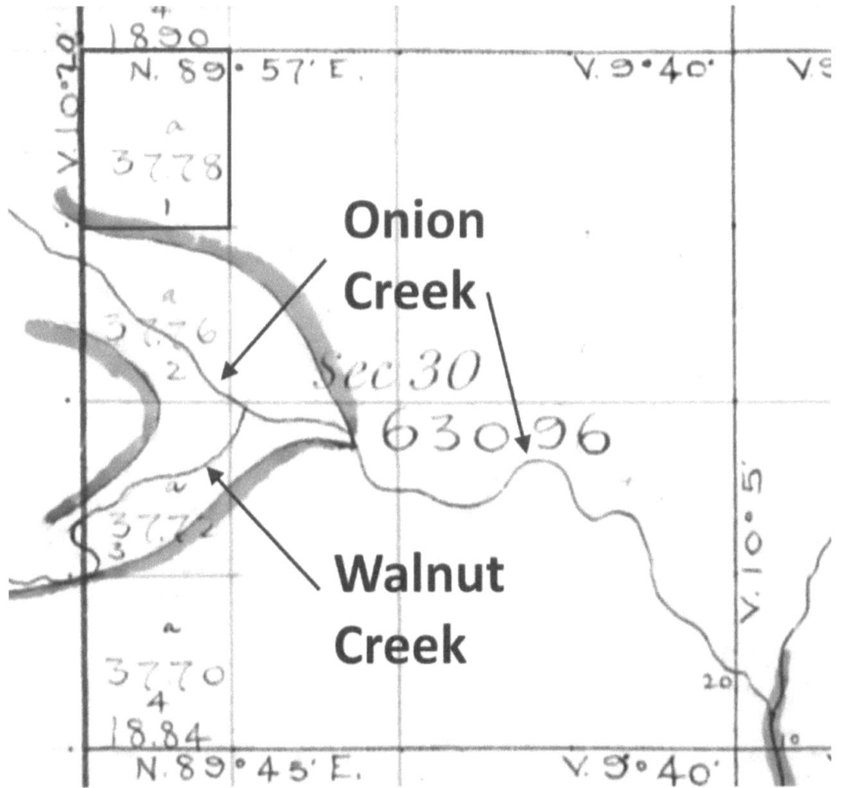

Figure 36 - Portion of the original 1871 survey plat map showing section 30 in T33S-R15E.

266

Osage Trust Land

THE UNITED STATES OF AMERICA,

CERTIFICATE
No. 5022

To all to whom these presents shall come, Greeting:

Whereas Edmund Mason, of Montgomery County, Kansas,

has deposited in the GENERAL LAND OFFICE of the United States, a Certificate of the REGISTER OF THE LAND OFFICE at Independence, Kansas, whereby it appears that full payment has been made by the said Edmund Mason,

according to the provisions of the Act of Congress of the 24th of April, 1820, entitled "An act making further provision for the sale of the Public Lands," for and the Act of the 15th of July 1870, for the North West quarter of the North West quarter, of Section Thirty, in Township Thirty three, South of Range Fifteen East, in the District of lands subject to sale at Independence, Kansas, containing Thirty seven acres and twenty eight hundredths of an acre,

according to the official plat of the Survey of the said Lands, returned to the General Land Office by the SURVEYOR GENERAL, which said tract has been purchased by the said Edmund Mason,

NOW KNOW YE, That the United States of America, in consideration of the premises, and in conformity with the several acts of Congress in such case made and provided, HAVE GIVEN AND GRANTED, and by these presents DO GIVE AND GRANT, unto the said Edmund Mason,

and to his heirs, the said tract above described: To have and to hold the same, together with all the rights, privileges, immunities, and appurtenances, of whatsoever nature, thereunto belonging, unto the said Edmund Mason,

and to his heirs and assigns forever.

In Testimony Whereof, I, Ulysses S. Grant

PRESIDENT OF THE UNITED STATES OF AMERICA, have caused these Letters to be made PATENT, and the SEAL of the GENERAL LAND OFFICE to be hereunto affixed.

GIVEN under my hand, at the CITY OF WASHINGTON, the first day of October in the year of our Lord one thousand eight hundred and seventy three and of the INDEPENDENCE OF THE UNITED STATES the Ninety eighth.

BY THE PRESIDENT: U.S. Grant

By S.D. Williamson Secretary.

L.K. Lippincott Recorder of the General Land Office.

Figure 37 - Federal patent granted to Edmund Mason for NW1/4 NW1/4 S30-T33S-R15E 6th P.M.

Records from the courthouse in Independence, Kansas, revealed Edmund's payment of $47.23 for this land ($1.25 per acre × 37.78 acres) was received in September of 1872, and officially recorded October 2, 1872, in Independence. Interestingly, the very next day, October 3, 1872, Edmund sold this land to John Craig for $175.00, making a profit of just over $127 (Montgomery Co., KS, Reg. of Deeds, 1872).

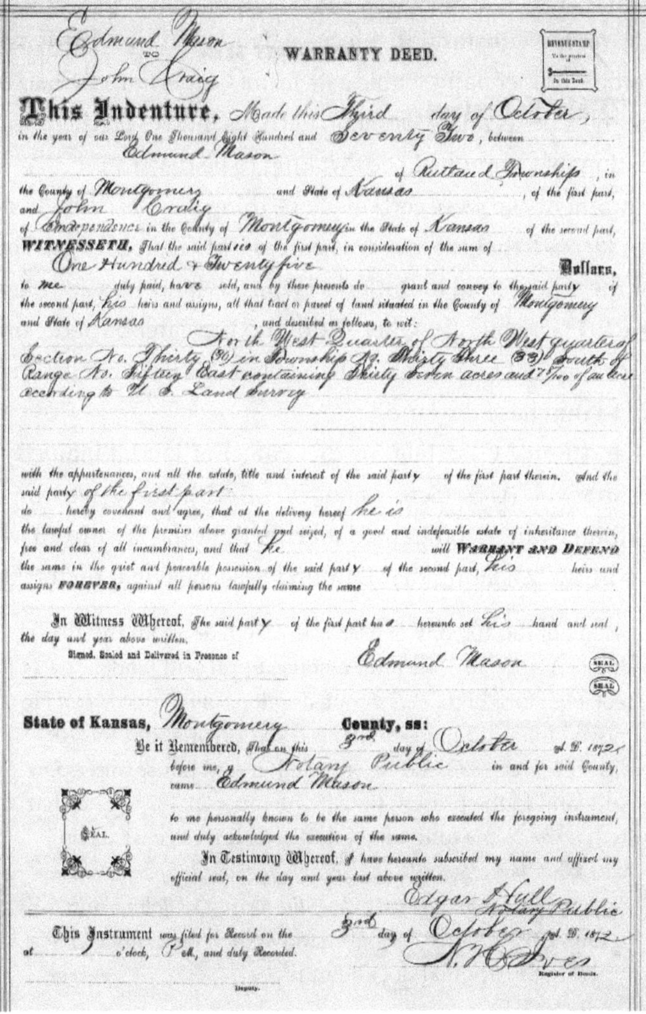

Edmund Mason
to
John Craig

WARRANTY DEED.

This Indenture, Made this Third day of October, in the year of our Lord One Thousand Eight Hundred and Seventy Two, between Edmund Mason of Rutland Township, in the County of Montgomery and State of Kansas, of the first part, and John Craig of Independence in the County of Montgomery in the State of Kansas of the second part,

WITNESSETH, That the said parties of the first part, in consideration of the sum of One Hundred & Twenty five Dollars, to me duly paid, have sold, and by these presents do grant and convey to the said party of the second part, his heirs and assigns, all that tract or parcel of land situated in the County of Montgomery and State of Kansas, and described as follows, to wit:

North West Quarter of North West quarter of Section No. Thirty (30) in Township No. Thirty three (33) South of Range No. Fifteen East containing Thirty seven acres and 78/100 of an acre according to U. S. Land Survey

with the appurtenances, and all the estate, title and interest of the said party of the first part therein. And the said party of the first part do hereby covenant and agree, that at the delivery hereof he is the lawful owner of the premises above granted and seized, of a good and indefeasible estate of inheritance therein, free and clear of all incumbrances, and that he will WARRANT AND DEFEND the same in the quiet and peaceable possession of the said party of the second part, his heirs and assigns FOREVER, against all persons lawfully claiming the same.

In Witness Whereof, The said party of the first part has hereunto set his hand and seal, the day and year above written.

Signed, Sealed and Delivered in Presence of

Edmund Mason (SEAL)

(SEAL)

State of Kansas, Montgomery **County, ss:**

Be it Remembered, That on this 3rd day of October A. D. 1872 before me, a Notary Public in and for said County, came Edmund Mason to me personally known to be the same person who executed the foregoing instrument, and duly acknowledged the execution of the same.

SEAL.

In Testimony Whereof, I have hereunto subscribed my name and affixed my official seal, on the day and year last above written.

Edgar Hull
Notary Public

This Instrument was filed for Record on the 3rd day of October A. D. 1872 at 1 o'clock, P M., and duly Recorded.

N. H. Ives
Register of Deeds.

Deputy.

Figure 38 - Warranty Deed: Edmund Mason to John Craig

This piece of land was sold a year before the actual patent was issued in Edmund's name (a typical occurrence as process times were often very slow) and well over a year after the Ingallses had returned to the big woods of Wisconsin. Why did he purchase and sell this land within a day? Perhaps John Craig didn't have a right to purchase land under the current land laws, such as length of settlement or age, and used Mason to acquire it on his behalf. Perhaps Mason had been living there, but wanted to move to another, more substantial, piece of land. This parcel wasn't large enough to be commercially viable as a farm. Or perhaps he had only ever purchased the land as an investment. Perhaps, however, there were other, more questionable, circumstances waiting to be discovered.

For the moment, we were certain of one thing . . . Mason owned the land in section 30, and that, alone, was important. Don't forget this patent wasn't for the school land in Rutland Twp., *this* land was in Independence Twp., close to Harrisonville, where Edmund was later buried. And to have qualified for this federal patent, he had to have *settled* on it before he could even *apply* to purchase the land.

In the Land Entry Case File for this parcel of land, obtained from the National Archives (U.S. Gen. Land Off., 1873), there was an affidavit signed by John Craig (who immediately bought the land from Mason) on September 21, 1872, stating that Edmund Mason settled on the land . . .

> . . . about the *10th* day of *March* 1872. On or about the 10th day of *March,* 1872 he built a house upon said land *12* by *14* feet, *one* story high, *Board* roof, *one* door, *no* window *and* He moved into said house with *his effects* on or about the *10th* day of *March* 1872 and has resided in said house and upon said land to the present time [September 21 1872], and that he has made the following additional improvements on said land: *has plowed [ ] in cultivation about [8?] acres of land, has a fence built on the east side of the forty.* / s/ *John Craig* (Craig, 1872) (Italics denotes handwritten text, other text is typed in the original document.)

Edmund's brother John also signed an affidavit acknowledging that the testimony of John Craig was "substantially correct" (Mason, 1872). At first glance, this seemed to discredit any relevance to our search. All these dates were after the Ingallses had left Kansas. And it was sworn to by not one, but two, men.

But not all such legal documents were accurate. As Laura pointed out in her own writings, some men on the frontier filed for claims or purchased land following all the rules. Other men, however, didn't. Some "played" the system to acquire land and the associated wealth. Was Mason one of these? The clues started to come together.

Despite seeming proof that Mason's section 30 land came into play too late to be of note, we couldn't shake the feeling that it was somehow important. Why? Its location was, effectively, identical to Laura's description: *almost exactly* two miles away from the little house site, *on the other side of Onion Creek* (as is clearly shown on the original plat map), *on the other side of a wood,* and *on the way to Independence.* Current aerial photographs confirm the area around Onion Creek is quite heavily wooded, too, just as Laura described. As trees grew near water sources, it's more than likely these woods would have been present at the time Edmund Mason patented this land. So, all the descriptors Laura used for Mr. Edwards land and its location just seemed to perfectly fit with this parcel of Mason's.

But was Edmund living on this land when the Ingalls family arrived in Kansas, which would coordinate with Laura's writings? Or did he just happen to purchase the parcel in addition to his land in Rutland Township? And did he obtain the Rutland Township land after selling the Independence Township land? It was important to find out what the historical records would reveal.

According to the patent for his section 30 property, he purchased the land under an Act of Congress, dated July 15, 1870 - Removal of Osage from Kansas - 16 Stat. 335, section 12. Do you remember the Indian Appropriation Bill we explained in an earlier chapter? This is when it comes into play. That Act governed the sale of the land of the Osage Diminished Reserve and required purchasers be "actual settlers only, said settlers being heads of families or over twenty-one years of age . . . ."

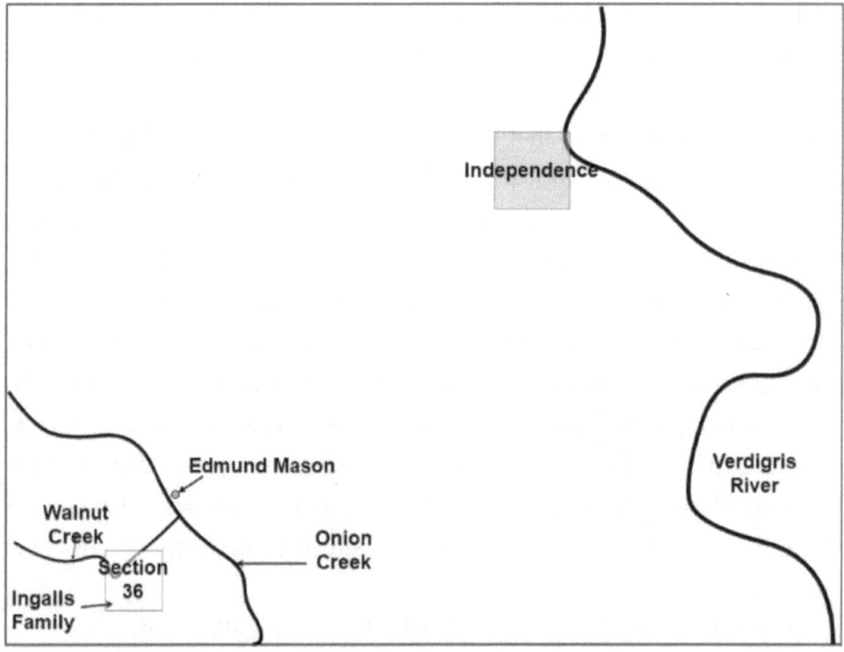

Figure 39 - Map showing locations of the Ingalls property and Edmund Mason's land in Independence Twp., and the approximate courses of Walnut Creek, Onion Creek, and the Verdigris River

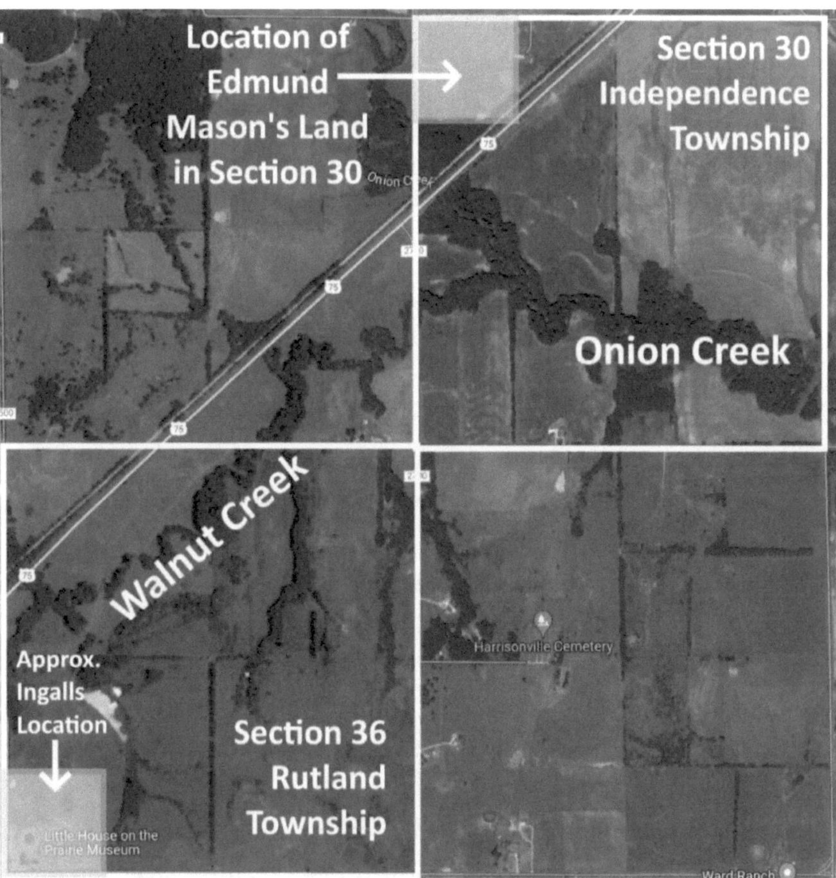

Figure 40 - Google Maps Satellite View from 2023 showing the locations of Walnut Creek, Onion Creek, Edmund Mason's land in Independence Twp., & the Ingalls family. Used with permission of Google. (Imagery ©2023 CNES / Airbus, Maxar Technologies, USDA/FFPAC/GEO)

Daniel Mulford Valentine, Associate Justice of the Supreme Court of Kansas, in an 1877 case, *Brake v. Ballou* (19 Kas. 397), explained who could actually purchase land there:

> Under this statute no one but an "actual settler" could purchase any of said land . . . [t]he government evidently intended not only that no one but actual settlers should get any portion of said Osage Diminished Reserve, but also that every quarter-section of such reserve *should be occupied by an actual settler*. There is no pretense that the plaintiff was ever an actual settler at all on the land in controversy. *Therefore he had no right himself to purchase said land from the government*. . . . If he could obtain title to lands [by fraud] it would be to cause the government to sell its lands to others than actual settlers in violation of its own laws. (*Brake v. Ballou*, 1877) (Our emphasis.)

The text of the governing Act, as clarified by this case from the Supreme Court of Kansas, made it abundantly clear that anyone, Edmund Mason included, wishing to purchase land in the Osage Diminished Reserve, must have "actually settled" on and occupied the land in order to legally purchase it. So, he had to have settled on, and occupied, this land prior to September of 1872, the date the Land Entry Case File noted the purchase. Being an "actual settler" implied both a significant length of time in residence, and improvements to the land. This had the potential of supporting the theory Mason had been living there at the time the Ingallses arrived rather than on his section 36 property.

But his section 36 land had its claims, too. Beyond the fact that the land was located within the Osage Diminished Reserve, this parcel had other parameters attached. It was in a "school" section and, therefore, had to be obtained differently than other sections. As we've mentioned, most western states reserved sections 16 and 36 for school land, which could not be homesteaded or preempted in the usual manner. Kansas was no different. The sale of school lands was governed by the provisions of an act of the Legislature of the State of Kansas approved on February 22, 1864, and entitled "An act to provide for the sale of School lands" as amended by later acts. This was handled separately from the federal land patents, such as Mason's section 30 parcel. Under the laws of Kansas at that time:

> Any person who has settled upon and improved any portion of school lands prior to the appraisement, may, within sixty days from its appraisement, file in the probate court of his county a petition, stating that he has settled upon and improved said lands; that the same have been appraised, and the amount of the appraisement, and asking that he be allowed to purchase the same. (Zabriskie, 1870, p. 734; Dassler, 1876, p. 934)

Once the petition was approved and the purchase price fully paid by the settler, the State of Kansas would issue a patent in the buyer's name. Edmund's patent wasn't issued until 1881, a full ten years after the Ingallses left Kansas, though his purchase date was February 24, 1872, nine years prior to receiving his patent.

Edmund's petition could not be located in Independence, nor at the Kansas State Historical Society, but we do know from the terms of the patent that he paid for the land in installments, with interest on his payments, and the purchase price was $560. The amount of land was 160 acres in the eastern half of the NW quarter and the western half of the NE quarter of section 36. The patent was recorded on the 24th of May in 1881, just eleven days after his final installment was paid.

Records of his payments are still available and, when they were recorded, the County thankfully noted the date of sale of the land. In Edmund's case, the land was sold to him on February 24, 1872, and he paid for it in nine installments, the final payment being in the amount of $226.25, with $24.65 of that sum being interest. This last payment seemed particularly high given the overall cost of the property, but that's what the records showed (Montgomery Co., KS, Clerk's Off., 1881).

But, if he had been "actually settling" on this section 36 piece of *state*-administered land in order to qualify to purchase the land in February of 1872, how could he also have been "actually settling" on the section 30 piece of *federally*-administered land in order to qualify to purchase it in

March of 1872? Something didn't add up. Mason couldn't have been in two places at once!

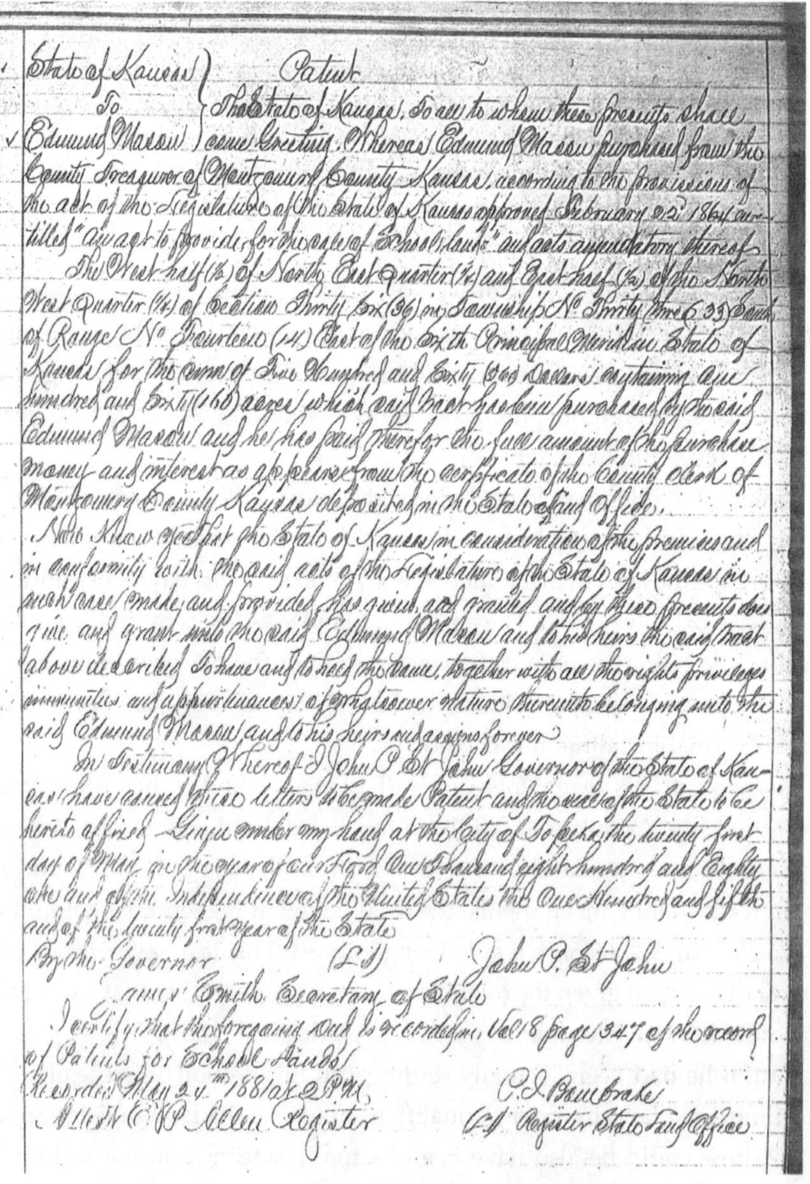
State of Kansas To Edmund Mason — Patent

The State of Kansas, To all to whom these presents shall come Greeting. Whereas Edmund Mason purchased from the County Treasurer of Montgomery County Kansas, according to the provisions of the act of the Legislature of the State of Kansas approved February 22 1864 entitled "an act to provide for the sale of School lands" and acts amendatory thereof

The West half (½) of North East quarter (¼) and East half (½) of the North West Quarter (¼) of Section Thirty Six (36) in Township No Thirty three (33) South of Range No Fourteen (14) East of the Sixth Principal Meridian State of Kansas for the sum of Five Hundred and Sixty (560) Dollars containing One hundred and Sixty (160) acres which said tract has been purchased by the said Edmund Mason and he has paid therefor the full amount of the purchase money and interest as appears from the certificate of the County Clerk of Montgomery County Kansas deposited in the State Land Office.

Now Know ye that the State of Kansas in consideration of the premises and in conformity with the said acts of the Legislature of the State of Kansas in such case made and provided has given and granted and by these presents does give and grant unto the said Edmund Mason and to his heirs the said tract above described To have and to hold the same, together with all the rights privileges immunities and appurtenances of whatsoever nature thereunto belonging unto the said Edmund Mason and to his heirs and assigns forever

In Testimony Whereof I John P. St John Governor of the State of Kansas have caused these letters to be made Patent and the seal of the State to be hereto affixed Given under my hand at the City of Topeka the twenty first day of May in the year of our Lord One thousand eight hundred and Eighty one and of the Independence of the United States the One Hundred and fifth and of the twenty first year of the State

By the Governor (L.S.) John P. St John

James Smith Secretary of State

I certify that the foregoing deed is recorded in Vol 8 page 347 of the record of Patents for School Lands

Recorded May 24th 1881 at 2 P.M.

C. J. Bembrake

Attest C. P. Allen Register

C.J. Register State Land Office

Figure 41 - Edmund Mason's State Patent

We found a possible answer in an unlikely spot. The agricultural schedule of the 1875 Kansas state census gave us a very important clue. This schedule detailed the number of acres of winter wheat or rye each farmer planted in the fall of 1874, the acreage of crops planted in 1875, and the total acreage of the farm. It contained entries for both Edmund and his brother, John, who arrived in Montgomery County about the same time. As they presumably settled on their land at about the same time, too, you'd assume they would have made fairly equal progress in the establishment of their farms.

The 1875 schedule indicated Edmund Mason then had 160 acres, which was the amount of land we know he owned in section 36 of Rutland Township. He didn't sow any winter wheat or rye in the fall of 1874 and had only planted ten acres of crops in 1875 (six of corn and four of Irish potatoes). On that same schedule, his brother, John, planted fifteen acres of winter wheat in fall 1874 and thirty acres of corn in 1875. Two years' worth of crops equaled only ten acres for Edmund, but forty-five for John.

Edmund had 150 rods (825 yards, just less than a half mile) of rail fencing, as compared to John's 320 (1,760 yards or 1 mile). He also owned $25 worth of farm equipment, compared to John's $40 worth, and had paid no wages for farm help during the year, compared to John's $50.

This data implied Mason was in the fairly early stages of establishing his farm during 1874 and 1875, as compared to his older brother. If he had arrived, and settled, on his section 36 piece of Kansas state land well prior to its purchase date of February 1872, why would he be so far behind his brother, who arrived at the exact same time Edmund did?

The evidence suggested one thing: Edmund might have purchased his section 36 piece of land earlier, but it doesn't appear he actually relocated there and started farming until about 1872–73, which was well after the Ingallses had left Kansas.

The almost parallel purchases of land, one from the state of Kansas, and the other from the federal government, seemed to point to only one conclusion: Edmund Mason had played the system. By claiming he "actually settled" two pieces of land at roughly the same time, he was probably banking on the separate state and federal processes to avoid detection. By what appears to be some less-than-accurate statements from his brother and the purchaser of his section 30 land, he was able to "double dip" with two properties.

John Craig and John Mason attested to Edmund having "settled" on his section 30 parcel in March of 1872, which is after his section 36 purchase date in February of 1872. This, technically, made it possible for Edmund to have bought his section 36 property and then immediately "settle" on the section 30 property. But that just didn't add up. You couldn't own a property you have settled and also be an "actual settler" elsewhere at the same time. So, clearly, something was afoot.

Further digging in the National Archives revealed an instructional letter from Willis Drummond, Commissioner of the General Land Office, which helped clarify the situation (Drummond and U.S. Dept. of the Interior, 1871, pp. 4–5). To summarize, anyone who had settled on their claim *before* the act of July 15, 1870, was only given until July 15, *1871,* to prove up and pay for the claim. Otherwise, you were given a year from your date of settlement *and* that date of settlement had to be after the date the land was surveyed. Mason's section 30 land was surveyed March 5–9, 1871, and approved by the Surveyor General's Office June 9, 1871. So, Mason couldn't have given a date of settlement before March (or maybe June) 1871 without forfeiting the land, and the later his specified date, the later he could prove up and pay. So, the date of settlement specified in his file, and affirmed by Craig and John Mason, was unlikely to reflect the real date of settlement at all.

Given Mason's actual settlement in section 30 by at least 1872, but probably earlier, and that he really hadn't established any significant farming operation on his section 36 land until around 1875, *and* the fact that his section 30 property fit Laura's description of Mr. Edwards' land perfectly, we had to come to one conclusion: If Edmund Mason was any part of our Tennessee Wildcat, he was almost certainly living on his land in section 30 when the Ingalls family arrived in Montgomery County.

Ironically, while our research all but debunked the notion Mason was living on his section 36 property when the Ingallses arrived, that fact doesn't make him less likely to have at least a sliver of the Mr. Edwards character . . . it actually made him slightly more likely! If nothing else, he was living right where Laura said Mr. Edwards lived.

The plot thickened.

Mr. Edwards as Santa's Helper

With Mason's likeliest location in fall of 1869 determined, we looked for other ways to connect him to "Mr. Edwards." We turned again to the Christmas story.

> . . . she heard Mr Edwards say he had carried his clothes on his head when he swam the creek. His teeth rattled and his voice quivered. He would be all right, he said, as soon as he got warm. . . . 'Your little ones had to have a Christmas,' Mr Edwards replied. 'No creek could stop me, after I fetched them their gifts from Independence.'
>
> . . . .
>
> So Santa Claus said, 'Hello Edwards! Last time I saw you, you were sleeping on a corn-shuck bed in Tennessee.' And Mr. Edwards well remembered the little pair of red-yarn mittens that Santa Claus had left for him that time.

This heart-warming Christmas chapter progressed in beautiful detail. Laura described how Mr. Edwards brought the family nine sweet potatoes from Independence, how he stayed for dinner, and, along with Ma and Pa, "sat by the fire and talked about Christmas times back in Tennessee and up north in the Big Woods."

This story reiterated the Tennessee origins of Mr. Edwards and implied his ongoing bachelor status as he didn't seem to have any family to spend the holiday with. We'd already established Mason's likeliest location would have put him across a significant creek from the Ingallses, but would Edmund Mason have chosen to spend Christmas with the Ingalls family in 1870? After a year living somewhat nearby, being less than two miles away no matter which property he was living on, they certainly could have been considered neighbors, and maybe even friends.

But, by this time, both John, and another of Edmund's brothers, Thomas Henry, were living in the area. It's unlikely Edmund would have chosen to spend Christmas with his neighbors rather than his brothers. If Edmund Mason was really our Christmas Mr. Edwards, and was close enough to have done the Ingalls family such a sweet, albeit dangerous, favor, wouldn't the Ingallses have known his brothers, too? Wouldn't they have invited *all* the Mason brothers to celebrate Christmas with them? If not, would Edmund have abandoned his brothers on the holiday?

And what about the grown-ups talking about Christmases past? Was Laura simply trying to make the story more interesting by turning Mr. Edwards into a "Tennessee wild-cat" who had slept on a corn-shuck bed and received red yarn mittens? If so, why would a story of a childhood in Tennessee be more interesting than if the very English Edmund Mason had been reminiscing with Ma and Pa "about Christmas times back in [England] and up north in the Big Woods?" It didn't seem likely that even a young Laura, or her adult parents in later discussions about Mr. Edwards, would have ignored his English origins, does it? It would seem stories from another country would hold as much, if not more, interest than those of a nearby state.

So, while Mason did live across a creek from the Ingallses, just about every other detail about this story didn't add up. Our conclusion? Mason very likely wasn't the hero of the Christmas story.

Going Out

Our final chance to connect Edmund Mason with Mr. Edwards was via Laura's story near the end of *LHOTP*, recounted in chapter 25, "Soldiers." It described how Pa decided to leave Kansas rather than being forced to leave by soldiers:

> Mr Scott started to speak, but Pa stopped him. 'Save your breath, Scott. It's no use to say another word. You can stay till the soldiers come if you want to. I'm going out now.'

> Mr Edwards said he was going too. He would not stay to be driven across the line like an ornery yellow hound.
>
> 'Ride out to Independence with us, Edwards,' Pa said. But Mr Edwards answered that he didn't care to go north. He would make a boat and go on down the river to some settlement farther south.
>
> 'Better come with us,' Pa urged him, 'and go down on foot through Missouri. . . . .
>
> But Mr Edwards said he had already seen Missouri . . .
>
> . . . .
>
> Mary said politely, 'Good-bye, Mr Edwards.' But Laura forgot to be polite. She said: 'Oh, Mr Edwards, I wish you wouldn't go away! Oh, Mr Edwards, thank you, thank you for going all the way to Independence to find Santa Claus for us.'

There were a few noteworthy points in this account, the most important being that Mr. Edwards left at the same time as the Ingallses. This may, of course, have simply been fiction, or a literary device aimed at amping up the drama. Or even a way of making it technically possible Mr. Edwards could reappear in later books. Laura did admit in her notes and letters that the story of Mr. Edwards helping Pa secure the De Smet claim wasn't true. Later, she had him briefly reappear once more, when the family was in De Smet, and assigned him the story of giving Mary $20 for college (Wilder, 2016, pp. 210-211,167).

Additionally, there was one phrase within this dialog that was particularly noteworthy: "an ornery yellow hound." The word "ornery" is an American word that English people did not use (Osmond, 2017). The English also rarely use the word "hound," except when talking about fox or hare hunting (as with horses and hounds). In most other cases, an Englishman would use the word "dog." But he wouldn't use the word "ornery." Admittedly, Edmund Mason had been in North America for about three to four years by this time, so he could have picked up some American vernacular, but it's unlikely this phrase would ever have been naturally spoken by a born-and-bred Englishman.

Other points of interest from this section were that the person Laura described here was the same person who met Santa Claus in Independence, which we've established was almost certainly not Mason. Also, his leaving Kansas by himself in this scene confirmed both his bachelorhood, and his apparent "aloneness." With Mason's brothers settled nearby, and the fact that he stayed in the area until his death, this clue definitely didn't fit.

Also important to consider was this: when Laura wrote about their leaving Kansas in *Pioneer Girl,* she gave quite a different account than the one that ended up in *LHOTP*. She didn't mention Mr. Edwards (or any other "Mr.") by name at all. Though she did briefly mention soldiers, she provided a different reason for their returning to Wisconsin:

> Soon after this Pa put the cover on the wagon again and hitched Pet and Patty to it. Then he and Ma took everything out of the house and put it in the wagon. Then we all got in the wagon and . . . drove away leaving our little house standing empty and lonely on the prairie. The soldiers were taking all the white people off the Indian's land.
>
> . . . .
>
> All the neighbors went with us for a while, then they scattered but we went on to Missouri.
>
> . . . .
>
> After driving for days and days . . . we came at last to the place we had left when we went west. The land was Pa's again because the man who bought it from him had not paid for it.

Summary

What did all this mean when we looked at Edmund Mason as a possible candidate for a full, or even partial, match for Laura's Mr. Edwards? Any kind of substantial case really doesn't hold together, does it?

The Edmund/Edwards name connection fell apart quickly. Men in those days used last names to address each other as is evidenced throughout

Laura's writing. And the names Mason and Edwards are not easily confused.

And, unfortunately, the location of Mason's land in section 30, wasn't substantial enough to make any real claim. Although this is, perhaps, the single closest "match" to our Tennessee Wildcat's list of clues, this one item just isn't enough to stand up against all the facts that discount Mason from at least full contention as Mr. Edwards.

Thinking about possibly helping Pa build the cabin, it wasn't probable the son of an established Devonshire farmer would have had the skills to build and American-style log cabin.

Also, while Mason was a bachelor during this time, he certainly wasn't alone. His brothers were there, too. Leaving family on a holiday to spend the day with very recent acquaintances doesn't feel plausible.

Physically, he could have been a match. But most homesteaders would have shared many physical characteristics: suntanned from working outdoors, lean from physical labor, roughened hands, etc. So, even this wasn't remotely convincing evidence.

It was also incredibly unlikely an English son of a successful farmer would have possessed the language, terms, mannerisms, habits (particularly spitting tobacco juice), or garb Laura described in enthusiastic detail.

And it was all but impossible that family stories told later could mix up an Englishman, with the associated accent and mannerisms, with a wild-cat from Tennessee.

Also, when we factor in far more probable suspects with names Laura used in early *LHOTP* and *Pioneer Girl* drafts, like Brown and Thompson, it's difficult to attribute any portion of Mr. Edwards to Edmund Mason, save him having land that closely matched the described location of Mr. Edwards.

Though he was an interesting man, the facts were very clear. Despite some folks' long-held beliefs, Edmund Mason was, at best, only a small fraction of the Mr. Edwards character. At worst? He wasn't a match at all.

– 12 –

Bringing It All Together

A Few Additional Discoveries and (Almost) the End of our Trail

MR. EDWARDS SURE led us on a wild chase, didn't he? Had Laura's prairie been as empty as she intimated in the *Little House* series, it wouldn't have been such a puzzle . . . or such a winding path to any concrete conclusions. But we learned very quickly into this hunt that a passel of potential suspects were milling about the area where the Ingallses settled . . . and that we needed to seriously consider each and every one of those numerous men.

Understanding the lay of the land—from the state of our country to the state of Kansas to the state of the immediate area surrounding the Ingallses' little house—was a critical step in forming our search area and piecing together the clues we began to uncover.

Realigning the search area to include all the reasonable land Mr. Edwards could have settled on was an important step, too. It put into play a lot more suspects . . . many of whom played important roles in our investigation. And many of whom hadn't been considered in the past.

When we finally assembled our search area, sharpened our research tools, and amassed the wealth of details Laura had provided in both her published books *and* her unpublished drafts, as well as her personal notes and letters, it was time to finalize our task. While the obvious goal was to hunt down our Tennessee Wildcat, the more specific goal was to discover this: was Mr. Edwards a real, verifiable man, a composite of several men, a loose collection of memory fragments, or pure fiction?

Very early on in the hunt, we had that break. There were too many facts, too many specific names, and too many versions of the same stories to convince us an experienced author like Laura Ingalls Wilder had simply created a fictitious character such as Mr. Edwards out of thin air. If that had been the case, Laura wouldn't have written so many versions of her anecdotes about him; she would just have deftly created his character, assigned his backstory, and moved into the writing portion of crafting her novel. But she didn't. As she worked to tease details out of her memory, writing and re-writing fragments about her family's time in Kansas, she clearly wasn't constructing a work of fiction. She was trying to remember *truth.* A wholly fictitious character is created, not remembered.

And Laura, herself, asserted several times that all she wrote about was true . . . though not always the whole truth (Koupal, 2017, p. 15). This was confirmed further by a letter Laura wrote to Ida Louise Raymond, her editor at Harper & Brothers, dated July 2, 1934: "it [*LHOTP*] is written from my own memories of what happened to us and how we lived . . . in Indian Territory in the years 1870 and 1871" (Wilder, 2016, p. 75).

So, before we even began our quest in earnest, it seemed far-fetched and rather illogical that Mr. Edwards would be the only main character in the whole *Little House* series who was pure fiction. She had written about dozens and dozens of actual people, so to add one, lone character who was purely made up just didn't make sense. So, we were more than grateful to determine Mr. Edwards almost certainly wasn't just a beautifully crafted work of Laura's imagination.

Of course, our *highest* hopes were that Mr. Edwards had been a real man who possessed that name and fit the bill in every conceivable way. Although unlikely, given the incredible amount of *Little House* research that had been accomplished prior to our attempt, we still had hopes we might uncover a Tennessee bachelor hiding among historical records. But after poring through hundreds of period documents, even in our realigned search area, we couldn't locate one man who fit enough of the established criteria to be a complete, or even substantial, match to our Tennessee Wildcat. We didn't find even one man who fit several of the various descriptors.

So, we had to conclude that Mr. Edwards wasn't fiction, nor was he a completely real person—in the sense that he wasn't just one verifiable man with the correct name and background, and possessing all the attributes and storylines Laura assigned him in her books.

This left our two remaining options, which were really just different versions of the same thing—either Mr. Edwards was a loose collection of memory fragments woven together via family lore, or he was a composite character. Though similar, there was an important difference between those two options: a loose collection of memories is hard to substantiate as they have a dream-like and fractured quality. It's hard to know what is fact and what is fiction (and what is somewhere in between) in this scenario. Facts are mixed in with fiction to build a story or character, but there is no real purpose other than to shore up the truth with enough filler to make something cohesive.

But a composite character shows more intent. It's creating a purposed character out of a number of real facts . . . for a specific reason. This option would mean Mr. Edwards was created to serve a specific literary function in *LHOTP*. And, as we discuss in a moment, we believe he absolutely did.

As we dove into our research, it became clear that Laura wasn't just dealing with a few fuzzy memories. Consistently accurate names, as well as some details of location and timing, were certainly an issue in each of her retellings of various stories. In her drafts, she told and retold specific tales with various names in various roles before finally settling on the published versions. But that process actually solidified our case: names (Brown, Thompson, Edwards, etc.) changed in various drafts, but the *stories* didn't. Pa *did* build the cabin with help. He *did* dig a well with help. He *did* go to Independence. Someone *did* bring Christmas presents. The name or names of the men associated with these narratives might have been unclear in Laura's mind (likely a product of Laura's very young age at the time she was writing about), but the stories, themselves, weren't.

And this left only one logical conclusion: Mr. Edwards was a composite character. Just as Nellie Oleson was a composite built from three girls who had a negative impact on Laura in her youth, Mr. Edwards was likely built from men who aided and supported the Ingalls family from the moment they rolled into Kansas. Our beloved Mr. Edwards, therefore, was almost certainly a compilation of helpers and heroes.

That fact put a little wind into our sails. If our inability to identify an actual wild Tennessean bachelor (who lived two miles northeast of the Ingallses, and with the name of Edwards and all the associated characteristics Laura noted) brought us down a peg or two, knowing that there *were* men who embodied the noble and endearing qualities of Mr. Edwards brought us right back up. As a result, we hoped more than ever to discover who these individual real men might have been.

Our curated list of "Mr. Edwards" clues from those Laura provided in her early drafts and letters certainly helped. Those identifiers were:

- Tanned (Caucasian)
- Wildcat (rough, uncultured)
- From Tennessee
- Bachelor
- Alone/lonely
- Lived beyond woods
- Lived two miles away
- Lived northeast of the Ingallses
- Lived across a significant creek
- Had carpentry skills
- Spent Christmas with the Ingallses
- Left Kansas, same time
- Had already seen Missouri
- After Kansas, went south by boat

Slowly and methodically, we compared all the potential suspects against this list. Our search area, which was quite different than that of previous researchers, was not only fairly large, but the prairie was packed with far more settlers than Laura had led us to believe within that newly-defined expanse. By the time the Ingallses left Kansas, more than eight thousand people resided in the immediate area.

Luckily for us, all these residents meant the frontier in Kansas was a little less "wild" than Laura had led us to believe, too. There was already a county in place, and copious amounts of period data were available in the form of land records, censuses, newspaper articles, atlases, and area histories. And into these resources we dove with vigor.

After letting go of the possibility Mr. Edwards was one verifiable man, we readjusted our objective. We turned our hopes toward finding clear-cut favorites for each aspect of our Wildcat. But even with that new goal, we had to conclude that many of our identified criteria were unfortunately common traits amongst dozens of men, especially the physical characteristics which were impossible to verify anyway. That meant our hunt wasn't going to be easy, quick, or entirely conclusive.

There were numerous bachelors in the area, all likely farming, for example. They wouldn't have settled on such large parcels of land unless that was their current or intended profession. One condition for getting land under the Homestead Act was having a portion of the land under cultivation, after all. Thus, these settlers were probably similarly built: lean and tanned from working hard outdoors. As bachelors, and thus without womenfolk to do their washing and mending, they were all probably a bit rough around the edges, too. Chewing tobacco, and the resulting spitting, wasn't uncommon either. And all the men establishing homesteads would have possessed either enough carpentry skills to build their own cabins and barns, or enough muscle to enlist a master carpenter like Pa to trade their physical help for his expert knowledge. No sensible man would have come to settle on bare land without at least some skill level in that department.

There were many men in the neighborhood from Tennessee, too, though we'll address that curious point in our wrap up later. And many of those men lived across creeks and beyond woods from the Ingallses.

Looking at the landscape, and the hundreds of inhabitants, the reality was, we were awash with possibilities for Mr. Edwards.

One bonus we didn't expect, however, as we forged ahead in examining our list of suspects, was that we made some interesting discoveries. The Johnsons, a couple who lived right next to Bennet Tann, and where his son, Dr. George Tann, resided, were likely renamed the "Scotts" by way of Laura misremembering them as the Robertsons.

In *LHOTP* chapter 20, "A Scream in the Night," Laura told the story of Pa hearing what sounded like a woman's scream and rushing out to head up the creek to the Scotts to see if they needed help. She also wrote that, at the time, the wind was howling and screeching. How could anyone hear a human voice in those conditions unless the home Pa hurried to was fairly nearby?

In her early manuscript, *Pioneer Girl*, Laura's description of Pa hearing a woman calling for help was "down the creek toward Robertson's" (Wilder, 2014, p. 11). Yet, it was the Johnson's home that was actually the closest to the Ingallses'. It was near Walnut Creek, next to the Tann place, and was the only real possibility to have been hurried to or heard from that distance. So, the "Scotts" from *LHOTP*, who started out as the "Robertson's" in *Pioneer Girl*, were almost certainly, in real life, the "Johnsons." The Johnsons' land was one of the few places Pa could have heard such a cry from, especially as it matched Laura's description of its location.

Given that Laura also mentioned the Robertson name in connection with Carrie's birth, we could also surmise Mrs. Johnson was likely the woman who helped Ma (assisting Dr. Tann, her neighbor) during labor. When Carrie arrived, Laura was gone on her day trip with Pa and Mary to the "Indian camp" where they hunted for beads, examined animal bones, and saw fringe prints in the dust. When they returned, "the black Dr. was there and Mrs Robertson . . ." (Wilder, 2014, p. 14). If our Mrs. Johnson was, indeed, who Laura misnamed "Mrs. Robertson," this made absolute sense. Dr. Tann and the Johnsons lived on adjoining properties, and both were among the Ingallses' closest neighbors. Knowing the name of the woman who almost certainly helped bring Carrie into the world was an unexpected, and welcome, nugget to have come across while looking for our Tennessee Wildcat.

In the research surrounding the Robertsons/Johnsons/Scotts connection, something else struck us . . . we believe the Scotts may have been a composite family just as Nellie Oleson was a composite character, and Mr. Edwards was shaping up to be, too. But that, of course, is a topic for another book.

And, similar to our bonus finds about the Robertsons, identifying the likeliest candidates for the two sets of bachelors Laura wrote about in *Pioneer Girl* was another pleasant discovery, as we discussed in our chapter on bachelors.

The Robertsons or the Gilmours?

The Gilmour family is the only other realistic possibility to be "the Scotts" from *LHOTP*. Part of the Gilmour property was closer to the Ingalls cabin than the location of the Johnson cabin (as shown in *The 1881 Atlas*). However, we don't know where on the Gilmour property their cabin was, so it could have been further away than the Johnsons'. In fact, because the school land appraisement record for this section lists *no* improvements on the Gilmour land, we cannot be sure they were actually residing there at all. Furthermore, the location of the Johnson cabin combined with its proximity to Dr. Tann—along with the more similar name to the one Laura used—resulted in our conclusion that the Johnsons were the more likely candidates for "the Scotts."

But, of course, as interesting as these unexpected *Little House* finds were, our main goal was to find our Mr. Edwards. With so many potential suspects for various aspects of Mr. Edwards roaming the prairie, however, how could we even begin to identify the likeliest of candidates? We went back to Laura's own words in her early drafts to sift through our clearest and most pertinent clues.

Before she fact-checked, and before she was tasked with pulling her notes together into a cohesive narrative—and before her daughter, Rose Wilder Lane, had any editorial input—Laura simply wrote out her best recollections of those shadowy days on the prairie as a toddler. Those pages of notes and names and remembrances were, and remain, our strongest clues. Why? Because they were her unfiltered impressions and remembered facts in their purest form. As such, and because she cycled through the same group of names even when she gave them different roles in her stories, those drafts represent the closest we could possibly come to the truth. And from that premise, we formed our final guesses as to who represented each part of the composite character of Mr. Edwards.

Building the Cabin

For all the reasons we stated in our section on "Mr. Thompson," we believe that C.M. Thompson and Charles M. Thompson were the same man. We believe he had a town job and a country property like many at that time had, including another bachelor we discussed, George A. Brown, who helped found Independence. It was common for men to work town jobs to earn enough money to buy equipment and seed until their country farms were flourishing enough to sustain themselves. And that is exactly what we believe Thompson did.

Laura wrote in one of her early drafts of *LHTOP* that, when Pa first met one of their neighbors, he was referred to as "an old batchelor [*sic*] and alone." Laura named this neighbor "Mr. Thompson" and said he helped Pa build the family cabin (Wilder, no date a, pp. 44–46).

And, in this case, we believe Laura had the correct name. Thompson's land was close enough to be a neighbor, in the correct location with regard to the Ingallses' land, and he was a bachelor who could, as Laura wrote in chapter 5, of *LHOTP*, "The House on the Prairie," "get along without a house better than [Ma] and the girls [could]."

But Thompson didn't just have the right name, a homestead in the area, or the fact that he was a bachelor going for him. For one, he was a carpenter by trade. So, who better to help Pa, also a master carpenter, build a solid family home? He had also arrived in the area at exactly the right time to both help Pa and to need help on his own cabin. Furthermore, he had a strong connection to another person Laura distinctly named in her early drafts: Mr. Brown.

Probably one of the most compelling arguments in his favor, however, was this: even if he didn't have the correct name, he checked *all* the boxes to be the best candidate for the bachelor who helped Pa build the family cabin: timeline, marital status, proximity, carpenter skillset, location in relation to the cabin, etc. So, when you add all those checked boxes with Laura's repeated use of the name "Mr. Thompson" in her early drafts, Charles M. Thompson emerged as our clear and definitive favorite for the hero of the cabin building story.

The Christmas Story

The tale of Mr. Edwards heroically crossing a frigid and dangerously high winter creek, simply to bring the Ingalls girls their Christmas presents from Independence, is probably the most endearing, and enduring, story in the *Little House* series. It was so captivating, it even made its way into the *Little House on the Prairie* television show ('Little House on the Prairie: The Pilot', 1974). When Laura first wrote about the event in *Pioneer Girl*, however, it was a "Mr. Brown" who performed that daring, and incredibly kind, deed.

> . . . when we waked on Christmas morning our stockings were hanging on the back of a chair by our bed and out of the top of each showed a bright shining new tin cup. Farther down was a long, flat stick of red and white striped peppermint candy all beautifully notched along each edge.
>
> Mr Brown the neighbor from across the creek stood looking at us. He said Santa Clause [*sic*] couldn't cross the creek the night before so left the presents with him and he swam over that morning. (Wilder, 2014, p. 16 n. 36)

After determining there were no other "Mr. Browns" who convincingly fit the clues left by Laura in her drafts and letters, we had to look creatively at the area data. When we did, we discovered a connection which birthed a rather fascinating hypothesis.

While our candidate for "Christmas Mr. Edwards" didn't own land across a creek from the Ingallses' land, his part-time roommate in Independence, and fellow carpenter, Charles M. Thompson, did.

Though this may seem like a bit of a leap, in the absence of any other "Mr. Browns" who matched Laura's story in any way to be seriously considered, Fred Brown became the one option that made reasonable sense. If we took Laura at her word that "Mr. Brown" was the correct name for the Christmas story hero, and added in the solid circumstantial evidence we uncovered, Fred emerged as more than plausible for this portion of Mr. Edwards.

After all, Thompson, who we believe helped Pa build the family cabin, was friends and roommates with Fred Brown at his town dwelling. Fred also hailed from the same state and shared the same profession Thompson did, which implied they might have even known each other before arriving in Kansas, bolstering their strong ties and likely solid connection. So, it wasn't a huge leap to believe Thompson could have enlisted Fred's help in building his own home and farm. And, if Pa and Thompson were trading building work as Laura described, it was also no stretch to assume Fred Brown also worked with Pa at some point during the building of either the Ingalls or Thompson cabins. Or both.

Neighbors working together certainly builds relationship, which would have almost certainly happened between Thompson and the Ingallses, especially if he happened to stay for dinner as Laura described, and if he had, indeed, sung "Old Dan Tucker" with the family as Laura fondly remembered. So, it's not a large further leap to imagine Thompson asking his friend and housemate, Fred Brown, to fetch the Ingalles' Christmas gifts if he was going to be coming out to his country farm near the Ingallses anyway. Whether Fred would have done it because he had also befriended Pa and the girls, or whether he simply did it as a favor to his own friend, Charles Thompson, who *did* know the Ingallses, we can't surmise.

But we do believe Fred Brown is the sweet hero of the Christmas Story. He had a connection to the Ingallses through Thompson, had a connection to Independence, had to cross a creek from his friend's house to get to the

Ingallses (and just to get directly from Independence to the Ingallses), was a bachelor free to take risks and spend the holiday with the family, and had the exact name Laura used in each of her earliest draft versions of the story as well as in connection with the name of Thompson. When you add it all together, and in the absence of any more suitable and probable candidate, Fred's our only logical choice for our Christmas Mr. Edwards.

The Perfect Location & Pa Going to Town

The location clues Laura offered us seemed like they would quickly preclude most of the Ingallses' neighbors. The version of Mr. Edwards who made it into *LHOTP* lived two miles across a creek, beyond woods, and in the direction of Independence, which was northeast of the Ingallses' land.

But with a couple of creek options in the area, and their associated woods, and the direction not being so important in a composite character, there were just too many potential candidates to come to any sort of definitive conclusion.

Let's pause there for a minute. Why wouldn't it be so important for any part of a composite character to be located where Laura originally indicated? Because once you have described a character, and set their location, attributes, and descriptors, any additional person you pour into that composite must fall under the original description. For example, Nellie Owens was the first "Nellie Oleson." If she had blond curls, but the subsequent girls had black or brown hair, the description of that composite character wouldn't change. Whatever you decide as the descriptors when we first meet a character, those descriptors stay.

The first time we met Mr. Edwards, he was helping Pa build the house, and his own home was described as being two miles away, beyond woods and a creek. After that was set, any new person being incorporated into the Mr. Edwards composite wouldn't change those established parameters. Instead, their associated story would be told as if the incorporated person had all the same attributes and lived in the same location. So, it is far more likely that the first person in the composite, Mr. Thompson, lived in the location Laura described, but not the rest. Even then, Laura could have used the location of a later member of that composite in tandem with the characteristics of the first person in that composite.

If Laura, who was, remember, an accomplished author by this time, had intended for Mr. Edwards to be a composite from the start, she could have assembled the various men she'd construct him out of, and pulled out the characteristics of each that best fit her narrative and purpose, including location, prior to beginning to write in earnest.

But if we trust at face value that Laura had the direction correct in this instance, meaning the described "Mr. Edwards" land had to be roughly two miles northeast of the Ingallses' cabin, and across a creek, there were only a couple of real possibilities. One of those was Oliver Carrow, whose parcel fit the bill rather nicely. His land was located in section 30 of Independence Township, just over two miles northeast of the Ingallses' land, across a large creek (Onion Creek) and beyond woods. It was on a great trajectory for Pa to easily stop to ask a neighbor if he'd be willing to check in on Ma and the girls during a trip to Independence, too. However, he was married . . . and Canadian.

Henry VanWinkle and James Sands were northeast too, in section 19 of Independence Twp. They were positioned equally well for Pa to pass right by their property on the way to Independence.

And, of course, this perfect location was also shared by a man who had, until now, been considered either the best, or only, possible "Mr. Edwards." We're referring, of course, to Edmund Mason.

Mason's land in section 30 of Independence Township was a far better option than his land nearer the Ingallses' property in section 36 of Rutland Township, if you go by Laura's descriptors. It was two miles away, across Onion Creek, and beyond woods. It was also almost perfectly in the right direction . . . between Pa's cabin and Independence.

We had two problems with a declaration that any man, Mason included, could be included in the Mr. Edwards' composite, however. One is that there were multiple men who fit this general location description. Especially if you consider that toddler Laura might not have known in which direction anyone lived. There were plenty of men about two miles away, across creeks, and beyond woods . . . both in the direction of Independence as well as in other directions.

The second large issue was this: we weren't even sure this story truly happened. In *LHOTP*, Pa's trip to Independence and back took several days. Why? Because Laura believed they were forty miles from town, which would have meant a several-day trip. Pa was a responsible man in Laura's eyes, so, of course he would have made sure the family was taken care of in his lengthy absence.

When Laura first researched where the cabin might have been, she originally believed the family had settled in northern Oklahoma. If they had, their home would have, indeed, been approximately forty miles from Independence. But she erred. Her family was much, much closer to Independence than she realized. Had she had access to the family bible at that time, she would have seen the notation of Carrie's birth, which was in Montgomery County, Kansas. But she clearly didn't, and guessed they had settled in northern Oklahoma. If they had, and the distance to Independence had been approximately forty miles, Pa might have eased Ma's concerns over being left alone for so long by asking a neighbor to check in. Though, frankly, we would have thought asking a married neighbor to do the checking up would have been a safer and more "proper" option.

A relatively quick trip to town, however, wasn't the same as leaving Ma and the girls for more than a week. Pa would have hustled into Independence, which was only about ten miles away, finished his business, and high-tailed it home. Especially as Ma was nervous about nearby Osage Indian camps. Because of this much closer location, and probability Pa was quick, it's unlikely he was gone for more than a night.

Even an ox team could make sixteen to eighteen miles in one day pulling an empty wagon in good conditions (Marcy, 1859, p. 45). So, an empty wagon pulled by good horses, which were quicker, could have traveled the distance to Independence and back in one day if pushed. And that would have meant Pa probably was only gone for one night at the very most. If he had ridden horseback, however, the trip would have meant he definitely wouldn't even have been gone overnight. If Laura remembered correctly that this was the trip in which Pa fetched supplies and glass for their windows, however, the trip was likely with a wagon. So, at most, Pa wasn't gone more than one night and two days. But would even an overnight trip warrant stopping in at a neighbor for assistance? Possibly. For the multi-day trip Laura wrote into her story? Absolutely. But a much shorter trip, perhaps even just one day? Unlikely.

So, even if this trip actually happened, and Pa did stop in to ask a neighbor to check in on the family, *and* Laura's stated distance of Mr. Edwards' property was correct, there were still many possible people this portion of the story could have been referring to. If she had the distance to Mr. Edwards' land wrong for this portion of the story, however, there were exponentially more people to factor in. As such, it was impossible to ascertain whether this trip actually happened, whether a neighbor was called into service to check on the family, and, if they were, who that neighbor might have been.

Other Literary Clues

There was absolutely no doubt Laura beautifully rendered Mr. Edwards. From an author's perspective, she paid close and careful attention to her depiction of this literary hero in an absolutely textbook way. His physical details, fleshed out backstory, and endearing quirks and characteristics gave her readers a clear visual, a sense of who he was, and a reason to fall in love with this Tennessee Wildcat.

Some of the clues Laura gave us, particularly his physical attributes (tall, lean, tanned (implying Caucasian), etc.), his dress sense (coon skin cap, ragged jumper, tall boots), and his mannerisms (wildcat-rough, uncultured, but polite in his manners with Ma, spit tobacco juice, and could sing "Old Dan Tucker"), are all beautiful, vivid details that helped the reader picture Mr. Edwards. But those details weren't the kind you could confirm via public land records, newspaper articles, or area histories. So, while they brought the composite Mr. Edwards wonderfully to life, they weren't a tremendous amount of help in our actual search.

Interesting Notes

As tempting as it was to try to locate Mr. Edwards based on Laura's various descriptors in *LHOTP*, her early drafts added some final large clues to her intentions with his character. And they were pretty important points.

- There was no Tennessean mentioned in any of the early drafts. *Not one.*
- And the only Mr. Edwards she mentioned in at least one early draft was married *and* died in the digging of his own well (Wilder, no date a, p. 122).

The combination of these two critical details was convincing evidence that Laura wasn't remembering one specific person, but rather a series of people she then molded into one character for a specific purpose.

An example of another time Laura did this was when writing *The Long Winter*. She wrote the family as struggling alone in Pa's store in town, huddled together and bravely making it through by their own resourcefulness and determination. That was, in fact, the overarching theme in all her books: A family alone in the wild frontier carving a life out of raw land and doing it pretty much by themselves.

But the family wasn't alone in Pa's storefront during that time. George Masters, his wife, and their infant were living with the Ingalls family during the long winter. In her letters to Rose and other drafts, Laura mentioned cutting the Masters out of the story to increase the sense of the family's isolation during that time (Wilder, 2014, pp. 204–205 n. 10, 2016, pp. 165–167). Likewise, she mentioned cutting several characters out of other stories to amplify the sense of self-reliance of pioneers, her family included. And, of course, she also wrote in her notes and letters about making three girls into the composite character of Nellie Oleson (Miller, 2016; Wilder, 2016, pp. 169, 177) in order to cull characters and keep the throughline of a nemesis.

Because we had her own words as evidence that cutting out and consolidating characters served her themes and the greater narrative arc, and she showed an acute understanding of how to use specific stories and characters to underpin those themes, to assume she knew exactly what she was doing when she crafted Mr. Edwards was no great leap. Laura clearly wanted to convey a sense of greater isolation on the Kansas prairie than there really was in practice. Therefore, keeping Mr. Edwards as a single character, comprised of several men, served multiple purposes: reducing the number of characters, increasing the idea of isolation on the prairie, and being able to pull all the stereotypical characteristics of a western bachelor homesteader into one person.

But why a "Tennessean Wildcat?" Had Laura heard the phrase somewhere and thought it a perfect option to elicit the image she was wanting for her Mr. Edwards: a rough and tumble frontiersman who epitomized the raw country they found themselves in, replete with horse-thieves, claim protection clubs, and wild, sparsely-populated land? Did she create the phrase herself? Had she known a man later in life who described himself this way, and it seemed poetically fitting to use as a summation of the kind of bachelor homesteaders the family lived among on the wild frontier?

We may never know, but the fact that the only Mr. Edwards she ever mentioned was both married and died was telling. As was the fact she never mentioned anyone from Tennessee at all.

Summing it all Up

Knowing Laura never mentioned a Tennessean, let alone one who was clearly a wildcat, in her earliest drafts, led us to the end of the trail and our final conclusions. Mr. Edwards was a beautifully rendered composite character, crafted from snippets of memory and family lore, and meant to serve an important literary function in *LHOTP*. He was ascribed stereotypical physical characteristics of period frontiersman, given a plausible backstory, and imbued with a handful of quirky, but memorable, attributes to flesh him out as a compelling character. He was meant to represent the kind of men who both tamed the west and who inhabited the raw land around the Ingallses.

While Nellie Oleson was a composite of three women who had a rather unpleasant effect on Laura's life, Mr. Edwards was a composite of another kind. In him, all those who aided and supported the Ingallses in their quest to establish a home in Kansas were represented. In this character, we saw sharing the work of building a home, possibly looking in on the family while Pa was away, and risking a frigid and raging creek to bring the Ingalls girls their simple Christmas gifts. In this Tennessee Wildcat, the best of the men who roamed the Kansas prairie was represented. Rough around the edges, maybe, but kind and decent, too.

Of all the possible suspects who held a potential claim to a sliver of Mr. Edwards, Charles M. Thompson was the person we believed likely set the standard. Helping the Ingallses build their cabin, to the sacrifice of building his own, was a pretty decent thing to do. Through his friendship with his Independence roommate, he may have had influence over the girls getting their Christmas gifts, too. And, for all we know, he might have been the one Charles asked to look in on the family.

We still lean toward that interesting connection between Thompson and Fred Brown . . . and are convinced he factored into the Christmas story as the Ingallses' benefactor at the very least. While we have established the incredible unlikelihood that Edmund Mason was any significant part of Mr. Edwards, it remains possible that he, along with dozens of other male neighbors, did tangentially contribute to the concept of Mr. Edwards' character.

Just like Ma explained once in *On the Banks of Plum Creek* when Laura questioned her about Santa Claus . . .

> "Ma!" she cried. "There IS a Santa Claus, isn't there?"
>
> "Of course there's a Santa Claus," said Ma. . . . .
>
> "The older you are, the more you know about Santa Claus," she said. "You are so big now, you know he can't be just one man, don't you? You know he is everywhere on Christmas Eve. He is in the Big Woods, and in Indian Territory, and far away in York State, and here. He comes down all the chimneys at the same time. You know that, don't you?"
>
> "Yes, Ma," said Mary and Laura.

> "Well," said Ma. "Then you see—"
>
> "I guess he is like angels," Mary said, slowly. And Laura could see that, just as well as Mary could (Wilder, 1992, p. 57).

We believe that's a little of what Laura was trying to achieve with Mr. Edwards. His character embodied a whole class of men who were part of the opening of the west. In that wild time, there were claim jumpers and horse thieves and men who got rowdy in saloons. But there were good men, too. Men who would step in to help a man secure his homestead claim amidst a crowd of jostling men or drop a twenty-dollar bill into a blind girl's lap. Men who went to great lengths to help each other, protect each other, and build strong, thriving communities out of strangers.

And Laura knew our Mr. Edwards, that Tennessee Wildcat, could represent them all.

The End of the Trail? What's Next?

One look at the resources we accessed and compiled during the research of this project should indicate we looked under every known rock (and a few previously unknown ones) for clues, information, and corroborating data. Do we think we did a thorough job? Yes. Do we hope there's more to discover? Absolutely!

Our intention with this project was to do exhaustive research into the available source material, getting creative along the way, to discover any possible clues we could about Mr. Edwards . . . or anything *Little House* related, really. Along the way we *did* uncover new information. Some of it corrected previously held beliefs or erroneous "facts." Some of it shed light on new possibilities. Some of it confirmed things we already knew.

It wasn't our goal to diminish previous research but to add to the body of *Little House* knowledge already available. But there are many questions we still have. And we'd love to see them eventually answered.

- What if the descendants of Charles M. Thompson or Fred Brown, who never even knew of their potential ties to Mr.

Edwards, poked around in their attics and uncovered some family letters or journals which could confirm our suspicions?

- What if previously lost histories or period records were suddenly found in the basement of a Kansas courthouse, museum, or newspaper?
- What if more Ingalls letters surfaced, sharing the specific names and details of those who aided the family during their time in Kansas?

We'd also love to learn more about Edmund Mason . . . partially because he was a rather fascinating man in his own right, and partially because we'd love to find proof of him living on that second piece of land we discovered in section 30. It wouldn't change our overall findings, but it would strengthen his bid to be considered for at least a sliver of Mr. Edwards.

The fact is, we'd welcome any new information that sheds light on Laura, the entire Ingalls family, or our beloved Mr. Edwards. To discover some hidden source of data, even if it changed our opinions, would be welcome. We've been on the hunt for the truth, after all.

So, we'll keep looking along the trail for any newly discovered rocks to peek under.

And we hope you will, too!

Epilogue
Edmund Mason After the Ingallses

THROUGH A CAREFUL review of the evidence, we discounted Edmund Mason as our full Mr. Edwards. Though, based only on the location of one of the parcels of land he owned and *may* have lived on, we do concede he *potentially* could have been part of the "Pa going to Independence" portion of our wildcat's composite, if that story ever actually happened. Our ultimate assessment and conclusions stand, however: he likely wasn't a significant part of Mr. Edwards, if he played any part at all.

But, at the same time, we can't deny Mason was a rather fascinating man in his own right. Because we'd gathered so much information in hopes of connecting him to Mr. Edwards, and because there has been so much speculation about Mason and his possible connection to the *Little House* books, we thought it a shame to shut all our collected data up in a file cabinet drawer just because he wasn't our man. So, we decided to offer it here to you in this epilogue. We hope you enjoy!

—o0o—

We've already addressed the early, British, years of Edmund Mason, as well as his travel via Canada to Kansas. So, we'll pick up his story there.

When the Ingalls family headed back to Pepin in the spring of 1871, Edmund Mason was a twenty-five-year-old bachelor and possibly residing on that almost-forty-acre plot in the northwest quarter of section 30 in Independence Township, roughly two miles from the cabin Pa built.

His brother, John Mason, was also still a bachelor and living three miles away from the Ingallses' cabin. Both men remained unmarried for the next three years. But in 1874, within a period of five months, the two brothers were joined in wedlock to two young sisters.

On the last day of May in 1874, sixteen-year-old Emily ("Emma") Howard married John Mason, who was almost twenty-four years older than his bride. Just under five months later, Edmund married Emma's younger sister, Mary Etta (generally known as "Etta"). Their wedding took place on October 22nd at Edmund's home which, by this time, was in section 36 of Rutland Township, very close to the property the Ingalls had settled on. Edmund was twenty-eight. His young bride was only fifteen.

Figure 42 – Portrait of Etta Howard Mason

The Howard sisters were daughters of Ephraim Howard and Jane Hopkins Howard, who had married in 1836 in Indiana, where their older children were also born. In the 1880 federal census, one of these older children, thirty-five-year-old Nancy, was classified as "idiotic" (as was their fourteen-year-old granddaughter, Isobel Howard, who was living next door with her parents, Thomas and Martha). Ephraim and Jane had ten children in total: seven girls and three boys.

By 1860, the Howards had left Indiana and were farming in Mound City Township, Linn County, KS, about twenty-five miles from Fort Scott. Ephraim had purchased eighty acres of land there in June of 1860. Within ten years, the family had moved to Sycamore Township, in Montgomery County, directly north of Independence Township and about ten to fifteen miles from Edmund's home. At the time of their wedding, however, Etta was described as being "of St. Paul," ('Marriage License for Edmund Mason and Mary E. Howard', 1874). The town of St. Paul no longer exists, but in the early 1870s it was "a small place . . . near the Cherokee line, on [the] Little Caney [river]" (Jones, 1870), west of the current city of Caney on the southern border of Montgomery County, about ten or eleven miles from Edmund's property. (And not to be confused with the current city of St. Paul, in Neosho County, Kansas, which was formerly named "Osage Mission" but renamed "St. Paul" in 1895 (acatholicmission.org, no date).)

Two months before Edmund and Etta's second wedding anniversary, their first child, William ("Willie") was born (he later married Josie Brown, the daughter of Andrew John Brown). Two years later, in October of 1878, their first daughter, Ida, arrived, followed by their second son, Ira, in April of 1881.

Edmund Mason and the Tann Family

There is a very interesting point of connection between Mason and Dr. Tann's family that also occurred in 1881, after the death of Dr. Tann's father, Bennet. *The Independence Kansan* printed this tidbit on February 16, 1881, p.1: "Quite a serious affair occurred near Mr. Hobson's place last Friday week. Mr. Ed. Mason went to Independence in the morning after a coffin in which to bury Mr. Tann, who died Thursday night" (The Independence Kansan, 1881).

Next came a son named Charles ("Charlie"). His headstone states he died September 17, 1888, aged just five years, four months, and two days, which would give his date of birth as May 15, 1883. Another son, Albert, is listed in the 1885 state census, aged ten months, but no further records related to Albert could be located. The available information indicates Albert and Charles might have been the same child (Albert Charles or Charles Albert Mason, perhaps), though the dates don't quite match up.

Therefore, he was probably a subsequent child who died either in infancy or toddlerhood.

Etta gave birth to another daughter, Stella, in September of 1885, followed in April of 1889 by their third daughter, Cordelia ("Delia"). Their fourth son, James, arrived in April of 1891. The final child born during the time of their marriage, and the fourth daughter, Anna, arrived in 1895 when Etta would have been around thirty-five, and Edmund would have been nearing fifty.

We don't know much about Edmund and Etta's life together, or whether their early marriage was a happy one. But we do know things definitely took a turn for the worse within a year of Anna's birth. It was then their union came to a rather acrimonious end.

In September of 1895, Etta filed for divorce one month before their twenty-first wedding anniversary. But "through the influence of friends the proceedings were stayed and the couple patched up their difficulties and have been living together" (*The Weekly Star and Kansan*, 1896c, p. 4). Their reconciliation was brief, however; Etta filed again for divorce just four months later, in January of 1896.

In response, Edmund published the following notice in a few different local newspapers:

> All persons are hereby warned against trusting my wife, Etta Mason, on my account as I shall pay no debts of her contraction. All persons who have accounts against her, made before the publication of this notice, will please present the same to me within 10 days. EDMUND MASON. (Mason, 1896)

This same newspaper also reported on the new divorce proceedings besides this notice of non-responsibility for Etta's debts. But why was Edmund so concerned about Etta racking up those debts? Such notices were standard practice in divorces at this time, to make sure the community knew the marital finances were now separate. It's possible, from the rather terse wording of being "warned against trusting" his wife, she had a habit of overspending on his account, as well. Whatever the reason, he clearly felt the need to legally "cover his back" against any debt his soon-to-be ex-wife might accrue.

Interestingly, John Mason had published a similar notice in his divorce proceedings nearly nine years earlier:

> All persons are hereby warned not to trust or credit Emma Mason, my wife who has left my bed and board, as I will not pay any debts of her contracting" (Mason, 1887).

This notice was published in several newspapers between September and November of 1887. Just over a year later, "Mrs. Emma Mason was convicted of keeping a bawdy house in the police court Tuesday, and fined $15 and costs, amounting to $38.35" (*The Weekly Star and Kansan*, 1888, p. 3). (Note: The writers in us couldn't help but hope the police court was where the conviction took place and not where she *kept* the "bawdy house!" It appears editors weren't as concerned with clarity in the late 1800's!)

It appears that John and Emma never formally divorced, as there was no notice of it in the newspaper, or in court documents. But Edmund and Etta's divorce hearing was held in March of 1896. Etta testified to Edmund's "neglect and abuse, which was partially corroborated by two other witnesses" (*The Weekly Star and Kansan*, 1896a, p. 4). Their divorce was granted in late March of 1896. Etta retained custody of their children as well as "about two-thirds of the property, which is supposed to be worth about $25,000" (*Independence Daily Reporter*, 1896, p. 2). The terms of the settlement were arranged between Edmund and Etta out of court, before the hearing, so it appears they were at least amicable enough to come to some sort of consensus about the division of the marital estate without involving a judge.

Following the divorce, Edmund went to live with his eldest daughter, Ida, who was then married to Barnabas Lindley, the son of a Quaker pastor, Rev. Isaac Lindley. Mason was enumerated with them in the 1900 census, along with their son, Rex. The entry stated Edmund was born on April 1, 1846 . . . and he was listed as divorced.

It's curious that Edmund came to live with Ida and Barnabas as he never belonged to any church in the area and did not appear to be particularly religious. He was never a member of any local church (*Independence Daily Reporter*, 1906, p. 1). So, it is somewhat surprising that his eldest daughter married the son of a preacher, and that Edmund chose to live with this particular daughter in the first place.

While the 1900 census confirmed his divorced status, it also raised a question. Why this birthdate? His verified birth certificate stated his actual birthdate was September 2, 1845. So, did he not celebrate his own birthday and, therefore, just didn't remember when it actually was? It wasn't tradition to celebrate birthdays until the latter half of the 1800's, so, despite it seeming odd to modern sensibilities, it wasn't unheard of for folks in this time period to be uncertain of their own birth years or dates. That said, it's also possible he was just being a little mischievous. April Fool's Day was well established by this time, having begun back in the 1500's in France, after all. So, he could have just been making a rather cheeky joke . . . at least with his birth month and day. And he probably just didn't know his real birth year.

Figure 43 - Barnabas and Ida Lindley, with their son, Rex

It might be prudent to note that some people have pointed to the information on Edmund's gravestone as if it's fact. Etched in stone, the date *September 14, 1846,* was listed as his birthdate. But that 1900 census gave a different date: April 1, 1846. And both of those differ from his actual birth certificate. A gravestone and a federal census should both be reliable sources of information. But, clearly, mistakes were made.

Though Edmund appeared with Barnabas and Ida, as well as their son Rex, in the 1900 census, the 1905 Kansas state census listed Edmund as living alone on a farm in Rutland Township. Whereas, in 1900, Etta was living on the Rutland Twp. property with seven of her children, and a twenty-four-year-old male servant named Louie Trent. There is no direct evidence that Edmund and Etta ever lived together after their divorce, but their post-divorce relationship is somewhat mysterious.

When Etta died in August of 1920, the *Independence Daily Reporter* referred to her as the "widow of the Late Edward [*sic*] Mason," despite their divorce six years earlier, which is odd (it also referred to her as "Ella" rather than "Etta") (*Independence Daily Reporter*, 1920, p. 5). We understand that some descendants of the Mason family believe they might never have actually divorced. But the newspaper notification of their proceedings, the 1900 Federal Census, and the divorce decree confirmed otherwise.

But there is another, possibly greater mystery too, and it relates to children Etta gave birth to *after* she and Edmund divorced.

Her obituary listed ten children (*The Coffeyville Daily Journal*, 1920, p. 9), but *his* obituary stated he and Etta had "eight children, one of whom is dead" (*Independence Daily Reporter*, 1906, p. 1). The three additional children mentioned in Etta's obituary were Henry, Opal, and Marie Mason.

Records indicate Henry was born in September of 1896, after the March 1896 divorce decree, and that his father was "Ed Mason." Likewise, Opal was born in June 1899; father "Edmund Mason." Marie (or Maria) was born in 1903, but no father is listed.

Did Etta name Edmund as Henry and Opal's father because she didn't want to admit to giving birth, while unmarried, to another man's children?

Or was Edmund embarrassed or unwilling to acknowledge children resulting from an ongoing, post-divorce relationship with Etta? Given her testimony accusing Edmund of neglect and abuse, and his notice about her debts, as well as the financial settlement in the divorce that likely meant Etta had no need to placate Edmund, it seems unlikely they would have continued to produce offspring.

In looking for additional evidence, we found the 1900 census listed Etta with seven of her children, including Henry and Opal (misspelled "Opia"). The birthplace of both Henry's and Opal's father is listed as "England." The 1910 census gives similar information for Henry, Opal, and Marie. So, was England really the birthplace of their actual father, and it was just a coincidence he was born in the same country as Edmund, or did Etta tell the census enumerator a little white lie to conceal a worse version of out-of-wedlock childbearing than having kids with her ex-husband? Or was Edmund actually the father of Henry and Opal, but not Marie? The 1920 and 1930 censuses, when Henry, Opal, and Marie were independent of their mother, provided more interesting tidbits.

Henry gave his father's birthplace as England in both censuses. Opal, on the other hand, listed Kansas in 1920 and England in 1930. Marie listed Kansas in 1920 and United States in 1930. She was the only one of the three who did not have Edmund specifically recorded as her father in the available birth records and who didn't state England as her father's birthplace on any document. Whether Edmund really was the father of Henry, Opal, or Marie remains a mystery, but one that may be able to be resolved through modern-day DNA testing and, possibly, recollections or letters via their descendants.

Following his divorce, Edmund lost much of his land, as well as his home, and lived most of the rest of his life with his daughter, Ida, and her husband. Perhaps his circumstances during this period, which also included periods of poor health, caused him to reflect on his life and his English roots, which then sparked a desire to see England once again.

Whatever the reason, in the last few years of his life, he returned not once, but twice, to his British childhood home. The first visit, accompanied by his brother John, took place in May of 1901, by which time his parents and siblings who had remained in England were all deceased, except his second-oldest sister, Thomasin Courtice (*The Coffeyville Weekly Journal*, 1901, p. 5).

He visited a second time in the summer of 1905, accompanied by Charles W. Canning (*The Daily Free Press and the Times*, 1906, p. 5). Charles was a fellow Englishman and Elks Lodge member, a successful businessman, a prominent resident of Independence Township, and a longstanding neighbor, having arrived in the area around 1870. Following their visit, Edmund and Charles returned to New York from Liverpool on the S.S. *Caronia*, a brand-new liner of the Cunard fleet, whose maiden voyage was earlier in 1905. The *Caronia* later became famous for sending one of the most significant iceberg warnings to RMS *Titanic* on the morning of April 14, 1912, the day before the infamous tragedy.

Edmund, however, arrived safely back on Ellis Island on September 27, 1905, after an eight-day journey. Just four months later, however, he was dead. He was preceded in death by his older brother, John, who died "after a protracted illness" fifty-five days after Edmund's return to Ellis Island, on November 21, 1905 (*The Evening Star*, 1905, p. 5). This illness is probably why he hadn't accompanied Edmund on his second trip to England.

Though Edmund's general health had been good while he traveled, he died on January 24, 1906, from the effects of an operation for a stomach ulcer. Two days later, his funeral was held in Bolton Church, and he was buried in Harrisonville cemetery. This cemetery, with a panoramic view of the surrounding country, was the final resting place of many of Edmund's family members, including his brother, John, and ex-wife, Etta.

At the time of Edmund's death, as the Independence *Evening Star* reported, "He had prospered in a worldly way and was the owner of much valuable property, among which is the building in which is located the Elks Home in this city" (*The Evening Star*, 1906a, p. 5). During his lifetime, he had progressed from owning one small parcel of land in Independence Township to becoming one of the largest real estate owners in the area, owning land and buildings in Independence itself, as well as in Rutland Township.

Edmund Mason's Death & Birth Dates

Official sources, and his gravestone, generally state he died January 25, 1906 but his death was reported in the *Independence Daily Reporter*, on Thursday, January 25, 1906, page 1, in which it states he died "last evening" and actually gives his death date as January 24th. As a newspaper shouldn't have reported a death that hadn't yet happened, it appears both the birth and death dates on his gravestone are incorrect.

According to *The 1903 History*, which was published two to three years before his death, Edmund "accumulated a large farm property, consisting of seven hundred and ninety acres, which he devotes largely to the raising of stock" (Duncan, 1903, p. 507). His knowledge of stock raising probably originated from his English farm upbringing in the village of Lifton, where a "large cattle fair is held in the village on the 13th of February, and a cattle show on the first Thursday in June" (White, 1850, p. 803). However he gained his knowledge, Edmund undeniably became a successful businessman. His farming success was reputedly "due wholly to his own efforts and the splendid judgment which he uses in the marketing of stock and the products of his farm" (Duncan, 1903, p. 507).

In addition to his substantial farming and real estate holdings, however, he had various diversified commercial interests. He was a stockholder for several years in the Commercial National Bank, the Citizens National Bank, and The Union Hardware and Implement Company, all in Independence. He also built a new, modern hotel in Independence in 1902 at an estimated cost of $10,000 for two stories and a basement.

His last will and testament contained the following real estate bequests, totaling just under 728 acres, all of them in Rutland Township, and showing he owned about two-thirds of section, 36, in which the Ingallses had lived, at the time of his death:

Ira Mason: About 88 acres in section 24.

James Mason: About 140 acres in section 24.

Cordelia Mason: 80 acres in section 26.
William Mason: 140 acres in section 36.
Stella Mason: About 140 acres in section 36.
Anna Mason: About 140 acres in section 36.

Edmund didn't bequeath any real estate to his oldest daughter, Ida Lindley, because he had already transferred lots 17 and 18 of Block 41 in the city of Independence to her, as well as ten shares of Citizens National Bank of Independence, Kansas, stock.

Edmund also bequeathed $50 cash to William, Stella, and Anna and gave instructions to have a house and barn built on the land given to Anna, with a total cost not to exceed $1,000. The remainder of his estate was to be divided equally among his seven surviving children.

That the remainder of his estate was to be "divided equally among [his] children," meant Ida Lindley, William Mason, Ira Mason, James Mason, Cordelia A. Mason, Stella Mason, and Anna Mason. In this will, Edmund appeared to make a clear and overt declaration that these were his *only* children, which is perhaps the strongest indicator that he was not the father of Henry, Opal, and Marie as Etta had both claimed and insinuated (Mason, 2015).

Part of the land bequeathed to Stella and Anna, the southern half of the southeast quarter of section 36, township 33, range 14 (immediately east of the old Ingalls land) was transferred to Edmund by Harry W. Talbott and others in 1898 for the sum of just $1 (*The Coffeyville Daily Journal*, 1898a, p. 4). In contrast, the land that was bequeathed to Cordelia was transferred to Edmund, also in 1898, for the much larger sum of $1,200 by John A. Sampson (*The Coffeyville Daily Journal*, 1898b, p. 4). In addition to the lots in Independence that were transferred to Ida, in 1903, H. O. Cavert and wife transferred lot 16, block 41 in Independence to Edmund (*The Coffeyville Daily Journal*, 1903, p. 3). Thus, at some point, Edmund owned at least lots 16, 17, and 18 in block 41.

Interestingly, an atlas of Montgomery County from 1916 shows Etta Mason as owning the property that Edmund had bequeathed to Stella and Anna, but their brother, William, owned his adjacent piece of land. At the time of their father's death, Anna was just eleven-years-old and Cordelia was sixteen, whereas William was nearly thirty, so perhaps their status as minors somehow impacted the situation. This land was particularly referenced in his will as being part of a "nunc pro tunc order in a case heretofore decided in District Court of Montgomery County Kansas in which Etta Mason was Pltf and Edmund Mason Deft" (Mason, 2015).

What's a *Nunc Pro Tunc* Order?

A *nunc pro tunc* order is a court order that has a retroactive effect, as of a specified date, for the purpose of correcting an error or omission in a prior court order. When a court issues a *nunc pro tunc* order, its effect is as if the order was in place at the earlier date. "Nunc pro tunc" is Latin for "now for then."

This was almost certainly referring to Edmund and Etta's divorce decree and it was therefore likely Etta was granted this land during divorce proceedings. Though, if so, Edmund clearly believed he still owned this land as his will was written less than two months before his death. There was no official record of who owned what, however. A notice of their divorce that appeared in a local newspaper on April 3, 1896, read simply, "Etta Mason vs. Edmund Mason. Divorce granted—property divided as per stipulation" (*The Weekly Star and Kansan*, 1896b, p. 4).

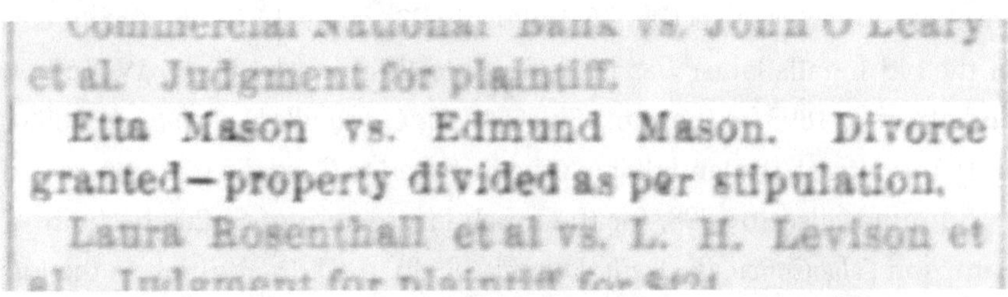
et al. Judgment for plaintiff.

Etta Mason vs. Edmund Mason. Divorce granted—property divided as per stipulation.

Laura Rosenthall et al vs. L. H. Levison et

Figure 44 - Notice of the granting of the divorce of Etta and Edmund Mason in The Weekly Star and Kansan

Not only did Edmund own lots in Independence, the "Mason Block," which he erected in 1902 in Block 41, still stands on the corner of Eighth and Main streets in Independence today, with the name "Mason" clearly visible near the top. These lots were probably the ones given to Ida shortly before his death.

When we began researching this project in earnest, part of the Mason building, not quite up to its former glory, housed a Chinese restaurant. But it was very elegant in its day, as this contemporary newspaper report describes:

> Here is a plain but handsome modern structure, neatly and substantially built and furnished with every convenience. The exterior is of our native vitrified pressed brick, which for beauty of tint and firmness of texture is unexcelled anywhere. On either side of the spacious front entrance, on Main street, are wide stretches of plate glass reaching to the sides of a room 45 feet in inside width; and this glass front is supplemented by another broad window on the Eighth street side. This room is 9[0] feet in length and is supplied with a lavatory and sewer . . . and water connections. It is . . . adapted for a dry goods or carriage display, or in fact for a big store of any kind, along modern lines.
>
> Back of this is a broad hallway opening directly on Eighth street, with a roomy stairway leading to the second story. In the rear of this, with another plate glass front on Eighth street, is another store room, 45x38, already occupied by Mr. John Henderson as a flour and feed store.
>
> The second floor has been leased by the Elks lodge for a term of five years, and thought not yet occupied by them was finished according to the plans suggested by Mayor Moses, who is at the head of the order here. The front room, 60x45 feet, has been fitted up for a lodge room, and is magnificently lighted by broad windows and high ceilings, which render it a most attractive place of resort for the members. Back of this we find a reception room, 22x28, for guests; a banquet room, 22x40, at the northeast corner; a well appointed kitchen; a reading room, 18x30, which will some time in the future be furnished with a couple of billiard tables; and convenient property rooms and spacious hallways and ante rooms connecting them all.

The entire building gives evidence of careful and painstaking workmanship, down to the smallest details, and reflects especial credit upon the architect who drew the plans and the builders who carried them out.

. . . .

When a hard-headed and practical farmer like Mr. Mason invests $10,000 in a business building of this kind, which is not only admirably adapted for the purposes for which it is designed but an ornament to the city as well, it shows that faith in the future of Independence is not confined to those who live here (*Independence Daily Reporter*, 1902, p. 3).

Figure 45 - The Mason Block as of July 2017

Although a substantiated connection between Edmund Mason and Laura Ingalls Wilder's Mr. Edwards doesn't appear to exist, Mason did lead an adventurous and, by financial standards at least, successful life. But it also held many curious and unexpected twists and turns. And we certainly hope there is more to learn about Mason . . . especially whether he fathered Etta's last three children!

– Appendix –
Understanding the Public Land Survey System

AS PROMISED, THIS appendix is an expanded and detailed description of the Public Land Survey System (PLSS) that was in place during the period of time before, during, and after the Ingallses were in Kansas.

Most of the land in the United States (except for the original thirteen states and Texas) was surveyed using this system, which divided areas of land into townships, sections, and quarter sections.

Meridians and Baselines

The PLSS was based on a series of north-south lines, similar to lines of longitude, called Principal Meridians. To complement these north-south lines, there was a set of shorter east-west lines called baselines. The PLSS was comprised of several regions, defined by the points where a meridian crossed a baseline (called an *initial point* or *origin*).

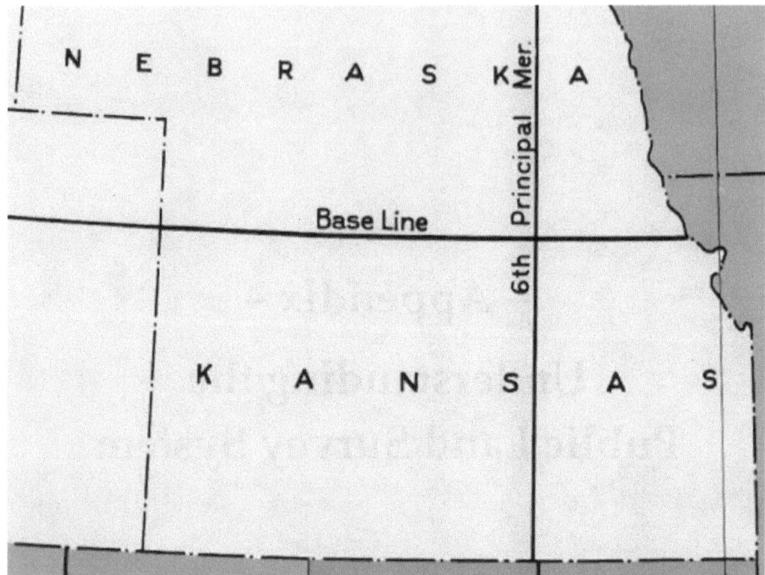

Figure 46 - Map showing the base line and principal meridian for surveying Kansas

Townships and Ranges

The basic unit of land within these regions was called a *township*, which was thirty-six square miles (six miles × six miles). A township was referenced by its position in the grid defined by the pertinent initial point. The term "township" was also used to define the position north-south of the baseline and "range" defined the position east-west of the principal meridian. So, for example, the township highlighted in the following diagram would be referenced as township 2 north, range 3 east.

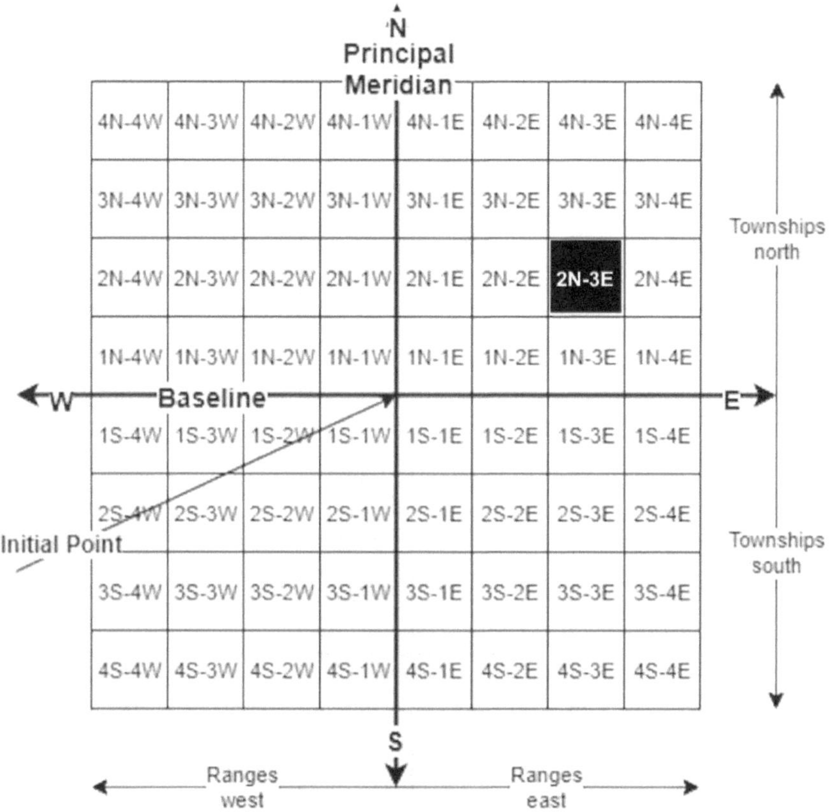

Figure 47 - Schematic diagram illustrating numbering of townships and ranges relative to a baseline and meridian

The correct legal description of this would be abbreviated as T.2 N, R.3 E. followed by an abbreviation for the relevant principal meridian. For the purposes of this book, we omitted the principal meridian reference (which was the 6th Principal Meridian for all of Kansas) and shortened the abbreviation to T2N-R3E.

Sections, Half Sections, and Quarter Sections

Townships were divided into units called *sections*, which were one square mile (one mile × one mile) or 640 acres. So, there were 36 sections in a township. Sections were further subdivided into half-sections, quarter-sections, etc. A quarter section was 160 acres, which was the amount of land available to be homesteaded under the Homestead Act. Sections within a township were numbered 1–36, beginning in the northeast corner, then zig-zagging west-south-east-south as follows:

6	5	4	3	2	1
7	8	9	10	11	12
18	17	16	15	14	13
19	20	21	22	23	24
30	29	28	27	26	25
31	32	33	34	35	36

Figure 48 - Order of section numbers within a township

When referencing a particular section in a legal land description, the section reference came before the township reference. Thus, for example, section 36 of township 2 north, range 3 east would be abbreviated: sec. 36, T.2 N., R.3 E. Again, for our purposes, we abbreviated this further to S36-T2N-R3E or 36-2N-3E.

Aliquot Divisions

Sections were usually further subdivided into half and quarter sections, which could be divided again into halves and quarters, and so on. These subdivisions, known as *aliquots,* were always referenced using the eight compass points: N, E, W, S, NW, NE, SW, and SE followed by "1/2" or "1/4" with the smallest subdivision coming first.

The following diagram helps to clarify this, as it shows various divisions of a single section.

<table>
<tr><td colspan="2" rowspan="2">NW1/4
(Northwest quarter)
160 acres</td><td colspan="2">N1/2NE1/4
(Northern half of the northeast quarter)
80 acres</td></tr>
<tr><td colspan="2">S1/2NE1/4
(Southern half of the northeast quarter)
80 acres</td></tr>
<tr><td rowspan="2">W1/2SW1/4
(Western half of the southwest quarter)
80 acres</td><td rowspan="2">E1/2SW1/4
(Eastern half of the southwest quarter)
80 acres</td><td>NW1/4SE1/4
(Northwest quarter of the southeast quarter)
40 acres</td><td>NE1/4SE1/4
(Northeast quarter of the southeast quarter)
40 acres</td></tr>
<tr><td>SW1/4SE1/4
(Southwest quarter of the southeast quarter)
40 acres</td><td>SE1/4SE1/4
(Southeast quarter of the southeast quarter)
40 acres</td></tr>
</table>

Figure 49 - Diagram showing aliquot divisions of a section

If a land description included land within more than one aliquot, the description was made up of multiple aliquots separated by commas, with the commas being read as "and."

For example, the land defined by the shaded area in Figure 50, overleaf, (comprising four aliquots) could be described as SE1/4 NW1/4, SW1/4 NE1/4, NW1/4 SE1/4, NE1/4 SW1/4 section 36, which means the south-east quarter of the northwest quarter *and* the southwest quarter of the northeast quarter *and* the northwest quarter of the southeast quarter *and* the northeast quarter of the southwest quarter of section 36.

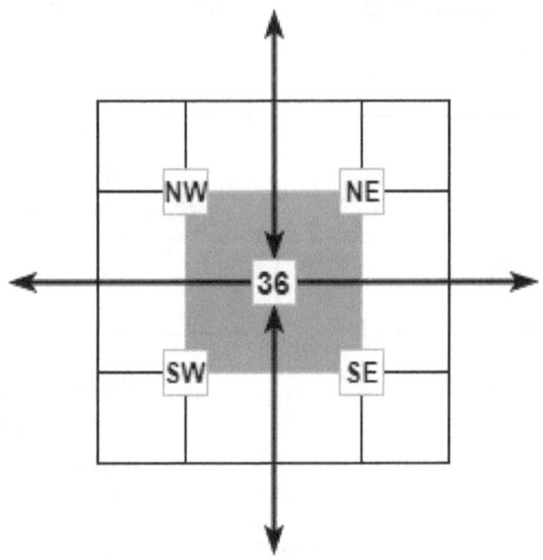

Figure 50 - Diagram illustrating a plot of land comprising four aliquots

Named Townships

So far, we've defined two versions of the term "township." As if that wasn't enough to confuse, there was a third usage of the term, which was "a named subdivision of a county." Just to make things yet more confusing, that version of the term may have or may not have corresponded exactly with the definition meaning a thirty-six-square-mile area of land. Sometimes it did. Usually, it did not.

In this book, we capitalized the word Township when referring to a named Township and used the lowercase word in both other cases. Also, note that "township" and "Township" were generally abbreviated twp. and Twp. respectively.

Montgomery County, Kansas, where the little house was located, was comprised of twelve named Townships (Louisburg, Sycamore, West Cherry, Cherry, Rutland, Independence, Drum Creek, Liberty, Caney, Fawn Creek, Parker, and Cherokee), which were themselves comprised of twelve complete townships and thirteen partial townships, as illustrated by the schematic map of Montgomery County, below.

Montgomery County

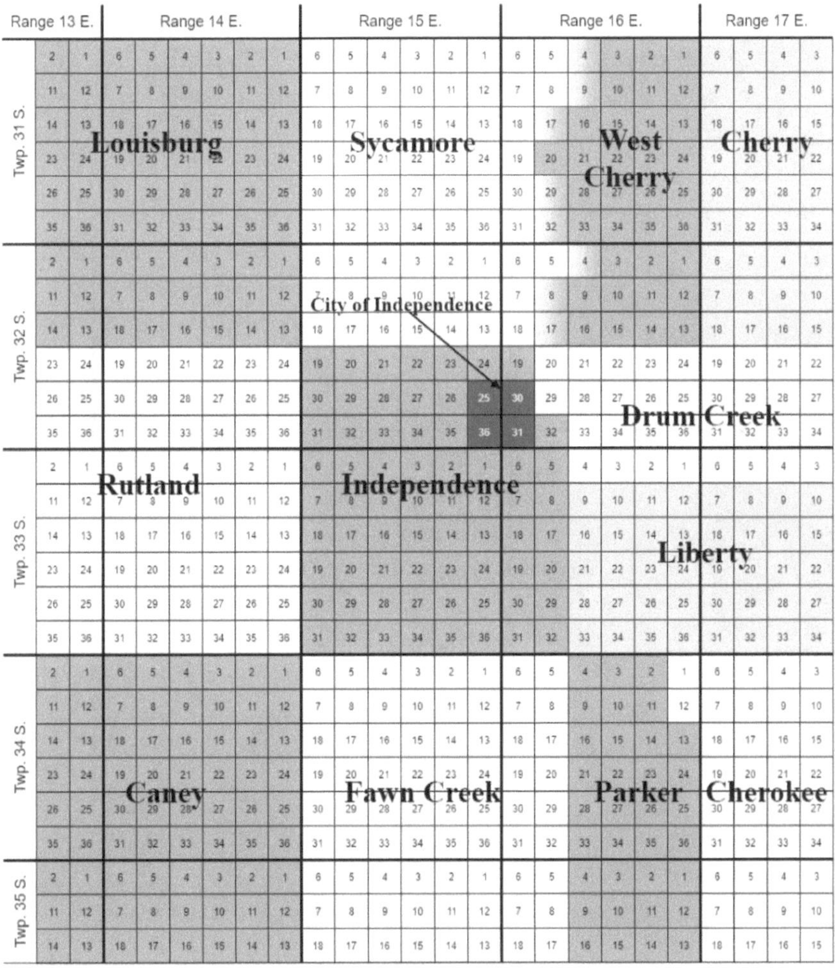

Figure 51 - Schematic map of Montgomery County showing townships and section numbers

Rutland Township, where the Ingalls family settled, and was the center of our search for Mr. Edwards, was comprised of portions of four (lower case) townships:

- All of township T33S-R14E
- The two easternmost "columns" of township T33S-R13E
- The three southernmost "rows" of township T32S-R14E
- Sections 23-26 & 35-36 of township T32S-R13E

	Range 13 E.		Range 14 E.					
	23	24	19	20	21	22	23	24
Twp. 32S	26	25	30	29	28	27	26	25
	35	36	31	32	33	34	35	36
	2	1	6	5	4	3	2	1
	11	12	7	8	9	10	11	12
	14	13	18	17	16	15	14	13
Twp. 33S	23	24	19	20	21	22	23	24
	26	25	30	26	28	27	26	25
	35	36	31	32	33	34	35	36

Figure 52 - Schematic diagram of Rutland Twp., showing townships, ranges, and section numbers

For the purposes of this book (and readability), references to "Rutland Township" generally referred to the shaded area (T33S-R14E), unless otherwise stated for clarity. Thus, for example, we referred to the section where the Ingalls family settled as "section 36 of Rutland Twp." even though there are four different sections 36 in Rutland Twp.

School Land Under the PLSS

In the original 1785 act, the PLSS designated section 16 as school land. If a school was built in the southeast corner, it was then centrally located within the township. This progressed such that, as a rule, both sections 16 and 36 were specifically reserved to be used for school land, whereas the other sections were available for homesteading. Section 36 was used to maintain the even spacing of the school sections, as illustrated below.

8	9	10	11	12	7	8	9	10	11	12	7	8	9
17	16	15	14	13	18	17	16	15	14	13	18	17	16
20	21	22	23	24	19	20	21	22	23	24	19	20	21
29	28	27	26	25	30	29	28	27	26	25	30	29	28
32	33	34	35	36	31	32	33	34	35	36	31	32	33
5	4	3	2	1	6	5	4	3	2	1	6	5	4
8	9	10	11	12	7	8	9	10	11	12	7	8	9
17	16	15	14	13	18	17	16	15	14	13	18	17	16
20	21	22	23	24	19	20	21	22	23	24	19	20	21
29	28	27	26	25	30	29	28	27	26	25	30	29	28
32	33	34	35	36	31	32	33	34	35	36	31	32	33
5	4	3	2	1	6	5	4	3	2	1	6	5	4
8	9	10	11	12	7	8	9	10	11	12	7	8	9
17	16	15	14	13	18	17	16	15	14	13	18	17	16

Figure 53 - Diagram illustrating the even spacing of school sections using sections 16 and 36

As we mentioned in the body of this book, section 36 being school land had a significant impact on our search for Mr. Edwards because the method by which a settler obtained land in that section (as well as section 16) was significantly different to other sections, which then impacted the type of historical land records kept and available for us to investigate.

The fact that the Ingalls family, and some of their neighbors, settled in one of these school sections in Rutland Township was further complicated by the fact that this all took place in Montgomery County, Kansas, which was located entirely within a portion of Osage Indian land known as the Osage Diminished Reserve.

Inline References

acatholicmission.org (no date) *Transition from Osage Mission to St. Paul, A Catholic Mission.* Available at: https://www.acatholicmission.org/12-transitions.html (Accessed: 12 August 2023).

Allen, D.R. (Lieut.) (1863) 'Muster Roll Entry for Longcor, George N.', in *Descriptive Roll of Captain Thomas H. Roseberry's Company (G) of Twenty-First Regiment Infantry Missouri Vols.*, p. 267 line 42. Available at: https://www.familysearch.org/ark:/61903/3:1:3QHV-J3DP-S9H2-G?i=266&cat=425623 (Accessed: 4 December 2020).

Brake v. Ballou (1877) *Kansas Reports.* Available at: https://books.google.com/books?id=2XVCAQAAMAAJ&pg=RA4-PA397#v=onepage&q&f=false (Accessed: 17 November 2020).

Brown, G.A. *et al.* (1869) 'Letter to the Hon. James M. Harvey, Governor of the State of Kansas regarding the disenfranchisement of voters in the election for the organization of Montgomery County', in *Montgomery County Organization Records*, pp. 48–51. Available at: https://www.kansasmemory.org/item/217033/page/48.

Buckner, Dr.B. (2004) *1850 U.S. Census Name Frequencies: Male First Names.* Available at: https://www.buckbd.com/genea/1850fnml.txt (Accessed: 3 November 2020).

Bur. of Land Mgmt. (2023) 'United States Bureau of Land Management Tract Books, 1800-c. 1955'. FamilySearch. Available at: https://www.familysearch.org/search/collection/2074276.

Bur. of Land Mgmt. (no date) 'Kansas S and E', in *United States Bureau of Land Management Tract Books.* Available at: https://www.familysearch.org/search/collection/2074276.

Cappello, N. (2019) 'The Bloody Benders: America's First Family of Serial Killers', *CrimeReads*, 19 August. Available at: https://crimereads.com/the-bloody-benders-americas-first-family-of-serial-killers/ (Accessed: 15 December 2020).

Chapman, B.B. (1938) *Removal of the Osages from Kansas, Part One. (The Kansas Historical Quarterly, vol. VII, no. 3, Aug. 1938, pp. 287–305), The Kansas Collection.* Translated by L.H. Nelson. Available at: http://www.kancoll.org/khq/1938/38_3_chapman.htm (Accessed: 20 July 2017).

'Christening Record for Edmund Mason' (1845). Available at: https://www.familysearch.org/ark:/61903/1:1:NTFT-58B.

Clarke, S. (1868) 'Report on the Treaty with the Great and Little Osage Indians', in *Congressional Globe.* 40th Cong., 2nd Sess., pp. 3256–3257. Available at: https://memory.loc.gov/cgi-bin/ampage?collId=llcg&fileName=082/llcg082.db&recNum=187 (Accessed: 23 June 2023).

Craig, J. (1872) 'Osage Trust Lands. Deposition in the Matter of the Application of Edmund Mason', in *Land Case Entry File no. 5022*. Land Office, Independence, Kansas.

Cutler, W.G. (1883) 'Montgomery County', in *History of the State of Kansas*. Chicago, Illinois: A. T. Andreas, p. 1563 et seq. Available at: https://hdl.handle.net/2027/umn.31951p010711602?urlappend=%3Bseq=519.

Dassler, C.F.W. (1876) 'Amendment to § 4, Kansas Sale of School Lands Act of 1864. "Privilege of purchasing, etc."', in *The General Statutes of Kansas*. St. Louis, MO: W. J. Gilbert, p. 934. Available at: https://www.google.com/books/edition/_/DUhMAQAAIAAJ (Accessed: 11 December 2020).

Drake, C.C. (1943) *Who's Who in Coffeyville, Kansas and Vicinity: A History of Kansas and Montgomery County, including the Cities of Coffeyville, Independence, Cherryvale, and Caney*. Coffeyville, Kansas. Available at: https://www.coffeyvillepl.org/wp-content/uploads/2018/08/Whos-Who.pdf (Accessed: 23 December 2020).

Drummond, W. and U.S. Dept. of the Interior (1871) 'Instructions Relating to Disposal of Osage Trust Land'. Available at: https://catalog.archives.gov/id/159146745 (Accessed: 4 November 2020).

Duncan, L.W. (1903) *History of Montgomery County, Kansas. By Its Own People.* Iola, Kansas: Press of Iola Register. Available at: http://archive.org/details/historyofmontgom00dunc (Accessed: 12 November 2020).

Easley, S. (2016–2017) 'Personal Communications re. Edmund Mason & Family'.

Edwards, J.P. (1881) *Historical Atlas of Montgomery County, Kansas.* Philadelphia. Available at: https://www.kansasmemory.org/item/224026 (Accessed: 19 August 2022).

Fitzpatrick, W.S. (Compiler) (ed.) (1895) 'Treaties and Laws of the Osage Nation as passed to November 26, 1890'. Press of the Cedar Vale Commercial. Available at: https://www.loc.gov/resource/llscd.02016475/?st=pdf (Accessed: 23 June 2023).

Foreman, G. (1933) 'Letter to Rose Wilder Lane', in *Little House on the Prairie-Background Material*. Iowa.

FreeBMD (no date) 'Edmund Mason Birth Index Entry', in *Civil Registration Index of Births (Sep Quarter 1845)*. Office for National Statistics. Available at: https://www.freebmd.org.uk/cgi/information.pl?cite=ev%2FHAw5hzUhLZvxjCbYUFg&scan=1 (Accessed: 4 December 2020).

Gen. Register Off. (1845) 'Edmund Mason Birth Certificate, 2 September 1845, application number 8447534-1.'

Gibson, I.T. (1872) 'No. 72.—Annual report of J. T. Gibson, agent Neosho Agency. Central Superintendency', in *Report of the Commissioner of Indian Affairs for the year 1871*. Washington: Government Printing Office, pp. 483–489. Available at: https://digitalcommons.csumb.edu/hornbeck_usa_2_e/9/ (Accessed: 23 June 2023).

Graves, W.W. (1916) *Life and Letters of Fathers Ponziglione, Schoenmakers and Other Early Jesuits at Osage Mission*. St. Paul, Kansas: W. W. Graves. Available at: https://archive.org/details/ponziglionescho00gravrich.

Graves, W.W. (1928) *Life and Letters of Rev. Father John Schoenmakers S.J.: Apostle to the Osages*. Parsons, Kansas: The Commerical Publishers. Available at: https://babel.hathitrust.org/cgi/pt?id=uc1.%24b306021.

Hairgrove, A. (1870) 'Note explaining why no real estate values were listed in the census schedules 1 & 3', in *United States Census, 1870. Kansas > Montgomery > Rutland > image 15 of 18*. FamilySearch. Available at: https://www.familysearch.org/ark:/61903/3:1:S3HT-64V9-5J4?i=14&wc=KGL5-C68%3A518653501%2C518914201%2C518835801&cc=1438024 (Accessed: 10 December 2020).

Harper, P.F. (1988) *Surely It Floweth with Milk and Honey: A History of Montgomery County, Kansas to 1930*. Independence, Kansas: Independence Community College Press.

Independence Daily Reporter (1896) 'Details of District Court Appearance in Etta Mason vs. Edward Mason ("About 6 p.m. the court heard the case of Etta Mason vs. Edward Mason, of Bolton . . .")', [Independence, Kansas], 22 March, p. 2.

Independence Daily Reporter (1902) 'A Modern Structure. Independence Adds Another to Her List of Elegant and Fashionable Business Blocks.', [Independence, Kansas], 25 July, p. 3.

Independence Daily Reporter (1906) 'Death of Edward Mason Last Night of Ulcer', [Independence, Kansas], 25 January, p. 1.

Independence Daily Reporter (1920) 'Death of Mrs. Ella Mason. Widow of the Late Edward Mason Passed Away This Afternoon', [Independence, Kansas], 6 August, p. 5.

Independence Pioneer (1870) 'Osage Treaty Accepted at Last', [Independence, Kansas], 17 September, pp. 2–3.

Jones, W.W. (1870) 'A Trip to the Verdigris and Caney Rivers', *The Girard Press*. [Girard, Kansas], 6 January, p. 1.

Koupal, N.T. (ed.) (2017) *Pioneer Girl Perspectives: Exploring Laura Ingalls Wilder*. Pierre: South Dakota Historical Society Press.

'Little House on the Prairie: The Pilot' (1974).

Mack, J.N. (2009) *Swords Into Ploughshares: The Struggle to Build an Ordered Community of Liberty on the southeast Kansas Frontier 1867-1876*. Ph.D. Dissertation (History). University of Kansas. Available at: https://kuscholarworks.ku.edu/handle/1808/5430 (Accessed: 25 March 2020).

Marcy, R.B. (1859) *The Prairie Traveler: A Hand-book for Overland Expeditions*. New York: Harper & Brothers.

'Marriage License for Edmund Mason and Mary E. Howard' (1874). Available at: https://www.familysearch.org/ark:/61903/3:1:939J-T83Q-GW?i=128.

Mason, E. (1896) 'Notice. ('All persons are hereby warned against trusting my wife, Etta Mason . . .')', *The Weekly Star and Kansan*. [Independence, Kansas], 31 January, p. 3.

Mason, E. (2015) 'Last Will and Testament of Edmund Mason'. Ancestry.com Operations, Inc. Available at: https://www.ancestry.com/search/collections/9065/.

Mason, J. (1872) 'Osage Trust Lands. Deposition in the Matter of the Application of Edmund Mason', in *Land Case Entry File no. 5022*. Land Office, Independence, Kansas.

Mason, J. (1887) 'Notice. ('All persons are hereby warned against trusting my wife, Emma Mason . . .')', *Independence Daily Reporter*. [Independence, Kansas], 19 October, p. 1.

Mason, T. (1866) 'Last Will and Testament of Thomas Mason'. Translated by S. Easley. Available at: https://probatesearch.service.gov.uk/#calendar (Accessed: 2 December 2020).

McFarland, H.M. (1933) 'Letter to Laura Ingalls Wilder', in *Little House on the Prairie-Background Material*. Iowa.

McVicar, P. and Kansas State Hist'l Soc. (1896) 'School Lands on the Osage Reservation. (An address delivered before the State Historical Society, at the annual meeting January 19, 1892)', in F.G. Adams (ed.)

Transactions of the Kansas State Historical Society, 1889-'96. Topeka: Press of the Kansas State Printing Co., pp. 69–71. Available at: https://archive.org/details/collections05kansuoft (Accessed: 11 December 2020).
Miller, R.E. (2016) *The Three Faces of Nellie*. Practical Pioneer Press.
Montgomery Co., KS, Clerk's Off. (1881) 'Sales of School Lands: Reports of Installments of Principal and Interest paid, for the six months ending June 30, 1881 (containing various payments for Sections 16 & 36 in townships 31-34, ranges 14-17)'.
Montgomery Co., KS, Reg. of Deeds (1872) 'Warranty Deed: Edmund Mason to John Craig', in *Montgomery County Deed Records*, p. 113.
Murdock, D.H. (1870) 'Letter to Adjutant Post of S.E. Kas. regarding assent of the Osages to sale of their [reservation] and removal to Indian Territory', in *Neosho Agency, 1831-1875: 1870-1871*, pp. 36–37. Available at: https://catalog.archives.gov/id/164143232 (Accessed: 7 December 2020).
Nobel, J. (2013) *Bloody Benders – The Forgotten Story of a Family of Pioneer Serial Killers, Digital Dying*. Available at: https://www.funeralwise.com/digital-dying/bloody-benders-the-forgotten-story-of-a-family-of-pioneer-serial-killers/ (Accessed: 15 December 2020).
Osmond, C. (2017) 'Ornery - Usage, Meaning & Examples', *Grammarist*, 18 October. Available at: https://grammarist.com/interesting-words/ornery/ (Accessed: 27 June 2023).
South Kansas Tribune (1871a) 'A suit has been instituted in the District Court of Allen county against the register and receiver of the United States Land Office, Humboldt', [Independence, Kansas], 27 September, p. 3.
South Kansas Tribune (1871b) 'From Humboldt. ('In conversation with Mr. C. M. Ralstin, . . .')', [Independence, Kansas], 26 July, p. 3.
South Kansas Tribune (1871c) 'Land Office Removed', [Independence, Kansas], 16 August, p. 2.
South Kansas Tribune (1871d) 'Notice of Contest: U.S. Land Office, Humboldt, Kansas, July 10th, 1871', [Independence, Kansas], 9 August, p. 3.
South Kansas Tribune (1871e) 'Our County. ("Among the numerous interesting localities of Montgomery county . . . is the valley of Onion Creek. . . .")', [Independence, Kansas], 17 May, p. 1.
The Border Sentinel (1873) 'The Cherryvale Horror: The Murders in Labette County', [Mound City, Kansas], 16 May, p. 2.

The Coffeyville Daily Journal (1898a) 'Real Estate Transfers. Harry W Talbott et al to Edmund Mason', [Coffeyville, Kansas], 17 May, p. 4.

The Coffeyville Daily Journal (1898b) 'Real Estate Transfers. John A. Sampson to Edmund Mason', [Coffeyville, Kansas], 22 November, p. 4.

The Coffeyville Daily Journal (1903) 'Real Estate Transfers. H. O. Cavert and wife to Edmund Mason', [Coffeyville, Kansas], 18 August, p. 3.

The Coffeyville Daily Journal (1914) 'A. K. Johnson Funeral details. Round About Coffeyville', [Coffeyville, Kansas], 17 October, p. 4.

The Coffeyville Daily Journal (1920) 'Mrs. Etta Mason (Obituary). 'Round About Coffeyville', [Coffeyville, Kansas], 7 August, p. 9.

The Coffeyville Weekly Journal (1901) 'Country Correspondence. Bolton. ('John and Ed Mason will start for their old home in England . . .')', [Coffeyville, Kansas], 17 May, p. 5.

The Daily Free Press and the Times (1906) 'Death of Edmund Mason', [Independence, Kansas], 26 January, p. 5.

The Evening Star (1905) 'A Pioneer Gone (John Mason Obituary)', [Independence, Kansas], 21 November, p. 5.

The Evening Star (1906a) 'Burial of Ed. Mason', [Independence, Kansas], 26 January, p. 5.

The Evening Star (1906b) 'J. L. James . . . Gets into Bitter Altercation over Division of Property', [Independence, Kansas], 2 August, p. 1.

The Independence Kansan (1878) 'We have been informed of the death of Frederick Brown . . .', [Independence, Kansas], 3 April, p. 3.

The Nat'l Archives (UK) (1851) 'Family of Thomas & Joanna Mason (1851). PRO /1884, Folio 225, Page 7, Schedule 16, Colmans: General Register Office: 1851 Census Returns database'. FreeCEN Free UK Genealogy. Available at: https://www.freecen.org.uk/search_records/597e8f27f4040b024a5d5e4f (Accessed: 26 November 2020).

The Nat'l Archives (UK) (1861) 'Family of Thomas & Joanna Mason (1861). PRO RG 9/1464, Folio 60, Page 1, Schedule 4: General Register Office: 1861 Census Returns database'. FreeCEN Free UK Genealogy. Available at: https://www.freecen.org.uk/search_records/5a148140f4040b9d6e7a3b00 (Accessed: 26 November 2020).

The Osage Mission Journal (1869) 'Legislative/Settlers Meeting', [Lawrence, Kansas], 7 January, p. 2.

The Times (1906) 'More About that Trouble at Wayside', [Independence, Kansas], 10 August, p. 4.

The Times (1907) 'J. L. James, of Wayside, dropped in yesterday . . .', [Independence, Kansas], 14 June, p. 5.

The Weekly Star and Kansan (1888) 'Mrs. Emma Mason was convicted . . .', [Independence, Kansas], 14 December, p. 3.

The Weekly Star and Kansan (1896a) 'Details of District Court Appearance in Etta Mason vs. Edward Mason ("About 6 p.m. the court heard the case of Etta Mason vs. Edward Mason, of Bolton . . .")', [Independence, Kansas], 27 March, p. 4.

The Weekly Star and Kansan (1896b) 'District Court Notes. Etta Mason vs. Edmund Mason. ('Divorce granted . . .')', [Independence, Kansas], 3 April, p. 4.

The Weekly Star and Kansan (1896c) 'The papers for a divorce suit were filed last week . . . for Mrs. Etta Mason against Edward Mason . . .', [Independence, Kansas], 31 January, p. 4.

U.S. Congress (1856) 'The Preemption Act of 1841. 5 Stat. 453. Sep 4, 1841', in *United States Statutes at Large*. Boston: Little, Brown, and Co., p. 453. Available at: https://tile.loc.gov/storage-services/service/ll/llsl//llsl-c27/llsl-c27.pdf (Accessed: 18 December 2020).

U.S. Congress (1870) 'Provision for the Removal of the Osage from Kansas. "And be it further enacted, That whenever the Great and Little Osage Indians shall agree thereto . . ." 16 Stat. 335 § 12', in *The Indian Appropriations Act of the 15th of July, 1870*, p. 362. Available at: https://www.loc.gov/resource/llsalvol.llsal_016/?sp=398 (Accessed: 18 December 2020).

U.S. Dept. of Agric. (1941) 'Aerial Photography Index for Montgomery County, Kansas, Sheet 3'. Available at: https://catalog.archives.gov/id/106759595 (Accessed: 10 December 2020).

U.S. Dept. of the Interior and Kansas State Hist'l Soc. (no date) *Records from Kansas Land Offices, Kansas Historical Society*. Available at: https://www.kshs.org/archives/193307 (Accessed: 24 November 2020).

U.S. Gen. Land Off. (1871) *Report of the Commissioner of General Land Office for the Year 1871*. Washington: Government Printing Office, Washington, p. 9,16,137,143. Available at: https://books.google.com/books?id=DK0yAQAAMAAJ.

U.S. Gen. Land Off. (1873) 'Edmund Mason (Independence, Kansas) Land Case Entry File no. 5022. Osage Trust & Diminished Reserve Lands.'

U.S. Gen. Land Off. (1874) 'Sarah E. Hunt (Montgomery County, Kansas) Land Patent no. 3504'. Available at: https://glorecords.blm.gov/details/patent/default.aspx?accession=KS1410__.008&docClass=STA&sid=fvd3yryx.m5q#patentDetailsTabIndex=1 (Accessed: 24 November 2020).

U.S. Geol. Survey (1886) 'Map of Kansas, Independence Sheet (Topographic)'. Department of the Interior/USGS. Available at: https://ngmdb.usgs.gov/ht-bin/tv_browse.pl?id=321e25091cbc351340beb26f61daccc4.

U.S. Geol. Survey (1894) 'Map of Kansas, Independence Sheet (Topographic)'. Department of the Interior/USGS. Available at: https://ngmdb.usgs.gov/ht-bin/tv_browse.pl?id=a849e0ba619c8da239446258a6fbc623.

U.S. Geol. Survey (1905) 'Map of Kansas, Independence Quadrangle (Topographic)'. Department of the Interior/USGS. Available at: https://ngmdb.usgs.gov/ht-bin/tv_browse.pl?id=7aa753f40d89359d8018cbe892371401.

U.S. Geol. Survey (1959) 'Map of Bolton Quadrangle, Kansas, Montgomery Co. (Topographic)'. Department of the Interior/USGS (7.5 Minute Series). Available at: https://ngmdb.usgs.gov/ht-bin/tv_browse.pl?id=91792d7908050064562e79a953a6b921 (Accessed: 29 June 2023).

White, W. (1850) 'Lifton Parish', in *History, Gazetteer & Directory of Devon, 1850*. Sheffield: Robert Leader (printer), pp. 803–804. Available at: https://specialcollections.le.ac.uk/digital/collection/p16445coll4/id/218254/ (Accessed: 16 November 2020).

Wilder, L.I. (1992) *On the Banks of Plum Creek*. Mammoth.

Wilder, L.I. (2014) *Pioneer Girl: The Annotated Autobiography*. Edited by P.S. Hill. Pierre, South Dakota: South Dakota Historical Society Press.

Wilder, L.I. (2016) *The Selected Letters of Laura Ingalls Wilder*. First edition. Edited by W. Anderson. New York, NY: Harper, an imprint of HarperCollins Publishers.

Wilder, L.I. (no date a) *Little House on the Prairie (Unpub. MS., Folder 14)*. Unpublished Manuscripts.

Wilder, L.I. (no date b) *Little House on the Prairie (Unpub. MS., Folder 15)*. Unpublished Manuscripts.

Wilder, L.I. (no date c) *Little House on the Prairie (Unpub. MS., Folder 16)*. Unpublished Manuscripts.

Wilder, L.I. (no date d) *Little House on the Prairie (Unpub. MS., Folder 17)*. Unpublished Manuscripts.

Wing, N. (2014) *A History of Tobacco in London, Londonist.* Available at: https://londonist.com/2014/11/london-a-history-in-tobacco (Accessed: 24 July 2017).

Zabriskie, J.C. (ed.) (1870) 'Kansas Sale of School Lands Act of 1864. "No. 160 E.-An Act to provide for the sale of the school lands." Feb 22, 1864. (Kansas. Legislative Acts)', in *The Public Land Laws of The United States*. San Francisco: H. H. Bancroft and Co., p. 734. Available at: https://www.google.com/books/edition/_/NDxHAQAAMAAJ (Accessed: 11 December 2020).

Zochert, D. (1976) *Laura: The Life of Laura Ingalls Wilder*. Avon.

Bibliography

"1841 Census of Lifton, Devon. Mason Families from Lifton and Kelly Parishes, Devon, England." *Our Family Past*, https://www.ourfamilypast.com/article/topic/945/1841-census-lifton-devon. Accessed 14 Dec. 2020.

1890 Veterans Schedules of the U.S. Federal Census for Washington F Roser. Ancestry.com Operations Inc, 2005, https://www.ancestry.com/search/collections/8667/. ancestry.com, 1890 Veterans Schedules of the U.S. Federal Census [database on-line].

"A. K. Johnson Funeral Details. Round About Coffeyville." *The Coffeyville Daily Journal*, [Coffeyville, Kansas], 17 Oct. 1914, p. 4. newspapers.com.

"A. K. Johnson of Bartlesville I.T., Passed through This City Yesterday . . ." *News-Broad-Ax*, [Coffeyville, Kansas], 28 May 1891, p. 5. newspapers.com.

"A Modern Structure. Independence Adds Another to Her List of Elegant and Fashionable Business Blocks." *Independence Daily Reporter*, [Independence, Kansas], 25 July 1902, p. 3. newspapers.com.

"A Narrow Chance. Mr. Ed. Mason Submits to a Serious Surgical Operation." *The Evening Star*, [Independence, Kansas], 23 Jan. 1906, p. 4. newspapers.com.

"A Pioneer Gone (John Mason Obituary)." *The Evening Star*, [Independence, Kansas], 21 Nov. 1905, p. 5. newspapers.com.

"A Resolution Enabling Bona Fide Settlers to Purchase Certain Lands Acquired from the Great and Little Osage Tribe of Indians, April 10, 1869 [No. 18]." *United States Statutes at Large*, vol. 16, Little, Brown, and Co., 1871, pp. 55–56, https://hdl.handle.net/2027/mdp.35112200623421?urlappend=%3Bseq=123. Hathi Trust Digital Library.

"A Strong Company (Ed. Mason Listed among Stockholders)." *The Weekly Star and Kansan*, [Independence, Kansas], 15 June 1894, p. 2. newspapers.com.

"A Suit Has Been Instituted in the District Court of Allen County against the Register and Receiver of the United States Land Office, Humboldt." *South Kansas Tribune*, [Independence, Kansas], 27 Sept. 1871, p. 3. newspapers.com.

Abel, Annie Heloise. *Indian Reservations in Kansas and the Extinguishment of Their Title*. University of Kansas, 1900, https://kuscholarworks.ku.edu/handle/1808/8221. KU ScholarWorks.

acatholicmission.org. "Transition from Osage Mission to St. Paul." *A Catholic Mission*, https://www.acatholicmission.org/12-transitions.html. Accessed 12 Aug. 2023.

Adelbert Streeter, Private, Company H, 58th Regiment, Illinois Infantry, Union. FamilySearch, United States Civil War Soldiers Index, 1861-1865, *Washington D.C.: Nat'l Archives and Recs. Admin.*, https://www.familysearch.org/ark:/61903/1:1:FSWJ-7ZW. Accessed 16 Dec. 2020.

"Administrator's Notices Regarding the Estate of Thomas H. Mason." *South Kansas Tribune*, [Independence, Kansas], 12 Mar. 1873, p. 3. newspapers.com.

Akright, Ora Frye. *Indian Land Cessions to the United States*. University of Kansas, 1924, https://kuscholarworks.ku.edu/handle/1808/21357. KU ScholarWorks.

Allen, Daniel R. (Lieut.). "Muster Roll Entry for Longcor, George N." *Descriptive Roll of Captain Thomas H. Roseberry's Company (G) of Twenty-First Regiment Infantry Missouri Vols.*, 1863, p. 267 line 42. FamilySearch, Military Records; 17th regiment infantry companies A-K 18th regiment infantry A-K 21st regiment infantry A-K 23rd regiment infantry A-K 24th regiment infantry A-K 25th regiment infantry A-K, *LDS film #1021082*, https://www.familysearch.org/ark:/61903/3:1:3QHV-J3DP-S9H2-G?i=266&cat=425623.

Anderson, William, editor. *A Little House Sampler*. Perennial Library, 1989.

---. *Laura Ingalls Wilder: A Biography*. 1st ed, HarperCollins, 1992.

---. *Laura Ingalls Wilder Country*. HarperPerennial, 1990.

Andes, L. D. "Letter Relinquishing SW1/4 S27-T34S-R13E in Montgomery County, Kansas, to Sutton McWhorter for $200." *Letters of Cancellation, Rejections and Suspensions*, 1871, pp. 351–52, https://catalog.archives.gov/id/140115204. National Archives, Letters of Cancellation, Rejections, and Suspensions, 5/19/1862 - 11/4/1871; Records of the Bureau of Land Management, 1685 - 2006 (RG49); National Archives at Kansas City (RM-KC), Kansas City, MO.

"Andrew John Brown (1846-1916) - Find A Grave Memorial." *Find A Grave*, https://www.findagrave.com/memorial/39096571/andrew-john-brown. Accessed 23 July 2017.

Baird, Alex H. "Letter to Hon J. D. Cox in Relation to Settlers Going upon Lands of the Osage Indians in Kansas." *Neosho Agency, 1831-1875: 1870-1871*, 1870, pp. 49–53, https://catalog.archives.gov/id/164143232. National Archives, M234 - Letters Received by the Office of Indian Affairs, 1824-1881; Letters Received, 1824 - 1880; Records of the Bureau of Indian Affairs, 1793 - 1999 (RG75); National Archives Building, Washington, DC.

Banns of Marriage between Thomas Mason & Joanna Mason. FamilySearch, 1831, https://www.familysearch.org/ark:/61903/3:1:939N-QPWV-S?i=14&cc=1804330&personaUrl=%2Fark%3A%2F61903%2F1%3A1%3AKCS6-G9P. FamilySearch, England, Devon, Parish Registers, 1538-1912. Dunterton Register of Banns of Marriage, p. 7, #14 (image 15).

"Bar Docket: Montgomery County District Court for the March Term Beginning March 3d, 1896. Court Docket. Etta Mason vs. Edmund Mason." *The Weekly Star and Kansan*, [Independence, Kansas], 28 Feb. 1896, p. 4. newspapers.com.

"Barnett Cemetery." *Kankakee Valley Genealogical Society*, http://www.kvgs.org/k3socemBARpics.html. Accessed 24 Nov. 2020.

Bass, N., et al. *Appointment of Appraisers to Appraise Section 36 Township 33 Range 14*. 15 Dec. 1871. State Archives Division, Kansas Historical Society, Copy in possession of author.

Becker, Sharon R., transcriber. "Ringgold County Iowa History Chapter Two ~ Out Of The Pathway Of Main Travel." *IAGenWeb Project. Ringgold County*, Jan. 2011, http://iagenweb.org/ringgold/history/1942/hist-1942_ChapTwo.html.

Becker, Sharon R., and Cathy Kilgore. "Ringgold County IAGenWeb Project ~ 'T-V' Surnames, Rose Hill Cemetery, Mount Ayr IA." *IAGenWeb Project. Ringgold County*, http://iagenweb.org/ringgold/cemeteries/tscrpts/rosehill/T-V.html#v. Accessed 24 Nov. 2020.

Bien, Morris. "The Public Lands of the United States." *The North American Review*, vol. 192, no. 658, Sept. 1910, pp. 387–402. JSTOR.

"Brake v. Ballou." *Kansas Reports*, vol. 19, 1877, p. 397, https://books.google.com/books?id=2XVCAQAAMAAJ&pg=RA4-PA397#v=onepage&q&f=false.

"Brake v. Ballou, 19 Kan. 397 (1877)." *Reports of Cases Argued and Determined in the Supreme Court of the State of Kansas*, 2nd Edition: Extra Annotated Edition, vol. 19, West Publishing, 1912, pp. 397–403, https://www.google.com/books/edition/Pacific_States_Reports_v_1_29_Kansas/2XVCAQAAMAAJ. Google Books, Pacific States Reports: v. 1- 29. Kansas.

"Branch No. 27 (Descendants of Thomas Latta)." *Latta Genealogy Society*, http://www.latta.org/Branches/Branch%2027.htm. Accessed 14 Feb. 2020.

Brown, George A., et al. "Letter to the Hon. James M. Harvey, Governor of the State of Kansas Regarding the Disenfranchisement of Voters in the Election for the Organization of Montgomery County." *Montgomery County Organization Records*, 1869, pp. 48–51,

https://www.kansasmemory.org/item/217033/page/48. Kansas Memory.
"Brown, Josiah J. (2 N.J. Inf.) Soldier Details." *The Civil War (U.S. National Park Service)*, https://www.nps.gov/civilwar/search-soldiers-detail.htm?soldierId=BE758B87-DC7A-DF11-BF36-B8AC6F5D926A. Accessed 15 Dec. 2020.
"Brown, Josiah J. (2 N.J. Vet. Inf.) Soldier Details." *The Civil War (U.S. National Park Service)*, https://www.nps.gov/civilwar/search-soldiers-detail.htm?soldierId=BD758B87-DC7A-DF11-BF36-B8AC6F5D926A. Accessed 15 Dec. 2020.
"Brown, Josiah J. (15 N.J. Inf.) Soldier Details." *The Civil War (U.S. National Park Service)*, https://www.nps.gov/civilwar/search-soldiers-detail.htm?soldierId=BF758B87-DC7A-DF11-BF36-B8AC6F5D926A. Accessed 15 Dec. 2020.
Buckner, Dr. Ben. *1850 U.S. Census Name Frequencies: Male First Names*. c 2004, https://www.buckbd.com/genea/1850fnml.txt.
Bur. of Land Mgmt. "Edmund Mason Tract Book Entry for NW1/4NW1/4 S30-T33-R15." *Kansas S and E*, vol. 41, p. 154, https://www.familysearch.org/ark:/61903/3:1:3QS7-89WS-YD3M?i=158. FamilySearch, United States Bureau of Land Management Tract Books, 1800-c. 1955; Kansas. Accessed 4 Dec. 2020.
---. "Frederick Brown Tract Book Entry for SE1/4NE1/4,NE1/4SE1/4 S20-T32-R15 & SW1/4NW1/4, NW1/4SW1/4 S21-T32-R15." *Kansas S and E*, vol. 41, p. 139, https://www.familysearch.org/ark:/61903/3:1:3QS7-99WS-Y8GN?i=140. FamilySearch, United States Bureau of Land Management Tract Books, 1800-c. 1955; Kansas. Accessed 17 Oct. 2022.
---. "Kansas S and E." *United States Bureau of Land Management Tract Books*, vol. 41, https://www.familysearch.org/search/collection/2074276. FamilySearch, "United States Bureau of Land Management Tract Books, 1800-c. 1955." Database with images.
---. "S. A. James Tract Book Entry for NW1/4SW1/4 S26-T33-R14." *Kansas S and E*, vol. 41, p. 45, https://www.familysearch.org/ark:/61903/3:1:3QS7-L9WS-Y63N?i=46. FamilySearch, United States Bureau of Land Management Tract Books, 1800-c. 1955; Kansas. Accessed 17 Oct. 2022.
"Burial of Ed. Mason." *The Evening Star*, [Independence, Kansas], 26 Jan. 1906, p. 5. newspapers.com.
Burns, Louis F. *A History of the Osage People*. University of Alabama Press, 2004.

Burr, Frank A., and Richard J. Hinton. *The Life of Gen. Philip H. Sheridan: Its Romance and Reality*. G. W. Lyon, 1889, https://www.google.com/books/edition/_/lGhHAQAAMAAJ?hl=en&gbpv=1&pg=PA3. Google Books.

Burrell, Howard A. "A. E. Sands." *History of Washington County Iowa From the First White Settlements to 1908*, vol. II, The S. J. Clarke Publishing Company, 1909, pp. 413–15, https://www.google.com/books/edition/_/TXcUAAAAYAAJ?hl=en&gbpv=1&pg=PA413. Google Books.

"Business References." *Historical Atlas of Montgomery County, Kansas*, 1881, p. 15.

"C. W. Canning." *History of Montgomery County, Kansas*, 1903, pp. 569–70, https://archive.org/details/historyofmontgom01dunc/page/568/mode/2up.

"Callahan's Present. ('Ed. Mason . . . Has Returned from a Protracted Visit at His Old Home in England. . . .')." *The Weekly Star and Kansan*, [Independence, Kansas], 5 Oct. 1905, p. 3. newspapers.com.

Cappello, Nile. "The Bloody Benders: America's First Family of Serial Killers." *CrimeReads*, 19 Aug. 2019, https://crimereads.com/the-bloody-benders-americas-first-family-of-serial-killers/.

Case, John F. "Let's Visit Mrs. Wilder." *Missouri Ruralist*, 20 Feb. 1918, p. 15. newspapers.com.

"Caught on the Wing. ('The Funeral of John Rowles . . .')." *The Wichita Daily Eagle*, [Wichita, Kansas], 29 Aug. 1915, p. 8. newspapers.com.

Chapman, Berlin B. "Removal of the Osages from Kansas, (Concluded). (The Kansas Historical Quarterly, Vol. VII, No. 4, Nov. 1938, Pp. 399–410)." *The Kansas Collection*, transcribed by Lynn H Nelson, Nov. 1938, http://www.kancoll.org/khq/1938/38_4_chapman.htm.

---. "Removal of the Osages from Kansas, Part One. (The Kansas Historical Quarterly, Vol. VII, No. 3, Aug. 1938, Pp. 287–305)." *The Kansas Collection*, transcribed by Lynn H Nelson, Aug. 1938, http://www.kancoll.org/khq/1938/38_3_chapman.htm.

Christening Record for Edmund Mason. 1845, https://www.familysearch.org/ark:/61903/1:1:NTFT-58B. FamilySearch, "England Births and Christenings, 1538-1975", database.

Christianson, James R. *A Study of Osage History Prior to 1876*. The University of Kansas, 1968, https://kuscholarworks.ku.edu/handle/1808/15010. KU ScholarWorks.

"Citizens National Bank, Independence, Kansas. Stockholders." *South Kansas Tribune*, [Independence, Kansas], 10 Apr. 1901, p. 1. newspapers.com.

Clarke, Frances M., and Rebecca Jo Plant. "No Minor Matter: Underage Soldiers, Parents, and the Nationalization of Habeas Corpus in Civil War America." *Law and History Review*, vol. 35, no. 4, Nov. 2017, pp. 881–927. *DOI.org (Crossref)*, https://doi.org/10.1017/S0738248017000414.

Clarke, Sidney. "Report on the Treaty with the Great and Little Osage Indians." *Congressional Globe*, 40th Cong., 2nd Sess., 1868, pp. 3256–57, https://memory.loc.gov/cgi-bin/ampage?collId=llcg&fileName=082/llcg082.db&recNum=187. Library of Congress, American Memory: U.S. Congressional Documents and Debates.

Clement, Margaret Gray. *Research on "Little House on the Prairie."* Independence Chamber of Commerce, 1972.

"Commercial National Bank, Independence, Kansas. Stock Holders." *South Kansas Tribune*, [Independence, Kansas], 10 Apr. 1901, p. 1. newspapers.com.

"Commercial National Bank, of Independence, Kas. Stockholders." *Independence Daily Reporter*, [Independence, Kansas], 4 Mar. 1893, p. 2. newspapers.com.

Congressional Globe. 40th Cong., 2nd Sess., 1868.

Connelley, William E. "Indians." *A Standard History of Kansas and Kansans*, vol. I, Lewis Publishing Company, 1919, pp. 226–28, https://babel.hathitrust.org/cgi/pt?id=hvd.32044086427754&view=1up&seq=290. Hathi Trust Digital Library.

Copp, Henry N., editor. *Public Land Laws Passed by Congress from March 4, 1869, to March 3, 1875*. A.L. Bancroft & Co., 1875, https://www.google.com/books/edition/Public_Land_Laws_Passed_by_Congress_from/0eQ9AAAAIAAJ. Google Books.

Cory, R. W., et al. *School Land Appraisement, State of Kansas, Montgomery County, Section 36 Township 33 South Range 14 East of the 6th P.M.* 18 Dec. 1871. State Archives Division, Kansas Historical Society, Copy in possession of author.

"Country Correspondence. Bolton. ('John and Ed Mason Will Start for Their Old Home in England . . .')." *The Coffeyville Weekly Journal*, [Coffeyville, Kansas], 17 May 1901, p. 5. newspapers.com.

"Covered Wagons." *The Oswego Weekly Register*, [Oswego, Kansas], Vol 1. No. 1., 13 May 1869, p. 2. newspapers.com.

Craig, John. "Osage Trust Lands. Deposition in the Matter of the Application of Edmund Mason." *Land Case Entry File No. 5022*, 1872.

Cutler, William G. "Montgomery County." *History of the State of Kansas*, A. T. Andreas, 1883, p. 1563 et seq., https://hdl.handle.net/2027/umn.31951p010711602?urlappend=%3Bseq=519. Hathi Trust Digital Library.

"Daniel B. Brown (1848-1878) - Find A Grave Memorial." *Find A Grave*, https://www.findagrave.com/memorial/151493854/daniel-b.-brown. Accessed 17 Aug. 2017.

"Daniel Everett (1836-1898) - Find A Grave Memorial." *Find A Grave*, https://www.findagrave.com/memorial/11338700/daniel-everett. Accessed 20 Mar. 2020.

Dassler, C. F. W. "Amendment to § 4, Kansas Sale of School Lands Act of 1864. 'Privilege of Purchasing, Etc.'" *The General Statutes of Kansas*, vol. 1, W. J. Gilbert, 1876, p. 934, https://www.google.com/books/edition/_/DUhMAQAAIAAJ. Google Books.

David H Mikel, 1884. 3 Apr. 2015, https://familysearch.org/ark:/61903/1:1:QVNS-BYQS. FamilySearch, United States General Index to Pension Files, 1861-1934.

"David Hugh Mikel (1841–1870), Sarah B. (1843–Deceased) Family Tree." *FamilySearch*, https://www.familysearch.org/tree/pedigree/landscape/KN8F-BWF. Accessed 14 Dec. 2020.

"Death Claimed Another Pioneer on Sunday in the Passing Away of Joseph L. James . . ." *South Kansas Tribune*, [Independence, Kansas], 5 July 1916, p. 5. newspapers.com.

"Death Claims Jos. L Jones. Another Old Settler Passed Away Yesterday (Joseph L. James)." *Independence Daily Reporter*, [Independence, Kansas], 3 July 1916, p. 2. newspapers.com.

"Death of Edmund Mason." *The Daily Free Press and the Times*, [Independence, Kansas], 26 Jan. 1906, p. 5. newspapers.com.

"Death of Edward Mason Last Night of Ulcer." *Independence Daily Reporter*, [Independence, Kansas], 25 Jan. 1906, p. 1. newspapers.com.

"Death of Mrs. Ella Mason. Widow of the Late Edward Mason Passed Away This Afternoon." *Independence Daily Reporter*, [Independence, Kansas], 6 Aug. 1920, p. 5. newspapers.com.

"Delinquent Tax List. Independence Township. John Thompson." *The Weekly Star and Kansan*, [Independence, Kansas], 27 July 1883, p. 4.

"Details of District Court Appearance in Etta Mason vs. Edward Mason ('About 6 p.m. the Court Heard the Case of Etta Mason vs. Edward Mason, of Bolton . . .')." *The Weekly Star and Kansan*, [Independence, Kansas], 27 Mar. 1896, p. 4. newspapers.com.

"---." *Independence Daily Reporter*, [Independence, Kansas], 22 Mar. 1896, p. 2. newspapers.com.

"Devon Census Populations Parishes I-M." *Footprints. Genealogy & Family History Research in Devon, England*, https://freepages.rootsweb.com/~footprints1/genealogy/dev2/census/i.htm. Accessed 4 Dec. 2020.

"Diogenes S. James." *History of Montgomery County, Kansas*, 1903, pp. 452–53, https://archive.org/details/historyofmontgom01dunc/page/452/mode/2up.

"District Court Notes. Etta Mason vs. Edmund Mason. ('Divorce Granted . . .')." *The Weekly Star and Kansan*, [Independence, Kansas], 3 Apr. 1896, p. 4. newspapers.com.

Dodge, Melvin Gilbert, editor. "Josiah Johnson Brown. (Rutgers Chapter. Rutgers College, New Brunswick N.J. Roll of Members, 1860)." *The Delta Upsilon Dicennial Catalogue*, Delta Upsilon Fraternity, 1902, p. 470, https://www.google.com/books/edition/The_Delta_Upsilon_Decennial_Catalogue_19/YN0CAAAAYAAJ. Google Books.

Drake, Charles Clayton. *Who's Who in Coffeyville, Kansas and Vicinity: A History of Kansas and Montgomery County, Including the Cities of Coffeyville, Independence, Cherryvale, and Caney*. 1943, https://www.coffeyvillepl.org/wp-content/uploads/2018/08/Whos-Who.pdf. Coffeyville Public Library.

Drummond, Willis and U.S. Dept. of the Interior. *Instructions Relating to Disposal of Osage Trust Land*. 28 Mar. 1871, https://catalog.archives.gov/id/159146745. National Archives, Instructions Relating to Disposal of Osage Trust Land, 3/28/1871 - 3/28/1871; Records of the Bureau of Land Management, 1685 - 2006 (RG 49); National Archives at Kansas City (RM-KC), Kansas City, MO.

Duncan, L. Wallace. *History of Montgomery County, Kansas. By Its Own People.* Press of Iola Register, 1903. archive.org, *Internet Archive*, http://archive.org/details/historyofmontgom00dunc.

"Early History of Montgomery County." *The Weekly Star and Kansan*, [Independence, Kansas], 27 Aug. 1897, p. 1. newspapers.com.

Easley, Sharon. *Personal Communications Re. Edmund Mason & Family*. 8 Dec. 2016–27 July 2017.

Eckles, Polly, transcriber. "1852 State Special Census of Iowa, Henry County." *Iowa State Census Project*, http://iagenweb.org/census/textdisplay.php?file=/census/henry/1852-IA-henry.txt. Accessed 21 Feb. 2020.

---, transcriber. "1854 State Census of Iowa, Henry County." *Iowa State Census Project*, http://iagenweb.org/census/textdisplay.php?file=/census/henry/1854/IA-1854Henry-Jefferson.txt. Accessed 21 Feb. 2020.

---, transcriber. "1856 State Census of Iowa, Henry County, Jefferson Township." *Iowa State Census Project*, http://iagenweb.org/census/textdisplay.php?file=/census/henry/1856-ia-henry-jefferson.txt. Accessed 21 Feb. 2020.

Eckles, Polly, and Marcia Arn, transcribers. "1854 State Census of Iowa - Washington County, All Townships." *Iowa State Census Project*, http://iagenweb.org/census/textdisplay.php?file=/census/washington/1854-ia-washington-all_twps.txt. Accessed 21 Feb. 2020.

"Edmund Mason." *History of Montgomery County, Kansas*, 1903, pp. 507–08, https://archive.org/details/historyofmontgom01dunc/page/506/mode/2up.

"Edmund Mason (1846-1906) - Find A Grave Memorial." *Find A Grave*, https://www.findagrave.com/memorial/8373663/edmund-mason. Accessed 17 Nov. 2020.

"Edmund Mason Erecting Building on the Corner of 8th and Main Streets. ('[The] Large and Substantial Building at the Corner of Eight and Main Sreets [*sic*] in This City . . .')." *The Evening Star*, [Independence, Kansas], 2 May 1902, p. 1. newspapers.com.

Edmund Mason (Montgomery County) Kansas State Land Patent for School Lands (W1/2NE1/4, E1/2NW1/4 S36-T33S-R14E 6th PM). 24 May 1881. Kansas Historical Society, Reference Services, State Archives Division, Topeka KS.

Edwards, John P. *Historical Atlas of Montgomery County, Kansas*. 1881, https://www.kansasmemory.org/item/224026. Kansas Memory.

Edwards, Richard, et al. *Homesteading the Plains: Toward a New History*. University of Nebraska Press, 2017.

"Everett, Daniel. Illinois Civil War Muster and Descriptive Rolls Detail Report." *Office of the Illinois Secretary of State. Illinois State Archives, Illinois Civil War Muster and Descriptive Rolls Database*, https://www.ilsos.gov/isaveterans/civilmustersrch.jsp [Search Criteria: 'Everett, Daniel']. Accessed 24 Nov. 2020.

"First Buildings in Independence: Judson House, First Log Hotel, Etc." *South Kansas Tribune*, [Independence, Kansas], Tribune Illustrated Edition, 24 July 1901, p. 41. newspapers.com.

"First Court House." *South Kansas Tribune*, [Independence, Kansas], 27 Aug. 1919, p. 12. newspapers.com.

Fitzpatrick, W. S. (Compiler), editor. *Treaties and Laws of the Osage Nation as Passed to November 26, 1890*. Press of the Cedar Vale Commercial, 1895, https://www.loc.gov/resource/llscd.02016475/?st=pdf. Law Library of Congress.

"Fleener, James A. Soldier Details." *The Civil War (U.S. National Park Service)*, https://www.nps.gov/civilwar/search-soldiers-detail.htm?soldierId=1283849D-DC7A-DF11-BF36-B8AC6F5D926A. Accessed 15 Dec. 2020.

Foreman, Grant. "Letter to Rose Wilder Lane." *Little House on the Prairie-Background Material*, 1933. National Archives, File 219; Box 14; Laura Ingalls Wilder Series; Rose Wilder Lane Papers; Herbert Hoover Presidential Library, West Branch, IA.

FreeBMD. "Edmund Mason Birth Index Entry." *Civil Registration Index of Births (Sep Quarter 1845)*, Office for National Statistics, https://www.freebmd.org.uk/cgi/information.pl?cite=ev%2FHAw5hzUhLZvxjCbYUFg&scan=1. FreeBMD. Accessed 4 Dec. 2020.

"From Humboldt. ('In Conversation with Mr. C. M. Ralstin, . . .')." *South Kansas Tribune*, [Independence, Kansas], 26 July 1871, p. 3. newspapers.com.

Garner, Bryan A., and Henry Campbell Black, editors. "Nunc pro Tunc." *Black's Law Dictionary*, 7th ed, West Group, 1999, p. 1097.

Gates, Paul W. *Fifty Million Acres: Conflicts Over Kansas Land Policy, 1854-1890*. Cornell University Press, 1954, http://archive.org/details/fiftymillionacre0000unse. Internet Archive.

Gen. Register Off. *Edmund Mason Birth Certificate, 2 September 1845, Application Number 8447534-1*. 1845. General Register Office for England and Wales (GRO), Tavistock Union, 1845 Sept Qtr, vol. 9, p. 462. Certified copy in possession of author.

General Highway Map, Montgomery County, Kansas. Kansas Dept. of Transportation, July 2017, http://wfs.ksdot.org/arcgis_web_adaptor/rest/directories/arcgisoutput/County/quarterInch/MontgomeryCountyQt.pdf.

"General Incidental Expenses of the Indian Service, § 12 Great and Little Osage Removal from Kansas. (Act of July 15, 1870)." *United States Statutes at Large*, vol. 16, Little, Brown, and Co., 1871, p. 362, https://hdl.handle.net/2027/mdp.35112200623421?urlappend=%3Bseq=450. Hathi Trust Digital Library.

"Geo. A. Brown, the Surveyor . . ." *South Kansas Tribune*, [Independence, Kansas], 7 Mar. 1894, p. 2. newspapers.com.

"George Andrew Brown (1844-1922) - Find A Grave Memorial." *Find A Grave*, https://www.findagrave.com/memorial/43877780/george-andrew-brown. Accessed 28 Mar. 2020.

"George Gilmour (1788-1835) - Find A Grave Memorial." *Find A Grave*, https://www.findagrave.com/memorial/42580735/george-gilmour. Accessed 20 Feb. 2020.

"George Newton Longcor (1842-1872) - Find A Grave Memorial." *Find A Grave*, https://www.findagrave.com/memorial/62444833/george-newton-longcor. Accessed 24 Nov. 2020.

"Georgia Ann 'Georgiana' Myers Streeter (1861-1907) - Find A Grave Memorial." *Find A Grave*, https://www.findagrave.com/memorial/90749714/georgia-ann-streeter. Accessed 1 Dec. 2020.

Gibson, Isaac T. "No. 72.—Annual Report of J. T. Gibson, Agent Neosho Agency. Central Superintendency." *Report of the Commissioner of Indian Affairs for the Year 1871*, Government Printing Office, 1872, pp. 483–89, https://digitalcommons.csumb.edu/hornbeck_usa_2_e/9/.

Gilmore, John S. "The Osage Indian and His Treaties." *History of Neosho and Wilson Counties, Kansas*, L. Wallace Duncan, 1902, pp. 838–46, https://www.google.com/books/edition/History_of_Neosho_and_Wilson_Counties_Ka/HjFEAQAAMAAJ. Google Books.

Golbez. *Map of the States and Territories of the United States as It Was from 1868 to 1876*. https://commons.wikimedia.org/wiki/File:United_States_1868-1876.png. Wikimedia Commons. Accessed 30 Nov. 2020.

Google. *Map of the SE Corner of Rutland Twp. & the SW Corner of Independence Twp., Montgomery County, KS*. Satellite Imagery, 2020. *Google Maps*, https://goo.gl/maps/UXfw3a8Z4uF6qaqb7.

---. *Map of the SE Corner of Rutland Twp. & the SW Corner of Independence Twp., Montgomery County, KS*. 2020. *Google Maps*, https://goo.gl/maps/hWZ7XBAcuDZ3oq4a9.

Graves, W. W. *Life and Letters of Fathers Ponziglione, Schoenmakers and Other Early Jesuits at Osage Mission*. W. W. Graves, 1916, https://archive.org/details/ponziglionescho00gravrich. archive.org.

---. *Life and Letters of Rev. Father John Schoenmakers S.J.: Apostle to the Osages*. The Commerical Publishers, 1928, https://babel.hathitrust.org/cgi/pt?id=uc1.%24b306021. Hathi Trust Digital Library.

Haines, Alanson A. "Josiah J. Brown." *History of the Fifteenth Regiment New Jersey Volunteers*, Jenkins & Thomas, 1883, pp. 248-9,384, https://archive.org/details/historyoffifteen00hain/page/n7/mode/2up. archive.org.

Hairgrove, Asa. "Note Explaining Why No Real Estate Values Were Listed in the Census Schedules 1 & 3." *United States Census, 1870. Kansas > Montgomery > Rutland > Image 15 of 18*, FamilySearch, 1870, https://www.familysearch.org/ark:/61903/3:1:S3HT-64V9-5J4?i=14&wc=KGL5-C68%3A518653501%2C518914201%2C518835801&cc=1438024. Washington, D.C.: Nat'l Archives and Recs. Admin., NARA microfilm publication M593.

Hamilton, John. "'From the Osage Country.' Letter to the Editor Regarding Treatment of the Osages by Settlers." *The Girard Press*, [Girard, Kansas], 3 Mar. 1870, p. 1. newspapers.com.

Hamilton, Samuel S., editor. *Indian Treaties, and Laws and Regulations Relating to Indian Affairs To Which Is Added an Appendix, Containing the Proceedings of the Old Congress, and Other Important State Papers, in Relation to Indian Affairs*. Way & Gideon, printers, 1826, https://www.google.com/books/edition/Indian_Treaties_and_Laws_and_Regulations/g3BBAAAAIAAJ. Google Books.

Hancock, Melanie. "TV Show Truths: Mr. Edwards." *Discover Laura*, https://discoverlaura.wordpress.com/2017/11/10/tv-show-truths-mr-edwards/. Accessed 10 Nov. 2017.

Harper, Paul F. *Surely It Floweth with Milk and Honey: A History of Montgomery County, Kansas to 1930*. Independence Community College Press, 1988.

"Harrisonville Cemetery Records, Montgomery County, Kansas." *Cemetery Records of Kansas*, vol. 12, pp. 22–41, https://www.familysearch.org/ark:/61903/3:1:3Q9M-CSSW-9QQD-C. FamilySearch, Kansas, Cemetery Abstracts. Accessed 16 Dec. 2020.

"Harrisonville Nuggets. (Quite a Serious Affair . . .')." *The Independence Kansan*, [Independence, Kansas], 16 Feb. 1881, p. 1. newspapers.com.

Hawkins, Kenneth. *Research in the Land Entry Files of the General Land Office: Reference Information Paper 114*. Nat'l Archives and Recs. Admin., Washington, DC, 2019, https://www.archives.gov/files/publications/ref-info-papers/rip114.pdf.

"Henry Alonzo VanWinkle (1847-1931) - Find A Grave Memorial." *Find A Grave*, https://www.findagrave.com/memorial/16668438/henry-alonzo-vanwinkle. Accessed 1 Dec. 2020.

Henthorn, Dick. "No Divorce for Uncle Wash by T. Clifford Morgan, Warsaw, MO, 1995." *Henthorn Genealogy News*, 23 Sept. 2009, https://henthorn-website-news.blogspot.com/2009/09/no-divorce-for-uncle-wash.html.

Hill, Pamela Smith. *Laura Ingalls Wilder: A Writer's Life*. South Dakota State Historical Society Press, 2007.

---. "Laura Ingalls Wilder Historical Timeline." *Little House on the Prairie*, 28 Dec. 2018, https://littlehouseontheprairie.com/history-timeline-of-laura-ingalls-wilder/.

History.com Editors. "Homestead Act." *HISTORY*, A&E Television Networks, 9 Nov. 2009, https://www.history.com/topics/american-civil-war/homestead-act.

---. "Kansas Enters the Union." *HISTORY*, A&E Television Networks, 13 Nov. 2009, https://www.history.com/this-day-in-history/kansas-enters-the-union.

Houdek Rule, Deb. *Laura Ingalls Wilder: Laura's Friends. Mr. Edwards.* http://www.dahoudek.com/liw/info/friends.aspx (Archived at: https://web.archive.org/web/20160208140945/http://www.dahoudek.com/liw/info/friends.aspx). Accessed 19 Jan. 2016.

"How To Enter Osage Lands." *The Lawrence Tribune*, [Lawrence, Kansas], 20 Apr. 1871, p. 2. newspapers.com.

Hutchings, C. F. "From Osage Mission: All Eyes Are Now Turned towards the Osage Diminished Reserve . . ." *The Daily Kansas Tribune*, [Lawrence, Kansas], 20 June 1869, p. 2. newspapers.com.

Ihrig, B. B. *History of Hickory County, Missouri*. 1970, http://www.familysearch.org/library/books/idurl/1/338765. FamilySearch Library.

"Illinois State Census, 1865." *Database with Images*, FamilySearch, https://www.familysearch.org/search/collection/1803971. Illinois State Archives, Springfield.

"Illustrations in 'Alone on the Plains. Notes of the Life the Pioneers Must Face.'" *The Smelter*, [Pittsburg, Kansas], 14 Sept. 1887, p. 7. newspapers.com.

"Immigration Still Continues to Pour In." *Independence Pioneer*, [Independence, Kansas], 13 Nov. 1869, p. 2. newspapers.com.

"Important to Settlers on Osage Lands." *The Leavenworth Times*, [Leavenworth, Kansas], 8 Apr. 1871, p. 3. newspapers.com.

"Important to Settlers on the Osage Lands." *The Daily Kansas Tribune*, [Lawrence, Kansas], 13 June 1869, p. 2. newspapers.com.

"In Memory of the Departed: Beautiful Memorial Services Held Yesterday by the Elks." *The Evening Star*, [Independence, Kansas], 7 Dec. 1908, p. 2. newspapers.com.

"Independence Is Growing . . ." *Independence Pioneer*, [Independence, Kansas], 1 Jan. 1870, p. 2. newspapers.com.

"Indian Land Cessions in the United States: Kansas 1." *Library of Congress, Washington, D.C. 20540 USA*, https://www.loc.gov/resource/g3701em.gct00002/?sp=26. Accessed 25 Oct. 2020.

"Injury Fatal to Aged Man: Joseph L. James Died Yesterday Afternoon." *The Evening Star*, [Independence, Kansas], 3 July 1916, p. 1. newspapers.com.

"Instructions for the Disposal of the Osage Indian Trust and Diminished Reserve Lands." *The Neodesha Citizen*, [Neodesha, Kansas], 21 Apr. 1871, p. 2. newspapers.com.

Iowa Adjutant General's Off. "Thirty-Fifth Regiment Iowa Volunteer Infantry." *Roster and Record of Soldiers in the War of the Rebellion Together with Historical Sketches of Volunteer Organizations 1861-1866*, vol. 5, Emory H. English, State Printer & E. D. Chassell, State Binder, 1911, pp. 507–612, https://hdl.handle.net/2027/hvd.hx2xt2?urlappend=%3Bseq=559. Hathi Trust Digital Library.

"Iowa, County Marriages, 1838-1934." *Database*, FamilySearch, https://www.familysearch.org/search/collection/1805551. County courthouses, Iowa.

"Iowa, Records of Persons Subject to Military Duty, 1862-1910." *Database with Images*, FamilySearch, https://www.familysearch.org/search/collection/2821291. State Historical Society, Des Moines.

"Iowa State Census, 1885." *Database with Images*, FamilySearch, https://www.familysearch.org/search/collection/1803643. Secretary of State. State Historical Society, Des Moines.

"Iowa State Census, 1895." *Database with Images*, FamilySearch, https://www.familysearch.org/search/collection/1803957. Secretary of State. State Historical Society, Des Moines.

"Iowa State Census, 1905." *Database with Images*, FamilySearch, https://www.familysearch.org/search/collection/2126961. State Historical Department, Des Moines.

"Iowa State Census, 1915." *Database with Images*, FamilySearch, https://www.familysearch.org/search/collection/2240483. Iowa State Historical Department, Des Moines.

"Iowa State Census, 1925." *Database with Images*, FamilySearch, https://www.familysearch.org/search/collection/2224537. Iowa State Historical Department, Des Moines.

"J. L. James . . . Gets into Bitter Altercation over Division of Property." *The Evening Star*, [Independence, Kansas], 2 Aug. 1906, p. 1. newspapers.com.

"J. L. James, of Wayside, Dropped in Yesterday . . ." *The Times*, [Independence, Kansas], 14 June 1907, p. 5. newspapers.com.

"J. S. Latta (1838-1894) - Find A Grave Memorial." *Find A Grave*, https://www.findagrave.com/memorial/174632245/j.-s.-latta. Accessed 14 Feb. 2020.

"James A Fleener (1846-1938) - Find A Grave Memorial." *Find A Grave*, https://www.findagrave.com/memorial/73665398/james-a-fleener. Accessed 4 Jan. 2021.

"James A. Flener." *History of Montgomery County, Kansas*, 1903, pp. 458–59, https://archive.org/details/historyofmontgom01dunc/page/458/mode/2up.

"James, Harvy Kiah (1944) (Obituary), Independence Daily Reporter, Independence, Kansas, 19 Aug 1944." *USGenWeb, Ohio County Kentucky Archives, Obituaries*, 5 Aug. 1999, http://files.usgwarchives.net/ky/ohio/obits/j/j520001.txt.

"James: Joseph L., b. 7 Mar. 1827. d. 2 July 1916." *Harrisonville Cemetery Records, Montgomery County, Kansas*, p. 30, https://www.familysearch.org/ark:/61903/3:1:3Q9M-CSSW-9QQ6-F. Accessed 16 Dec. 2020.

"James: Martha A. d. 25 Oct. 1892 . . . Wife of J. L. James." *Harrisonville Cemetery Records, Montgomery County, Kansas*, p. 30, https://www.familysearch.org/ark:/61903/3:1:3Q9M-CSSW-9QQ6-F. Accessed 16 Dec. 2020.

"James Mason (1853-1900) - Find A Grave Memorial." *Find A Grave*, https://www.findagrave.com/memorial/116707772/james-mason. Accessed 16 Dec. 2020.

"James Nathaniel Sands (1850–1924)." *FamilySearch*, https://www.familysearch.org/tree/person/details/LHN1-RX7. Accessed 23 Nov. 2020.

"James W Thompson - Find A Grave Memorial." *Find A Grave*, https://www.findagrave.com/memorial/43012332/james-w-thompson. Accessed 30 Nov. 2020.

"James W. Thompson (Death Notice)." *The Weekly Star and Kansan*, [Independence, Kansas], 2 Apr. 1897, p. 3. newspapers.com.

"John Mason." *History of Montgomery County, Kansas*, 1903, pp. 759–60, https://archive.org/details/historyofmontgom01dunc/page/758/mode/2up.

John R. Newman. Declaratory Statements for Claimants on Osage Indian Lands. #204. Department of the Interior. General Land Office. Humboldt (Kansas) Land Office, 10 July 1871, https://catalog.archives.gov/id/140114747. National Archives., Record Group 49. National Archives Identifier: 140114747, image #110.

"John Stephen Latta I (1838-1894)." *WikiTree*, https://www.wikitree.com/wiki/Latta-221. Accessed 14 Feb. 2020.

"John Thompson (Unknown-1895) - Find A Grave Memorial." *Find A Grave*, https://www.findagrave.com/memorial/35520265/john-thompson. Accessed 1 Dec. 2020.

"John Wilson Gilmour." *Portrait and Biographical Record of the Willamette Valley Oregon Containing Original Sketches of Many Well Known Citizens of the Past and Present, Illustrated, Part 2*, Chapman Publishing Company, 1903, p. 1279, https://www.google.com/books/edition/Portrait_and_Biographical_Record_of_the/uPg0AQAAMAAJ?gbpv=0. Google Books.

"Johnson, Alexander. Marriage Index Listing." *Office of the Illinois Secretary of State. Illinois State Archives. Illinois Statewide Marriage Index, 1763-1900,* https://www.ilsos.gov/isavital/marriageSearch.do [Search Criteria: Groom's Name, 'Johnson'; Bride's Name, 'Parkhill']. Accessed 15 Dec. 2020.

Jones, W. W. "A Trip to the Verdigris and Caney Rivers." *The Girard Press,* [Girard, Kansas], 6 Jan. 1870, p. 1. newspapers.com.

"Joseph Kelly Johnson (Unknown-1859) - Find A Grave Memorial." *Find A Grave,* https://www.findagrave.com/memorial/167757107/joseph-kelly-johnson. Accessed 4 Jan. 2021.

"Joseph L. James." *History of Montgomery County, Kansas,* 1903, pp. 364–66, https://archive.org/details/historyofmontgom01dunc/page/364/mode/2up.

"Joseph Lee James (1827-1916) - Find A Grave Memorial." *Find A Grave,* https://www.findagrave.com/memorial/71039183/joseph-lee-james. Accessed 11 Dec. 2020.

"Joseph Paine Sands (1843-1923) - Find A Grave Memorial." *Find A Grave,* https://www.findagrave.com/memorial/117737163/joseph-paine-sands. Accessed 16 Dec. 2020.

"Josiah Johnson Brown (1839-1936) - Find A Grave Memorial." *Find A Grave,* https://www.findagrave.com/memorial/127102996/josiah-johnson-brown. Accessed 10 Dec. 2020.

"Kansas State Census, 1875." *Database with Images,* FamilySearch, https://www.familysearch.org/search/collection/1825178. Kansas State Historical Society, Topeka.

"Kansas State Census, 1875. Montgomery > Rutland Township > 2 Agriculture > Image 1 of 4." *Database with Images,* FamilySearch, https://familysearch.org/ark:/61903/3:1:3Q9M-CS3B-DS9R-T?cc=1825178&wc=WD7G-VVC%3A1597272664%2C1597282320%2C1597262301. Kansas State Historical Society, Topeka. Accessed 10 Dec. 2020.

"Kansas State Census, 1885." *Images,* FamilySearch, https://www.familysearch.org/search/collection/1825188. Kansas State Historical Society, Topeka.

"Kansas State Census, 1885. Montgomery > Rutland Township > 2 Agriculture." *Database with Images,* FamilySearch, https://www.familysearch.org/ark:/61903/3:1:3Q9M-CSQ3-QCTP?i=62&wc=W8BZ-D7M%3A1597342342%2C1597342503&cc=1825188. Kansas State Historical Society, Topeka, (Images 63-92). Accessed 10 Dec. 2020.

"Kansas State Census, 1895." *Database with Images*, FamilySearch, https://www.familysearch.org/search/collection/1825178. Kansas State Historical Society, Topeka.

"Kansas State Census, 1905." *Database with Images*, FamilySearch, https://www.familysearch.org/search/collection/2659394. Kansas State Historical Society, Topeka.

Kansas State Hist'l Soc. *Kansas Tract Book Guide. Kansas Federal Land Records, MS-321 Thru MS-359, MS-363 Thru MS-367.* https://www.kshs.org/government/landsrvy/pdfs/kansas_tract_book_guide.pdf. Accessed 11 Dec. 2020.

"Kansas Surveying History." *Kansas Society of Land Surveyors*, https://ksls.com/Kansas-Surveying-History. Accessed 11 Mar. 2020.

"Kansas-Nebraska Act." *10 U.S. Statutes at Large 277, Ch. 59*, 30 May 1854, https://www.loc.gov/law/help/statutes-at-large/33rd-congress/session-1/c33s1ch59.pdf.

Kaye, Frances W. "Little Squatter on the Osage Diminished Reserve: Reading Laura Ingalls Wilder's Kansas Indians." *Great Plains Quarterly*, vol. 20, no. 2, May 2000, https://digitalcommons.unl.edu/cgi/viewcontent.cgi?article=1022&context=greatplainsquarterly.

Kidwell, Barbara. "The Montgomery County Chronicle: Leaving the Banks of Drum Creek." *KSGenWeb*, http://www.ksgenweb.org/montgome/chron6.htm. Accessed 10 Dec. 2020.

Koupal, Nancy Tystad, editor. *Pioneer Girl Perspectives: Exploring Laura Ingalls Wilder*. South Dakota Historical Society Press, 2017.

"Land Acts." *Genealogy Fair*, National Archives and Records Administration, Washington, DC, 2014, https://www.archives.gov/files/calendar/genealogy-fair/2014/handouts/session-11-handout-5of5-martinez-land-other-land-acts.pdf.

"Land Entry Case Files." *Time Passages Genealogy*, https://time-passages.com/land-entry-case-files/. Accessed 26 Feb. 2020.

"Land Office Removed." *South Kansas Tribune*, [Independence, Kansas], 16 Aug. 1871, p. 2. newspapers.com.

"Land Office Swindle." *South Kansas Tribune*, [Independence, Kansas], 26 July 1871, p. 2. newspapers.com.

laurasprairiehouse.com. "Mr. Edwards - Biography." *Laura Ingalls Wilder Little House on the Prairie Definitive Guide*, https://laurasprairiehouse.com/family-friends/mr-edwards-biography/. Accessed 27 June 2023.

Lee, Dr. Paul. *Failure to Act: The Titanic and the Ice Warnings*. http://www.paullee.com/titanic/icewarnings.php. Accessed 26 Feb. 2018.

Leeson, Michael A. "History of Potter County. Chapter IX—Eulalia Township—Borough of Coudersport." *History of the Counties of McKean, Elk, Cameron and Potter, Pennsylvania*, J.H. Beers & Co., 1890, pp. 1044–70, https://hdl.handle.net/2027/coo1.ark:/13960/t9k36c09r?urlappend=%3Bseq=1094. Hathi Trust Digital Library.

"Legislative/Settlers Meeting." *The Osage Mission Journal*, [Lawrence, Kansas], 7 Jan. 1869, p. 2. newspapers.com.

"Let Us Celebrate." *The Weekly Star and Kansan*, [Independence, Kansas], 20 Aug. 1886, p. 3. newspapers.com.

Linsenmeyer, Penny T. "Kansas Settlers on the Osage Diminished Reserve: A Study of Laura Ingalls Wilder's Little House on the Prairie." *Kansas History*, vol. 24, no. 3, 2001, p. 18.

"List of Patrons for the Atlas of Montgomery County, Kansas." *Historical Atlas of Montgomery County, Kansas*, 1881, p. 10.

"List or Manifest of Alien Passengers for the U.S. Immigration Officer at Port of Arrival. SS. Caronia, Sailing from Liverpool 19 Sep 1905, Arriving at Port of New York, Sept 27, 1905. Sheet B." *Statue of Liberty & Ellis Island*, 1905, https://heritage.statueofliberty.org/show-manifest-big-image/czoxNzoidDcxNS0wNjI1MDMwOS5qcGciOw==/1.

Little House Discussed: Who Was Mr. Edwards? http://littlehousediscussion.blogspot.com/2015/02/who-was-mr-edwards.html. Accessed 27 June 2023.

Little House on the Prairie: The Pilot. Directed by Michael Landon, 30 Mar. 1974.

Little House on the Prairie-Background Material. 1933. National Archives, File 219; Box 14; Laura Ingalls Wilder Series; Rose Wilder Lane Papers; Herbert Hoover Presidential Library, West Branch, IA.

Little, Marietta. "A Lonesome Girl in 1870." *South Kansas Tribune*, [Independence, Kansas], Illustrated Edition, 24 July 1901, p. 40. newspapers.com.

"Local Dashes. ('Mrs. Etta Mason, of Bolton, Has Commenced Suit for Divorce . . .')." *The Weekly Star and Kansan*, [Independence, Kansas], 20 Sept. 1895, p. 3. newspapers.com.

"Local News. ('A Suit for Divorce Was Filed . . . by Etta Mason . . .')." *Independence Daily Reporter*, [Independence, Kansas], 20 Sept. 1895, p. 3. newspapers.com.

Mack, John N. *Swords Into Ploughshares: The Struggle to Build an Ordered Community of Liberty on the Southeast Kansas Frontier 1867-1876*. University of Kansas, 21 Apr. 2009, https://kuscholarworks.ku.edu/handle/1808/5430. KU ScholarWorks.

"Manuscript Group 291, Guide to the Baldwin-Brown-Coe Family (Newark, NJ) Papers 1776-1893 (Bulk Dates: 1800-1845). Biographical Note." *The New Jersey Historical Society*, https://jerseyhistory.org/guide-to-the-baldwin-brown-coe-family-newark-njpapers-1776-1893-bulk-dates-1800-1845mg-291/. Accessed 11 Dec. 2020.

"Marcelous Adelbert 'Albert' Streeter (1846-1899) - Find A Grave Memorial." *Find A Grave*, https://www.findagrave.com/memorial/31008676/marcelous-adelbert-streeter. Accessed 24 Nov. 2020.

Marcy, Randolph B. *The Prairie Traveler: A Hand-Book for Overland Expeditions*. Harper & Brothers, 1859.

Marriage Bond of James A. Fleenor Re. His Intended Marriage to Margaret M. James. 20 Oct. 1866, https://www.familysearch.org/ark:/61903/3:1:33S7-L1GK-9RKL?i=98. FamilySearch, Kentucky, County Marriages, 1797-1954; Ohio County, Kentucky Marriage Bonds vol. J, 1866-67, p.151 (image 99).

Marriage License for Edmund Mason and Mary E. Howard. 22 Oct. 1874, https://www.familysearch.org/ark:/61903/3:1:939J-T83Q-GW?i=128. FamilySearch, Kansas County Marriages, 1855-1911; Marriage licenses, 1872-1878, vol. B p. 147 (image 129).

Marriage License for Henry Vanwinkle and Sarah Jane Dawson. 7 Feb. 1871, https://www.familysearch.org/ark:/61903/3:1:939J-T837-RF?i=47&cc=1851040. FamilySearch, Kansas County Marriages, 1855-1911; Marriage licenses, 1870-1873, vol. A p. 32 (image 48).

Marriage License for James M. Thompson and Mary D. Means. 17 Aug. 1878, https://www.familysearch.org/ark:/61903/3:1:939J-T83W-FC?i=283. FamilySearch, Kansas County Marriages, 1855-1911; Marriage licenses, 1872-1878, vol. B p. 147.

Marriage License for Joshua Edwards and Sarah A. Auldridge. 9 July 1874, https://www.familysearch.org/ark:/61903/3:1:939J-T83Q-KQ?i=117. FamilySearch, Kansas County Marriages, 1855-1911; Marriage licenses, 1872-1878, vol. B p. 126 (image 118).

Marriage License for M. A. Streeter and George Annie Myers. 20 Mar. 1877, https://www.familysearch.org/ark:/61903/3:1:939J-T83W-ZZ?i=229. FamilySearch, Kansas County Marriages, 1855-1911; Marriage licenses, 1872-1878, vol. B p. 347 (image 230).

"Marriage of George A. Brown and Minnie Bowman." *South Kansas Tribune*, [Independence, Kansas], 10 Apr. 1872, p. 3. newspapers.com.

Marriage of Joseph Sands and Lucinda Van Winkle. https://www.familysearch.org/ark:/61903/1:1:XJH9-63D. FamilySearch, Iowa, County Marriages, 1838-1934. Accessed 16 Dec. 2020.

Marriage Record for W. Reeser & C. Miller. Ancestry.com Operations Inc, 2008, https://www.ancestry.com/search/collections/1169/. ancestry.com, Tennessee, U.S., Marriage Records, 1780-2002 [database on-line].

Marriage Register Entry for Thomas Mason & Joanna Mason. https://www.familysearch.org/ark:/61903/3:1:939N-QP99-W?i=7. FamilySearch, England, Devon, Parish Registers, 1538-1912; Dunterton Marriage Register June 1813-May 1836, p. 8, #22 (image 8).

"Mary Jane Gilmour Longcor (1849-1871) - Find A Grave Memorial." *Find A Grave*, https://www.findagrave.com/memorial/99744238/mary-jane-longcor. Accessed 24 Nov. 2020.

"Mason: Charlie, Son of E. Mason and E. . . ." *Harrisonville Cemetery Records, Montgomery County, Kansas*, p. 32, https://www.familysearch.org/ark:/61903/3:1:3Q9M-CSSW-9QQ5-V. Accessed 16 Dec. 2020.

"Mason: Edmond, b. 14 Sept. 1846. d. 25 Jan. 1906. B.P.O.E." *Harrisonville Cemetery Records, Montgomery County, Kansas*, p. 32, https://www.familysearch.org/ark:/61903/3:1:3Q9M-CSSW-9QQ5-V. Accessed 16 Dec. 2020.

Mason, Edmund. "Affidavit Required of Claimants for Osage Indian Lands." *Land Case Entry File No. 5022*, 1872.

---. *Last Will and Testament of Edmund Mason*. Ancestry.com Operations, Inc., 2015, https://www.ancestry.com/search/collections/9065/. ancestry.com, Kansas, U.S., Wills and Probate Records, 1803-1987 [database on-line].

---. "Notice. ('All Persons Are Hereby Warned against Trusting My Wife, Etta Mason . . .')." *The Weekly Star and Kansan*, [Independence, Kansas], 31 Jan. 1896, p. 3. newspapers.com.

"Mason: James, d. 15 Feb. 1900. Ae. 47 Yrs." *Harrisonville Cemetery Records, Montgomery County, Kansas*, p. 33, https://www.familysearch.org/ark:/61903/3:1:3Q9M-CSSW-9QQ7-X. Accessed 16 Dec. 2020.

Mason, Joanna. *Last Will and Testament of Joanna Mason*. Transcribed by Sharon Easley, 2 Feb. 1882, https://probatesearch.service.gov.uk/#calendar. gov.uk. Wills and Probate 1858-1996, [Date of Probate: 10 May 1888, Date of Death: 14 Apr 1888, Principal Registry, Folio 459].

Mason, John. "Notice. ('All Persons Are Hereby Warned against Trusting My Wife, Emma Mason . . .')." *Independence Daily Reporter*, [Independence, Kansas], 19 Oct. 1887, p. 1. newspapers.com.

---. "Osage Trust Lands. Deposition in the Matter of the Application of Edmund Mason." *Land Case Entry File No. 5022*, 1872.

"Mason: John, b. 31 Dec. 1834. d. 21 Nov. 1905. (B.P.O.E.)." *Harrisonville Cemetery Records, Montgomery County, Kansas*, p. 33, https://www.familysearch.org/ark:/61903/3:1:3Q9M-CSSW-9QQ7-X. Accessed 16 Dec. 2020.

"Mason: Mary Etta, b. 1860. d. 1920. Wife of Edmond Mason." *Harrisonville Cemetery Records, Montgomery County, Kansas*, p. 33, https://www.familysearch.org/ark:/61903/3:1:3Q9M-CSSW-9QQ7-X. Accessed 16 Dec. 2020.

Mason, Thomas. *Last Will and Testament of Thomas Mason*. Transcribed by Sharon Easley, 1 Mar. 1866, https://probatesearch.service.gov.uk/#calendar. gov.uk. Wills and Probate 1858-1996, [Date of Probate: 18 Aug 1866, Date of Death: 22 Mar 1866, Principal Registry, Folio 534].

McClure, Rhonda R. "What Is an 'Idiot' in the Census?" *Genealogy.Com*, 26 Apr. 2001, https://www.genealogy.com/articles/over/heard042601.html.

McFarland, Helen M. "Letter to Laura Ingalls Wilder." *Little House on the Prairie-Background Material*, 1933. National Archives, File 219; Box 14; Laura Ingalls Wilder Series; Rose Wilder Lane Papers; Herbert Hoover Presidential Library, West Branch, IA.

McVicar, Peter and Kansas State Hist'l Soc. "School Lands on the Osage Reservation. (An Address Delivered before the State Historical Society, at the Annual Meeting January 19, 1892)." *Transactions of the Kansas State Historical Society, 1889-'96*, edited by F. G. Adams, vol. V, Press of the Kansas State Printing Co., 1896, pp. 69–71, https://archive.org/details/collections05kansuoft. archive.org.

"Memorials in Barnett Cemetery." *Find A Grave*, https://www.findagrave.com/cemetery/104637/memorial-search?firstName=&lastName=&page=1#sr-11331613. Accessed 24 Nov. 2020.

"Mikel, David H. Illinois Civil War Muster and Descriptive Rolls Detail Report." *Office of the Illinois Secretary of State. Illinois State Archives, Illinois Civil War Muster and Descriptive Rolls Database*, https://www.ilsos.gov/isaveterans/civilmustersrch.jsp [Search Criteria: 'Mikel, David H']. Accessed 21 Nov. 2020.

Mikel, David H. Pension Record. 1884, https://www.familysearch.org/ark:/61903/1:1:QVNS-BYQS. FamilySearch, United States General Index to Pension Files, 1861-1934.

"Mikel, David H. Soldier Details." *The Civil War (U.S. National Park Service)*, https://www.nps.gov/civilwar/search-soldiers-detail.htm?soldierId=A5FBCFBA-DC7A-DF11-BF36-B8AC6F5D926A. Accessed 1 Dec. 2020.

Miller, Robynne Elizabeth. *The Three Faces of Nellie*. Practical Pioneer Press, 2016.

Miner, H. Craig, and William E. Unrau. *The End of Indian Kansas: A Study in Cultural Revolution, 1854 - 1871*. Univ. Press of Kansas, 1978.

Montgomery Co., KS, Clerk's Off. *Sales of School Lands: Reports of Installments of Principal and Interest Paid, for the Six Months Ending June 30, 1881 (Containing Various Payments for Sections 16 & 36 in Townships 31-34, Ranges 14-17)*. 1881. State Archives Division, Kansas Historical Society, Copy in possession of author.

Montgomery Co., KS, Reg. of Deeds. "Warranty Deed: Edmund Mason to John Craig." *Montgomery County Deed Records*, vol. D, 1872, p. 113. Montgomery County, Kansas.

"Montgomery County Organization Records." *Kansas Memory*, https://www.kansasmemory.org/item/display.php?item_id=217033&f=00149913. Accessed 15 Nov. 2020.

"More About That Trouble at Wayside." *The Times*, [Independence, Kansas], 10 Aug. 1906, p. 4. newspapers.com.

"Mr. Edwards Poll. What Is Your Opinion about the Character of Mr. Edwards?" *Laura Ingalls Wilder, Frontier Girl*, 10 June 2008, http://frontiergirl.proboards.com/thread/659/edwards-poll.

"Mr G A Brown and Wife . . . Have Removed to Central City, Colorado." *South Kansas Tribune*, [Independence, Kansas], 25 Sept. 1872, p. 3. newspapers.com.

"Mr. Geo. A. Brown and Wife Have Returned from Colorado . . ." *South Kansas Tribune*, [Independence, Kansas], 21 Apr. 1875, p. 3. newspapers.com.

"Mr. W. P. Brown (Death Notice)." *The Weekly Star and Kansan*, [Independence, Kansas], 13 Oct. 1881, p. 4. newspapers.com.

"Mrs. Emma Mason Was Convicted . . ." *The Weekly Star and Kansan*, [Independence, Kansas], 14 Dec. 1888, p. 3. newspapers.com.

"Mrs. Etta Mason (Obituary). 'Round About Coffeyville." *The Coffeyville Daily Journal*, [Coffeyville, Kansas], 7 Aug. 1920, p. 9. newspapers.com.

Murdock, D. H. "Letter to Adjutant Post of S.E. Kas. Regarding Assent of the Osages to Sale of Their [Reservation] and Removal to Indian Territory." *Neosho Agency, 1831-1875: 1870-1871*, 1870, pp. 36–37, https://catalog.archives.gov/id/164143232. National Archives, M234 - Letters Received by the Office of Indian Affairs, 1824-1881; Letters Received, 1824 - 1880; Records of the Bureau of Indian Affairs, 1793 - 1999 (RG75); National Archives Building, Washington, DC.

Musser, Karl. *Map of Oklahoma and Indian Territory*. https://commons.wikimedia.org/wiki/File:Okterritory.png. Wikimedia Commons. Accessed 30 Nov. 2020.

"Mysterious Disappearance. ('Last Fall a Mr. Geo. W. Lonchor, of Onion Creek, . . .')." *South Kansas Tribune*, [Independence, Kansas], 12 Mar. 1873, p. 2. newspapers.com.

Naylor, Chris. "'You Have the Body': Habeas Corpus Case Records of the U.S. Circuit Court for the District of Columbia, 1820-1863." *National Archives*, 15 Aug. 2016, https://www.archives.gov/publications/prologue/2005/fall/habeas-corpus.html.

nebraskastudies.org. *U.S. Government Land Laws in Nebraska, 1854-1904*. http://nebraskastudies.org/documents/535/7._U.S._Government_Land_Laws_in_Nebraska_1854-1904.pdf. Accessed 13 Aug. 2023.

New Jersey Deaths and Burials, 1720-1988. FamilySearch, https://www.familysearch.org/search/collection/1675445. Index based upon data collected by the Genealogical Society of Utah, Salt Lake City.

New Jersey Marriages, 1678-1985. FamilySearch, https://www.familysearch.org/search/collection/1675446. Index based upon data collected by the Genealogical Society of Utah, Salt Lake City.

Nobel, Justin. "Bloody Benders – The Forgotten Story of a Family of Pioneer Serial Killers." *Digital Dying*, 16 Nov. 2013, https://www.funeralwise.com/digital-dying/bloody-benders-the-forgotten-story-of-a-family-of-pioneer-serial-killers/.

"Notice of Contest: U.S. Land Office, Humboldt, Kansas, July 10th, 1871." *South Kansas Tribune*, [Independence, Kansas], 9 Aug. 1871, p. 3. newspapers.com.

"Now For A New Hotel. Work on a Modern Structure to Be Commenced at Once." *Independence Daily Reporter*, [Independence, Kansas], 13 Jan. 1902, p. 3. newspapers.com.

Nye, Eric W. *Pounds Sterling to Dollars: Historical Conversion of Currency*. https://www.uwyo.edu/numimage/currency.htm. Accessed 17 Dec. 2020.

"Obituary. Mrs. Edwin Mason." *Independence Daily Reporter*, [Independence, Kansas], 17 Aug. 1920, p. 4. newspapers.com.

Off. of Indian Affairs. *Report of the Commissioner of Indian Affairs for the Year 1869*. Government Printing Office, Washington, 1870, https://digitalcommons.csumb.edu/hornbeck_usa_2_e/8/. Digital Commons @ CSUMB, US and Indian Relations. 8.

---. *Report of the Commissioner of Indian Affairs for the Year 1870*. Government Printing Office, Washington, 1870, https://digitalcommons.csumb.edu/hornbeck_usa_2_e/45/. Digital Commons @ CSUMB, US and Indian Relations. 45.

---. *Report of the Commissioner of Indian Affairs for the Year 1871.* Government Printing Office, Washington, 1872, https://digitalcommons.csumb.edu/hornbeck_usa_2_e/9/. Digital Commons @ CSUMB, US and Indian Relations. 9.

"Old Settlers Reunion. ('The Same Year, 1869, Came . . . John Mason of England.')." *The Evening Star*, [Independence, Kansas], 13 Sept. 1904, p. 5. newspapers.com.

"Oliver Cairo (Carow) m Rachel McKune." Ancestry.Com Message Boards, 24 Apr. 2008, https://www.ancestry.com/boards/surnames.carow/36?viewType=FLAT_VIEW.

"On Sunday Last Was Buried Mr. Frederick Brown . . ." *South Kansas Tribune*, [Independence, Kansas], 3 Apr. 1878, p. 3. newspapers.com.

"Oregon Township." *Atlas of Washington County, Iowa*, The Iowa Pub. Co., 1906, p. 31, https://digital.lib.uiowa.edu/islandora/object/ui%3Aatlases_12121. Iowa Digital Library, Iowa Counties Historic Atlases.

"---." *Atlas of Washington County, Iowa*, Harrison & Warner, 1874, p. 11, https://digital.lib.uiowa.edu/islandora/object/ui%3Aatlases_6590. Iowa Digital Library, Iowa Counties Historic Atlases.

"Osage - Treaties With the United States." *Kansapedia - Kansas Historical Society*, Sept. 2015, https://www.kshs.org/kansapedia/osage-treaties-with-the-united-states/19293.

"Osage Lands. ('By a Recent Law of Congress the Whole Osage Reservation Is to Be Sold . . .')." *The Girard Press*, [Girard, Kansas], 16 June 1870, p. 2. newspapers.com.

"Osage Lands. ('The Osage Indians Have Accepted the Terms of the Recent Congressional Law Disposing of Their Lands, . . .')." *The Girard Press*, [Girard, Kansas], 22 Sept. 1870, p. 2. newspapers.com.

"Osage Treaty Accepted at Last." *Independence Pioneer*, [Independence, Kansas], 17 Sept. 1870, pp. 2–3. newspapers.com.

Osmond, Candace. "Ornery - Usage, Meaning & Examples." *Grammarist*, 18 Oct. 2017, https://grammarist.com/interesting-words/ornery/.

"Our County. ('Among the Numerous Interesting Localities of Montgomery County . . . Is the Valley of Onion Creek. . . .')." *South Kansas Tribune*, [Independence, Kansas], 17 May 1871, p. 1. newspapers.com.

"Our History—First Presbyterian Church." *First Presbyterian Church, Independence, Kansas*, http://fpc-indy-ks.org/new-page. Accessed 23 July 2017.

"Past Mayors of Independence, Kansas." *Independence, KS*, https://www.independenceks.gov/gallery.aspx?AID=3. Accessed 22 Oct. 2020.

"Personal Mention. ('James W. Thompson, Who Lived Five Miles Southwest of Town . . .')." *Independence Daily Reporter*, [Independence, Kansas], 31 Mar. 1897, p. 3. newspapers.com.

"Person:Moses Van Winkle (2) - Genealogy." *WeRelate*, https://www.werelate.org/wiki/Person:Moses_Van_Winkle_(2). Accessed 24 Nov. 2020.

"Philadelphia Home Missionary Society. Rev. D. B. Brown." *The Home Missionary*, vol. 21–23, Executive Committee of the American Home Missionary Society, 1849, pp. 112–13, https://www.google.com/books/edition/_/gJ4PAAAAIAAJ. Google Books.

Photograph of Isaac T. Gibson with Chetopah and Sam Bevenue, c. 1868-1872. https://gateway.okhistory.org/ark:/67531/metadc1619009/. Gateway to Oklahoma History, Oklahoma Historical Society, Oklahoma Historical Society Photograph Collection. Accessed 22 Oct. 2020.

"Polly Terrell Gilmour (Hickman) (1792 - 1829)." *Geni*, https://www.geni.com/people/Polly-Gilmour/6000000042965739925. Accessed 22 Nov. 2020.

"Principal Meridians and Base Lines." *Bureau of Land Management*, https://www.blm.gov/sites/blm.gov/files/meridianmap09_0.jpg. Accessed 2 June 2020.

Pyle, Roger, transcriber. "Personal Memoirs of Watson Stewart-Section 7: The Osages." *The Kansas Collection*, http://www.kancoll.org/articles/stewart/ws_section07.htm. Accessed 17 Nov. 2020.

"Re: Levi McKune." *Ancestry.Com Message Boards*, May 2008, https://www.ancestry.com/boards/surnames.mckune/48.2.1.1.1.1.1.1.3.

"Real Estate Transfers. Edmund Mason to Ida Lundley." *The Coffeyville Daily Journal*, [Coffeyville, Kansas], 31 Jan. 1906, p. 5. newspapers.com.

"Real Estate Transfers. H. O. Cavert and Wife to Edmund Mason." *The Coffeyville Daily Journal*, [Coffeyville, Kansas], 18 Aug. 1903, p. 3. newspapers.com.

"Real Estate Transfers. Harry W Talbott et al to Edmund Mason." *The Coffeyville Daily Journal*, [Coffeyville, Kansas], 17 May 1898, p. 4. newspapers.com.

"Real Estate Transfers. J M Thompson to Henry Sears." *The Weekly Star and Kansan*, [Independence, Kansas], 23 Dec. 1881, p. 5. newspapers.com.

"Real Estate Transfers. John A. Sampson to Edmund Mason." *The Coffeyville Daily Journal*, [Coffeyville, Kansas], 22 Nov. 1898, p. 4. newspapers.com.

Reece, J. N., editor. "Company H. One Hundred and Thirteenth Infantry." *Report of the Adjutant General of the State of Illinois. Volume VI. Containing Reports for the Years 1861-66*, Journal Company, Printers and Binders, 1900, p. 192, https://archive.org/details/reportofadjutant06illi1/page/192/mode/2up. Internet Archive.

Reynolds, William C. *Reynolds's Political Map of the United States, Designed to Exhibit the Comparative Area of the Free and Slave States and the Territory Open to Slavery or Freedom by the Repeal of the Missouri Compromise.* Wm. C. Reynolds and J.C. Jones, 1856, https://www.loc.gov/resource/g3701e.ct000604/. Library of Congress, Geography and Map Division.

"Robert Bronaugh Gilmour (1821-1882) - Find A Grave Memorial." *Find A Grave*, https://www.findagrave.com/memorial/35818785/robert-bronaugh-gilmour. Accessed 20 Feb. 2020.

Robinson, Edgar Sutton, editor. "Brown, Josiah Johnson." *The Ministerial Directory Of the Ministers in the Presbyterian Church in the United States (Southern), and in the Presbyterian Church in the United States of America (Northern)*, vol. 1, The Ministerial Directory Company, 1898, p. 188, https://www.google.com/books/edition/The_Ministerial_Directory/9WXozG4cLPIC. Google Books.

"Samuel Daniel Best (1829-1907) - Find A Grave Memorial." *Find A Grave*, https://www.findagrave.com/memorial/28844861/samuel-daniel-best. Accessed 28 July 2017.

"Samuel David Best - Facts. Black-Hurley Family Tree." *Ancestry*, https://www.ancestry.com/family-tree/person/tree/25010268/person/13944952795/facts. Accessed 28 July 2017.

"Samuel David Daniel Best - Facts. Best Family Tree." *Ancestry*, https://www.ancestry.com/family-tree/person/tree/80363377/person/44436515172/facts. Accessed 28 July 2017.

"Samuel M Riddle (1833-1884) - Find A Grave Memorial." *Find A Grave*, https://www.findagrave.com/memorial/83255473/samuel-m-riddle. Accessed 13 Dec. 2020.

"Search - BLM GLO Records." *Bureau of Land Management, General Land Office Records*, https://glorecords.blm.gov/search/. Accessed 24 Nov. 2020.

Shaw, William H. "Chapter XV. Essex County in the War of 1861-1865. (Continued.)." *History of Essex and Hudson Counties, New Jersey*, vol. I, Everts & Peck, 1884, pp. 61–93, https://www.google.com/books/

edition/History_of_Essex_and_Hudson_Counties_New/N0UWAAAAYAAJ. Google Books.
"Sheridan, Philip (1831-1888)." *Encyclopedia of the Great Plains*, http://plainshumanities.unl.edu/encyclopedia/doc/egp.war.042. Accessed 21 June 2023.
"Signing of the Osage Treaty. Early Settlement, Farewell Address by Konsakahala, Chief Osage Counsellor." *South Kansas Tribune*, [Independence, Kansas], 24 July 1901, p. 36. newspapers.com.
Sisson, John R. *Map of Washington County, Iowa*. Lewis W. Vale, 1859, https://digital.lib.uiowa.edu/islandora/object/ui%3Aatlases_6590. Iowa Digital Library, Iowa Historic Sheet Maps.
Smithsonian in the Classroom, Fall 2010. Final Farewells, Signing a Yearbook on the Eve of the Civil War. Smithsonian Institution, 2010, http://www.smithsonianeducation.org/educators/lesson_plans/yearbook/smithsonian_siyc_fall2010.pdf.
Snell, Kevin, transcriber. "Roster of Company C 8th Illinois Infantry (Three Years Service)." *The Illinois Civil War Project*, https://civilwar.illinoisgenweb.org/r050/008-c-in.html. Accessed 11 Dec. 2020.
Snow, G. C. "Letter to Thomas Murphy Regarding Conflict between Settlers and the Osage on the Diminished Reserve." *Neosho Agency, 1831-1875: 1868-1869*, 1869, pp. 923–26, https://catalog.archives.gov/id/164142200. National Archives, M234 - Letters Received by the Office of Indian Affairs, 1824-1881; Letters Received, 1824 - 1880; Records of the Bureau of Indian Affairs, 1793 - 1999 (RG75); National Archives Building, Washington, DC.
Standard Certificate of Death for Washington F. Reser. Missouri Secretary of State: State Archives, 11 Oct. 1942, https://www.sos.mo.gov/images/archives/deathcerts/1942/1942_00034130.PDF. Missouri Digital Heritage, Missouri Death Certificates, 1910 - 1969.
Stanton, Neil, transcriber. "Lifton: From White's Devonshire Directory of 1850." *GENUKI: UK & Ireland Genealogy*, https://www.genuki.org.uk/big/eng/DEV/Lifton/Lifton1850. Accessed 16 Nov. 2020.
Stark, Joey, transcriber. "1851 State Census of Iowa, Washington County, All Townships." *Iowa State Census Project*, http://iagenweb.org/census/textdisplay.php?file=/census/washington/1851-ia-washington-all.txt. Accessed 21 Feb. 2020.
---, transcriber. "Marriages. Mr. John S. Latta and Miss Charlotte Croft. March 12, 1868, Fairfield Ledger." *The IAGenWeb Project*, http://iagenweb.org/jefferson/Weekly_Ledger/1868_pages/Mar_12.html. Accessed 14 Feb. 2020.

"Streeter, Adelbert. Illinois Civil War Muster and Descriptive Rolls Detail Report." *Office of the Illinois Secretary of State. Illinois State Archives, Illinois Civil War Muster and Descriptive Rolls Database*, https://www.ilsos.gov/isaveterans/civilmustersrch.jsp [Search Criteria: 'Streeter, Adelbert']. Accessed 24 Nov. 2020.

"Streeter, Zeno. Marriage Index Listing." *Office of the Illinois Secretary of State. Illinois State Archives. Illinois Statewide Marriage Index, 1763-1900*, https://www.ilsos.gov/isavital/marriageSearch.do [Search Criteria: 'Streeter, Zeno']. Accessed 24 Nov. 2020.

Surveyor General's Off. *Survey Plat for Township No. 33 South Range 14 East of 6th Principal Meridian, Kansas (Rutland Twp.)*. 9 June 1871, https://glorecords.blm.gov/details/survey/default.aspx?dm_id=421495&sid=wiaqly3f.wll#surveyDetailsTabIndex=1. BLM General Land Office Records.

---. *Survey Plat for Township No. 33 South Range 15 East of 6th Principal Meridian, Kansas (Independence Twp.)*. 9 June 1871, https://glorecords.blm.gov/details/survey/default.aspx?dm_id=421974&sid=gupxmrnv.4vq&surveyDetailsTabIndex=1. BLM General Land Office Records.

---. *Survey Plat for Township No. 34 South Range 14 East of 6th Principal Meridian, Kansas (Caney Twp.)*. 9 June 1871, https://glorecords.blm.gov/details/survey/default.aspx?dm_id=421497&sid=ztd04sij.e5c&surveyDetailsTabIndex=1. BLM General Land Office Records.

---. *Survey Plat for Township No. 34 South Range 15 East of 6th Principal Meridian, Kansas (Fawn Creek Twp.)*. 9 June 1871, https://glorecords.blm.gov/details/survey/default.aspx?dm_id=421977&sid=fkfttsjk.qwg#surveyDetailsTabIndex=1. BLM General Land Office Records.

"The Cherryvale Horror: The Murders in Labette County." *The Border Sentinel*, [Mound City, Kansas], 16 May 1873, p. 2. newspapers.com.

"The Elks At Festal Board, After Initiating Four Candidates The B.P.O.E. Enjoy a Finely Appointed Banquet, Edward Mason Is Honored." *The Evening Star*, [Independence, Kansas], 26 Aug. 1904, p. 5. newspapers.com.

"'The First' in Independence; A Highly Interesting List of Early Day Features; A Collection of Facts from a Scrap Book of the Long, Long Ago." *Independence Daily Reporter*, [Independence, Kansas], 11 July 1919, p. 1. newspapers.com.

"The Homestead Act of 1862. 'An Act to Secure Homesteads to Actual Settlers on the Public Domain.' 12 Stat. 392. May 20, 1862, 37th Cong. Sess. II. Ch. 75." *United States Statutes at Large*, vol. 12, Little, Brown, and Co., 1863, p. 392, https://www.loc.gov/law/help/statutes-at-large/37th-congress/session-2/c37s2ch75.pdf. Law Library of Congress.

"The Indian Appropriations Act of the 15th of July, 1870. 'An Act Making Appropriations for the Current and Contingent Expenses of the Indian Department.' 16 Stat. 335. July 15, 1870, 41st Cong. Sess. II. Ch. 296." *United States Statutes at Large*, vol. 16, Little, Brown, and Co., 1871, p. 335, https://www.loc.gov/resource/llsalvol.llsal_016/?sp=371. Law Library of Congress.

"The Land Act of 1820. 'An Act Making Further Provision for the Sale of the Public Lands.' 3 Stat. 566. Apr 24, 1820, 16th Cong. Sess. I. Ch. 51." *United States Statutes at Large*, vol. 3, Charles C. Little and James Brown, 1846, p. 566, https://www.loc.gov/law/help/statutes-at-large/16th-congress/session-1/c16s1ch51.pdf. Law Library of Congress.

The Nat'l Archives (UK). *Family of Thomas & Joanna Mason (1841). PRO HO 107/1, Folio 11, Page 18, Colmans: General Register Office: 1841 Census Returns Database*. FreeCEN Free UK Genealogy, https://www.freecen.org.uk/search_records/5a1453fbf4040b9d6e47ae19. Accessed 26 Nov. 2020.

---. *Family of Thomas & Joanna Mason (1851). PRO /1884, Folio 225, Page 7, Schedule 16, Colmans: General Register Office: 1851 Census Returns Database*. FreeCEN Free UK Genealogy, 1851, https://www.freecen.org.uk/search_records/597e8f27f4040b024a5d5e4f.

---. *Family of Thomas & Joanna Mason (1861). PRO RG 9/1464, Folio 60, Page 1, Schedule 4: General Register Office: 1861 Census Returns Database*. FreeCEN Free UK Genealogy, 1861, https://www.freecen.org.uk/search_records/5a148140f4040b9d6e7a3b00.

"The Osage Lands ('The Parker Record of the 15th Is Justly Jubilant at the Conclusion of the Treaty of Sale of These Lands to Actual Settlers. . . .')." *Atchison Weekly Patriot*, [Atchison, Kansas], 24 Sept. 1870, p. 2. newspapers.com.

"The Osage Lands. ('Washington, June 8.—The Osage Indian Reservation Question Was Disposed of to-Day, in the Senate . . .')." *The Girard Press*, [Girard, Kansas], 16 June 1870, p. 2. newspapers.com.

"The Osage Leave Their Kansas Reserve." *A Catholic Mission*, http://www.acatholicmission.org/9-the-osage-leave-kansas.html. Accessed 1 Dec. 2020.

"The Papers for a Divorce Suit Were Filed Last Week . . . for Mrs. Etta Mason against Edward Mason . . ." *The Weekly Star and Kansan*, [Independence, Kansas], 31 Jan. 1896, p. 4. newspapers.com.

"The Treaty Rejected." *Independence Pioneer*, [Independence, Kansas], 2 July 1870, p. 2. newspapers.com.

"Thomas J Brown (Unknown-1900) - Find A Grave Memorial." *Find A Grave*, https://www.findagrave.com/memorial/87316709/thomas-j-brown. Accessed 30 Nov. 2020.

"Thomas Mason and Joanna Mason. Mason Families from Lifton and Kelly Parishes, Devon, England." *Our Family Past*, https://www.ourfamilypast.com/article/topic/949/thomas-mason-and-joanna-mason. Accessed 13 July 2016.

"Thompson, John. Soldier Details." *The Civil War (U.S. National Park Service)*, https://www.nps.gov/civilwar/search-soldiers-detail.htm?soldierId=30C0EAD8-DC7A-DF11-BF36-B8AC6F5D926A. Accessed 1 Dec. 2020.

Townsend, E. D. "Letter to Comdg. Genl. Dept. of Mo. Giving Him Discretionary Authority in Removal of Settlers from within Osage Reservation." *Neosho Agency, 1831-1875: 1870-1871*, 1870, pp. 44–46, https://catalog.archives.gov/id/164143232. National Archives, M234 - Letters Received by the Office of Indian Affairs, 1824-1881; Letters Received, 1824 - 1880; Records of the Bureau of Indian Affairs, 1793 - 1999 (RG75); National Archives Building, Washington, DC.

"Treaty With The Osage, 1825." *Wikisource*, 17 Apr. 2012, https://en.wikisource.org/wiki/Treaty_With_The_Osage,_1825.

"Union Iowa Volunteers, 35th Regiment, Iowa Infantry, Battle Unit Details." *The Civil War (U.S. National Park Service)*, https://www.nps.gov/civilwar/search-battle-units-detail.htm?battleUnitCode=UIA0035RI. Accessed 24 July 2017.

Union Theol. Seminary (New York, N.Y.). "Brown, Josiah Johnson. (Alumni, 1868)." *Alumni Catalogue of the Union Theological Seminary in the City of New York, 1836-1936*, Electronic Reproduction, Columbia University Libraries, 2007, 1937, p. 44, http://www.columbia.edu/cu/lweb/digital/collections/cul/texts/ldpd_5998059_000/pages/ldpd_5998059_000_00000108.html. Columbia University Libraries Electronic Books. 2006., Master copy stored locally on 5 DVDs#: ldpd_5998059_000 01 to 05.

United States Bureau of Land Management Tract Books, 1800-c. 1955. Database with images, FamilySearch, 16 June 2023, https://www.familysearch.org/search/collection/2074276. Bur. of Land Mgmt.

United States Census, 1830. Database with images, FamilySearch, https://www.familysearch.org/search/collection/1803958. National Archives and Records Administration. Washington, D.C., NARA microfilm publication M19.

United States Census, 1840. Database with images, FamilySearch, https://www.familysearch.org/search/collection/1786457. Nat'l Archives and Recs. Admin.. Washington, D.C., NARA microfilm publication M704.

United States Census, 1850. Database with images, FamilySearch, https://www.familysearch.org/search/collection/1401638. National Archives and Records Administration. Washington, D.C., NARA microfilm publication M432.

United States Census, 1860. Database with images, FamilySearch, https://www.familysearch.org/search/collection/1473181. Nat'l Archives and Recs. Admin.. Washington, D.C., NARA microfilm publication M653.

United States Census, 1870. Database with images, FamilySearch, https://www.familysearch.org/search/collection/1438024. National Archives and Records Administration. Washington, D.C., NARA microfilm publication M593.

United States Census, 1880. Database with images, FamilySearch, https://www.familysearch.org/search/collection/1417683. Nat'l Archives and Recs. Admin.. Washington, D.C., NARA microfilm publication T9.

United States Census, 1900. Database with images, FamilySearch, https://www.familysearch.org/search/collection/1325221. National Archives and Records Administration. Washington, D.C., NARA microfilm publication T623.

United States Census, 1910. Database with images, FamilySearch, https://www.familysearch.org/search/collection/1727033. National Archives and Records Administration. Washington, D.C., NARA microfilm publication T624.

United States Census, 1920. Database with images, FamilySearch, https://www.familysearch.org/search/collection/1488411. Nat'l Archives and Recs. Admin.. Washington, D.C., NARA microfilm publication T625.

United States Census, 1930. Database with images, FamilySearch, https://www.familysearch.org/search/collection/1810731. Nat'l Archives and Recs. Admin.. Washington, D.C., NARA microfilm publication T626.

United States Census (Mortality Schedule), 1850. Database with images, FamilySearch, https://www.familysearch.org/search/collection/1420441. NARA microfilm publication T655. Washington, D.C.: Nat'l Archives and Recs. Admin., n.d.

U.S. Congress. "Provision for the Removal of the Osage from Kansas. 'And Be It Further Enacted, That Whenever the Great and Little Osage Indians Shall Agree Thereto . . .' 16 Stat. 335 § 12." *The Indian Appropriations Act of the 15th of July, 1870*, 1870, p. 362, https://www.loc.gov/resource/llsalvol.llsal_016/?sp=398. Law Library of Congress.

---. "The Preemption Act of 1830. 4 Stat. 420. May 29, 1830." *United States Statutes at Large*, vol. 4, Charles C. Little and James Brown, 1846, p. 420, https://tile.loc.gov/storage-services/service/ll/llsl//llsl-c21/llsl-c21.pdf. Law Library of Congress.

---. "The Preemption Act of 1838. 5 Stat. 251. Jun 22, 1838." *United States Statutes at Large*, vol. 5, Little, Brown, and Co., 1856, p. 251, https://tile.loc.gov/storage-services/service/ll/llsl//llsl-c25/llsl-c25.pdf. Law Library of Congress.

---. "The Preemption Act of 1841. 5 Stat. 453. Sep 4, 1841." *United States Statutes at Large*, vol. 5, Little, Brown, and Co., 1856, p. 453, https://tile.loc.gov/storage-services/service/ll/llsl//llsl-c27/llsl-c27.pdf. Law Library of Congress.

U.S. Dept. of Agric. *Aerial Photography Index for Montgomery County, Kansas, Sheet 3*. 7 Nov. 1941, https://catalog.archives.gov/id/106759595. National Archives, 1941 Indexes to Aerial Photography of Montgomery County, Kansas; Indexes to Aerial Photographs of the United States, 1953 - 1957; Records of the Farm Service Agency, 1904 - 1983 (RG 145); National Archives at College Park - Cartographic (RDSC), College Park, MD.

U.S. Dept. of the Interior and Kansas State Hist'l Soc. "Records from Kansas Land Offices." *Kansas Historical Society*, https://www.kshs.org/archives/193307. Accessed 24 Nov. 2020.

U.S. Gen. Land Off. *Alexander K. Johnson (Montgomery County, Kansas) Land Patent No. 3354*. 15 July 1873, https://glorecords.blm.gov/details/patent/default.aspx?accession=KS1350__.301&docClass=STA&sid=n1ami11b.m2d#patentDetailsTabIndex=1. BLM GLO Records, Land Patent Search (digital images).

---. *Bennet Tann (Montgomery County, Kansas) Land Patent No. 3044*. 1 Aug. 1873, https://glorecords.blm.gov/details/patent/default.aspx?accession=KS1360__.318&docClass=STA&sid=ofdhmiyh.5tc#patentDetailsTabIndex=1. BLM GLO Records, Land Patent Search (digital images).

---. *Charles A. Thompson (Montgomery County, Kansas) Land Patent No. 2410*. 10 May 1873, https://glorecords.blm.gov/details/patent/default.aspx?accession=KS1340__.412&docClass=STA&sid=ax2nzbti.

wxp#patentDetailsTabIndex=1. BLM GLO Records, Land Patent Search (digital images).
---. *Circular from the General Land Office, Showing the Manner of Proceeding to Obtain Title to Public Lands, by Purchase, by Location with Warrants or Agricultural College Scrip, by Pre-Emption and Homestead*. Govt. Printing Off., 1870, https://lccn.loc.gov/08028828. Library of Congress.
---. *Circular from the General Land Office, Showing the Manner of Proceeding to Obtain Title to Public Lands, by Purchase, by Location with Warrants or Agricultural College Scrip, by Pre-Emption and Homestead*. Govt. Printing Off., 1867, https://lccn.loc.gov/09034430. Library of Congress.
---. *Daniel Everitt (Montgomery County, Kansas) Land Patent No. 3046*. 1 July 1873, https://glorecords.blm.gov/details/patent/default.aspx?accession=KS1350__.150&docClass=STA&sid=f1dwhnwm.ugs#patentDetailsTabIndex=1. BLM GLO Records, Land Patent Search (digital images).
---. *David Everitt (McHenry County, Illinois) Land Patent No. 8796*. 10 Mar. 1843, https://glorecords.blm.gov/details/patent/default.aspx?accession=IL0880__.174&docClass=STA&sid=kdxt10xq.s5q#patentDetailsTabIndex=1. BLM GLO Records, Land Patent Search (digital images).
---. *David Everitt (McHenry County, Illinois) Land Patent No. 13887*. 1 Oct. 1844, https://glorecords.blm.gov/details/patent/default.aspx?accession=IL0980__.189&docClass=STA&sid=kdxt10xq.s5q#patentDetailsTabIndex=1. BLM GLO Records, Land Patent Search (digital images).
---. *Edmund Mason (Independence, Kansas) Land Case Entry File No. 5022. Osage Trust & Diminished Reserve Lands.* 12 July 1873. Records of the Bureau of Land Management; National Archives, Washington, D.C., Record Group 49.
---. *Edmund Mason (Montgomery County, Kansas) Land Patent No. 5022*. 1 Oct. 1873, https://glorecords.blm.gov/details/patent/default.aspx?accession=KS1380__.266&docClass=STA&sid=lqxcscks.cpf#patentDetailsTabIndex=1. BLM GLO Records, Land Patent Search (digital images).
---. *Edward E. Edwards (Montgomery County, Kansas) Land Patent No. 5720*. 15 Dec. 1873, https://glorecords.blm.gov/details/patent/default.aspx?accession=KS1400__.323&docClass=STA&sid=hgsxx4qx.3sj#patentDetailsTabIndex=1. BLM GLO Records, Land Patent Search (digital images).
---. *Frederick Brown (Montgomery County, Kansas) Land Patent No. 3536*. 15 July 1873, https://glorecords.blm.gov/details/patent/default.aspx?accession=KS1360__.107&docClass=STA&sid=hcuulqro.don#

patentDetailsTabIndex=1. BLM GLO Records, Land Patent Search (digital images).

---. *George A. Tann (Montgomery County, Kansas) Land Patent No. 3628*. 15 July 1873, https://glorecords.blm.gov/details/patent/default.aspx?accession=KS1360__.150&docClass=STA&sid=ofdhmiyh.5tc#patentDetailsTabIndex=1. BLM GLO Records, Land Patent Search (digital images).

---. *George N. Longcor (Montgomery County, Kansas) Land Patent No. 3553*. 15 July 1873, https://glorecords.blm.gov/details/patent/default.aspx?accession=KS1350__.302&docClass=STA&sid=y0vuk2or.pee#patentDetailsTabIndex=1. BLM GLO Records, Land Patent Search (digital images).

---. *J. N. Sands (Montgomery County, Kansas) Land Patent No. 5077*. 1 Oct. 1873, https://glorecords.blm.gov/details/patent/default.aspx?accession=KS1380__.316&docClass=STA&sid=o5dwgcm0.avp#patentDetailsTabIndex=1. BLM GLO Records, Land Patent Search (digital images).

---. *Jacob S. Reser (Dallas County, Missouri) Military Bounty Land Warrant No. 5224*. 2 Oct. 1854. BLM GLO Records, Land Patent Search (digital images), *Military Bounty Land Warrant Vol. 816*, https://glorecords.blm.gov/details/patent/default.aspx?accession=0816-376&docClass=MW&sid=vgdfb2fn.diu#patentDetailsTabIndex=1.

---. *John Brown (Montgomery County, Kansas) Land Patent No. 3779*. 15 Apr. 1875, https://glorecords.blm.gov/details/patent/default.aspx?accession=KS1420__.495&docClass=STA&sid=nyo3x0dc.kep#patentDetailsTabIndex=1. BLM GLO Records, Land Patent Search (digital images).

---. *John Brown (Montgomery County, Kansas) Land Patent No. 6776*. 1 Apr. 1876, https://glorecords.blm.gov/details/patent/default.aspx?accession=KS1440__.113&docClass=STA&sid=cba1dkoc.hxf#patentDetailsTabIndex=1. BLM GLO Records, Land Patent Search (digital images).

---. *John Edwards (Montgomery County, Kansas) Land Patent No. 5566*. 1 Oct. 1873, https://glorecords.blm.gov/details/patent/default.aspx?accession=KS1390__.333&docClass=STA&sid=hgsxx4qx.3sj#patentDetailsTabIndex=1. BLM GLO Records, Land Patent Search (digital images).

---. *John L. Rowles (Montgomery County, Kansas) Land Patent No. 2917*. 20 May 1874, https://glorecords.blm.gov/details/patent/default.aspx?accession=KS1400__.473&docClass=STA&sid=izbik3n2.php#

patentDetailsTabIndex=1. BLM GLO Records, Land Patent Search (digital images).

---. *John S. Latta (Montgomery County, Kansas) Land Patent No. 1815*. 15 Mar. 1873, https://glorecords.blm.gov/details/patent/default.aspx?accession=KS1340__.119&docClass=STA&sid=1feswfp1.1jr#patentDetailsTabIndex=1. BLM GLO Records, Land Patent Search (digital images).

---. *Joseph B. Streeter (McHenry County, Illinois) Land Patent No. 10769*. 10 July 1844, https://glorecords.blm.gov/details/patent/default.aspx?accession=IL0910__.343&docClass=STA&sid=htjpanum.b3u#patentDetailsTabIndex=1. BLM GLO Records, Land Patent Search (digital images).

---. *Joseph L. James (Montgomery County, Kansas) Land Patent No. 3178*. 1 July 1873, https://glorecords.blm.gov/details/patent/default.aspx?accession=KS1350__.228&docClass=STA&sid=drhwkalm.ft3#patentDetailsTabIndex=1. BLM GLO Records, Land Patent Search (digital images).

---. *Joshua Edwards (Montgomery County, Kansas) Land Patent No. 1768*. 1 Aug. 1873, https://glorecords.blm.gov/details/patent/default.aspx?accession=KS1360__.234&docClass=STA&sid=hgsxx4qx.3sj#patentDetailsTabIndex=1. BLM GLO Records, Land Patent Search (digital images).

---. *Legal Description and Land Status: A Self Study Guide*. 2000, http://jay.law.ou.edu/faculty/Hampton/Mineral%20Title%20Examination/Spring%202012/Legal%20Land%20Descriptions_BLM(2000).pdf.

---. *M. A. Streeter (Montgomery County, Kansas) Land Patent No. 2047*. 15 Mar. 1873, https://glorecords.blm.gov/details/patent/default.aspx?accession=KS1340__.210&docClass=STA&sid=5qyw4qvr.z0n#patentDetailsTabIndex=1. BLM GLO Records, Land Patent Search (digital images).

---. *Oliver Carrow (Montgomery County, Kansas) Land Patent No. 2091*. 15 Mar. 1873, https://glorecords.blm.gov/details/patent/default.aspx?accession=KS1340__.224&docClass=STA&sid=arxwxlov.fqw#patentDetailsTabIndex=1. BLM GLO Records, Land Patent Search (digital images).

---. *Report of the Commissioner of General Land Office for the Year 1871*. Government Printing Office, Washington, 1871, p. 9,16,137,143, https://books.google.com/books?id=DK0yAQAAMAAJ. Google Books.

---. *S. A. James (Montgomery County, Kansas) Land Patent No. 6645*. 15 Jan. 1876, https://glorecords.blm.gov/details/patent/default.aspx?

accession=KS1430__.469&docClass=STA&sid=vjl2tbtn.ucw#patentDetailsTabIndex=1. BLM GLO Records, Land Patent Search (digital images).

---. *Samuel Riddle (Montgomery County, Kansas) Land Patent No. 3345*. 15 July 1873, https://glorecords.blm.gov/details/patent/default.aspx?accession=KS1350__.309&docClass=STA&sid=ccv42ki5.ijx#patentDetailsTabIndex=1. BLM GLO Records, Land Patent Search (digital images).

---. *Sarah E. Hunt (Montgomery County, Kansas) Land Patent No. 3504*. 1 June 1874, https://glorecords.blm.gov/details/patent/default.aspx?accession=KS1410__.008&docClass=STA&sid=fvd3yryx.m5q#patentDetailsTabIndex=1. BLM GLO Records, Land Patent Search (digital images).

---. *William F. Johns (Montgomery County, Kansas) Land Patent No. 4041*. 1 Sept. 1873, https://glorecords.blm.gov/details/patent/default.aspx?accession=KS1370__.008&docClass=STA&sid=2kg5a3mj.ggt#patentDetailsTabIndex=1. BLM GLO Records, Land Patent Search (digital images).

---. *Zenas Streeter (McHenry County, Illinois) Land Patent No. 23420*. 1 Mar. 1848, https://glorecords.blm.gov/details/patent/default.aspx?accession=IL1170__.143&docClass=STA&sid=htjpanum.b3u#patentDetailsTabIndex=1. BLM GLO Records, Land Patent Search (digital images).

U.S. Geol. Survey. *Map of Bolton Quadrangle, Kansas, Montgomery Co. (Topographic)*. Department of the Interior/USGS, 1959, https://ngmdb.usgs.gov/ht-bin/tv_browse.pl?id=91792d7908050064562e79a953a6b921.

---. *Map of Kansas, Independence Quadrangle (Topographic)*. Department of the Interior/USGS, Feb. 1905, https://ngmdb.usgs.gov/ht-bin/tv_browse.pl?id=7aa753f40d89359d8018cbe892371401.

---. *Map of Kansas, Independence Sheet (Topographic)*. Department of the Interior/USGS, Jan. 1894, https://ngmdb.usgs.gov/ht-bin/tv_browse.pl?id=7fbd16eeb00f5c51e13fd26d9998b5dc.

---. *Map of Kansas, Independence Sheet (Topographic)*. Department of the Interior/USGS, Apr. 1886, https://ngmdb.usgs.gov/ht-bin/tv_browse.pl?id=321e25091cbc351340beb26f61daccc4.

"U.S., Selected Federal Census Non-Population Schedules, 1850-1880." *Database*, Ancestry.com Operations, Inc., https://www.ancestry.com/search/collections/1276/. ancestry.com.

"Verdigris City ('This Is the Name of a New Town in Montgomery County. . . .')." *The Daily Kansas Tribune*, [Lawrence, Kansas], 18 June 1869, p. 2. newspapers.com.

"W. E. Brown (Obituary)." *Independence Daily Reporter*, [Independence, Kansas], 5 Apr. 1890, p. 3. newspapers.com.

Walker, Francis A. "Population by Counties—1790-1870. State of Kansas." *The Statistics of the Population of the United States, From the Original Returns of the Ninth Census (June 1, 1870)*, vol. 1, Government Printing Office, 1872, pp. 29–30, https://www2.census.gov/library/publications/decennial/1870/population/1870a-06.pdf. The United States Census Bureau.

Washington F. Reser: U.S. Postmaster Appointments. Ancestry.com Operations, Inc., 2010, https://www.ancestry.com/search/collections/1932/. ancestry.com, U.S., Appointments of U. S. Postmasters, 1832-1971 [database on-line].

"Washington Fain Reser (1816-1880) - Find A Grave Memorial." *Find A Grave*, https://www.findagrave.com/memorial/46850634/washington-fain-reser. Accessed 22 Dec. 2020.

"Washington Fain Reser (1849-1942) - Find A Grave Memorial." *Find A Grave*, https://www.findagrave.com/memorial/31499387/washington-fain-reser. Accessed 22 Dec. 2020.

"We Have Been Informed of the Death of Frederick Brown . . ." *The Independence Kansan*, [Independence, Kansas], 3 Apr. 1878, p. 3. newspapers.com.

White, William. "Lifton Parish." *History, Gazetteer & Directory of Devon, 1850*, Robert Leader (printer), 1850, pp. 803–04, https://specialcollections.le.ac.uk/digital/collection/p16445coll4/id/218254/.

"Who Was Mr. Edwards?" *Little House Discussed*, 10 Feb. 2015, http://littlehousediscussion.blogspot.com/2015/02/who-was-mr-edwards.html.

Wilder, Daniel Webster. "United States Census (Summary Table)." *The Annals of Kansas*, G. W. Martin, 1875, p. 522, https://www.google.com/books/edition/The_Annals_of_Kansas/-o8-AAAAYAAJ. Google Books.

Wilder, Laura Ingalls. *By the Shores of Silver Lake*. Full color collector's ed, HarperTrophy, 2004.

---. *Little House on the Prairie (Unpub. MS., Folder 14)*. Unpublished Manuscripts. The State Historical Society of Missouri, Folders 14-18; Laura Ingalls Wilder Papers, 1894-1943 (C3633); Columbia Manuscript Collections; Columbia Research Center; Center for Missouri Studies; Columbia, MO.

---. *Little House on the Prairie (Unpub. MS., Folder 15)*. Unpublished Manuscripts. The State Historical Society of Missouri, Folders 14-18; Laura Ingalls Wilder Papers, 1894-1943 (C3633); Columbia Manuscript Collections; Columbia Research Center; Center for Missouri Studies; Columbia, MO.

---. *Little House on the Prairie (Unpub. MS., Folder 16)*. Unpublished Manuscripts. The State Historical Society of Missouri, Folders 14-18; Laura Ingalls Wilder Papers, 1894-1943 (C3633); Columbia Manuscript Collections; Columbia Research Center; Center for Missouri Studies; Columbia, MO.

---. *Little House on the Prairie (Unpub. MS., Folder 17)*. Unpublished Manuscripts. The State Historical Society of Missouri, Folders 14-18; Laura Ingalls Wilder Papers, 1894-1943 (C3633); Columbia Manuscript Collections; Columbia Research Center; Center for Missouri Studies; Columbia, MO.

---. *Little House on the Prairie (Unpub. MS., Folder 18)*. Unpublished Manuscripts. The State Historical Society of Missouri, Folders 14-18; Laura Ingalls Wilder Papers, 1894-1943 (C3633); Columbia Manuscript Collections; Columbia Research Center; Center for Missouri Studies; Columbia, MO.

---. *Little House on the Prairie*. Newly illustrated uniform edition, Harper & Row, 1953.

---. *On the Banks of Plum Creek*. Mammoth, 1992.

---. *Pioneer Girl*. Brandt Copy, 1930. National Archives, Files 205-206; Box 14; Rose Wilder Lane Papers; Herbert Hoover Presidential Library, West Branch, IA.

---. *Pioneer Girl*. Bye Copy, 1930. National Archives, Files 209-210; Box 14; Rose Wilder Lane Papers; Herbert Hoover Presidential Library, West Branch, IA.

---. *Pioneer Girl*. Fragment sent to Carl Brandt, 1930. National Archives, File 212; Box 14; Rose Wilder Lane Papers; Herbert Hoover Presidential Library, West Branch, IA.

---. *Pioneer Girl*. Revised Draft, 1930. National Archives, Files 207-208; Box 14; Rose Wilder Lane Papers; Herbert Hoover Presidential Library, West Branch, IA.

---. *Pioneer Girl: The Annotated Autobiography*. Edited by Pamela Smith Hill, South Dakota Historical Society Press, 2014.

---. *The Long Winter*. Penguin Books, 1977.

---. *The Selected Letters of Laura Ingalls Wilder*. Edited by William Anderson, First edition, Harper, an imprint of HarperCollins Publishers, 2016.

---. *These Happy Golden Years*. Newly illustrated uniform edition, Harper & Row, 1971.

"William E. Brown (1809-1890) - Find A Grave Memorial." *Find A Grave*, https://www.findagrave.com/memorial/30045627/william-e.-brown. Accessed 15 Dec. 2020.

"William E. Brown (Obituary)." *The Weekly Star and Kansan*, [Independence, Kansas], 4 Apr. 1890, p. 3. newspapers.com.

"William M 'Willie' MASON - Facts. Mason in West Devon." *Ancestry*, https://www.ancestry.com/family-tree/person/tree/4974046/person/-1515392109/facts. Accessed 23 July 2017.

"William Perry Brown (1842-1881) - Find A Grave Memorial." *Find A Grave*, https://www.findagrave.com/memorial/30045548/william-perry-brown. Accessed 2 Dec. 2020.

"William Van Winkle (Abt.1848-)." *WikiTree*, https://www.wikitree.com/wiki/Van_Winkle-592. Accessed 24 Nov. 2020.

"William VanWinkle (1857-1935) - Find A Grave Memorial." *Find A Grave*, https://www.findagrave.com/memorial/16897903/william-vanwinkle. Accessed 1 Dec. 2020.

Willison, Jim, transcriber. "Roster of Company H 113th Illinois Infantry." *The ILGenWeb Project. The Illinois Civil War Project.*, https://civilwar.illinoisgenweb.org/r155/113-h-in.html. Accessed 21 Mar. 2020.

Wilson, Ebenezer E. "History of Montgomery County, Kansas." *Historical Atlas of Montgomery County, Kansas*, 1881, pp. 7–9.

Wilson, F. Marion. *Wilson's History of Hickory County*. 1909, https://archive.org/details/wilsonshistoryof00wils. archive.org.

Wing, Nic. "A History of Tobacco in London." *Londonist*, 28 Nov. 2014, https://londonist.com/2014/11/london-a-history-in-tobacco.

Zabriskie, James C., editor. "Kansas Sale of School Lands Act of 1864. 'No. 160 E.-An Act to Provide for the Sale of the School Lands.' Feb 22, 1864. (Kansas. Legislative Acts)." *The Public Land Laws of The United States*, H. H. Bancroft and Co., 1870, p. 734, https://www.google.com/books/edition/_/NDxHAQAAMAAJ. Google Books.

"Zeno Streeter (1821-1882) - Find A Grave Memorial." *Find A Grave*, https://www.findagrave.com/memorial/11337974/zeno-streeter. Accessed 24 Nov. 2020.

Zochert, Donald. *Laura: The Life of Laura Ingalls Wilder*. Avon, 1976.

Meet the Authors

Robynne Elizabeth Miller is wife to an amazing Brit and mother to a glorious brood of adopted, biological, and foster kids. A dual citizen of America and the UK, she's lived at length in both countries. Now, she makes her home in the Pacific Northwest. Passionate about her family, faith, music, travel, and cooking, she writes about the pioneers who formed our country and things that move her heart.

She has authored numerous nonfiction books, articles, and essays, mostly relating to pioneer life or the *Little House* series, including *The Three Faces of Nellie, Pioneer Mixology,* and *From the Mouth of Ma.* An experienced speaker, editor, and writing/publishing coach, Robynne teaches at conferences and writer's workshops and speaks at *Little House* sites and historic venues throughout the U.S. She is also the director of the Vision Christian Writers Conference at Mount Hermon, California.

She completed her MFA in Creative Nonfiction and Fiction through Ashland University, Ashland, Ohio, and holds a B.A. in English Literature from Westmont College, Santa Barbara, CA. Her MFA critical thesis was: *Nonfiction, Memoir, or Fiction? Dissecting the Works of Laura Ingalls Wilder* (June 2017). Her creative thesis was *Little Girl Rising* (2018).

On quieter days, Robynne can be found meandering back roads, singing at the top of her lungs, or making bacon from scratch.

J.D. Rushmore is a history and genealogy buff, with a particular interest in American history before 1900. He's enamored with the opening of the west, pioneers, the gold rush, the Oregon trail, etc. He's particularly passionate about researching historical mysteries, especially when they relate to the *Little House* series of books.

He is a musician in his spare time, as well as an "at everything" father, husband, and friend. He prefers the smell of historic archives to fresh air (unless it involves poking around a remote historic cemetery!) and has a knack for reading handwriting on historical documents that is illegible to others. Nothing thrills him more than finding the one tiny detail that, after being overlooked for decades, or even centuries, changes EVERYTHING.

Also by Robynne Elizabeth Miller

The Three Faces of Nellie

Whether you love her, hate her, or love to hate her, Nellie Oleson is one of most recognizable literary figures of the 20th century. But Laura Ingalls Wilder had a secret . . . Nellie wasn't a real person. Instead, she was a composite character created from three girls Laura knew from childhood: Nellie Owens, Genevieve Masters, and Estella Gilbert.

The character of Nellie Oleson is one-dimensional: snobbish, selfish, and thoroughly unpleasant. But the real women behind Laura's creation? An intriguing mix of the not-so-nice and the unexpectedly redeemable.

Laura Ingalls Wilder did a masterful job of creating the character of Nellie Oleson. But the three real-life women behind that iconic character are infinitely more intriguing.

From the Mouth of Ma

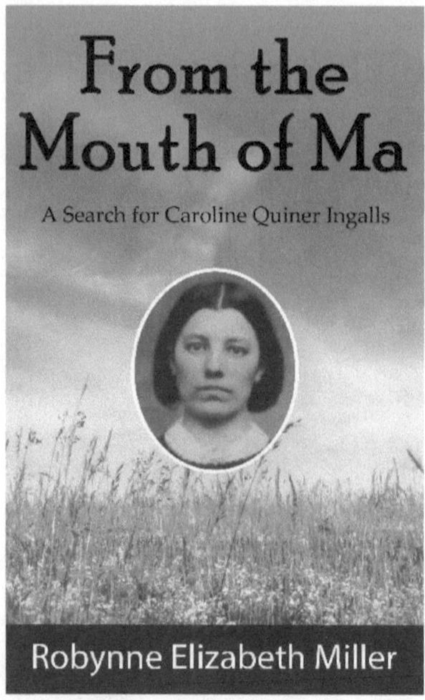

There's not a whole lot written about Caroline Quiner Ingalls, the mother of famed Little House on the Prairie author, Laura Ingalls Wilder. And I always wondered why. So, I set about looking for her. . .in family letters, bits of biography and, mostly, through the words she spoke throughout the Little House series. The Ma I thought I'd find wasn't the one I discovered. Would you like to meet her? I think you'll be happy that you did.

Pioneer Mixology:
Switchel, Sack Posset and Shrub

A quirky survey of Pioneer beverages. Recipes, tips, and a bit of history explaining the how and why behind what the settlers drank. From clarifying coffee with the swim bladder of a fish (um, YUCK!) to making coffee substitutes with everything from grape seeds to sweet potatoes, this book examines period beverages and how many of them came into being. A fun, sometimes irreverent (but extremely well-researched) book perfect for history buffs, homesteaders, beverage aficionados, fans of the prairie lifestyle.

Nonfiction, Memoir, or Fiction?:
Dissecting the Works of Laura Ingalls Wilder

This project is a critical paper partially fulfilling the requirements for a Masters of Fine Arts Degree in Creative Nonfiction and Fiction at Ashland University. It examines the works of beloved pioneer author Laura Ingalls Wilder, teasing out the elements of her stories that were Nonfiction, Memoir, or Fiction, and entering into a discussion about the impact using these various writing techniques had on her individual stories and her narrative arc as a whole.

Slightly Strange *Savory* Pioneer Recipes (that actually taste good!)

Think the pioneers had a monotonous diet? Not so! With a little creativity and a few basic staples, early settlers pulled together many incredibly interesting concoctions. And while some of them may sound a little dodgy at first (Chicken Mull and Egg Gravy, anyone?), they're actually very tasty. These recipes are authentic to the time period (Laura Ingalls Wilder's Ma and Pa would have either eaten or been exposed to these foods!), easy to make in our modern kitchens, beautifully adaptable to our contemporary palates, and a fun taste of history past! Don't be surprised if you add a few of these to your regular meal plans!

Slightly Strange *Sweet* Pioneer Recipes (that are delicious!)

A collection of pioneer recipes that are sweet, but slightly strange in name, use of odd ingredients, or in the method of cooking. But don't let that fool you, these easy recipes are delicious, even if they might seem a little weird at first!

Super Simple *Savory* Pioneer Recipes (five ingredients or less!)

Out of a love for *Little House on the Prairie* and Laura Ingalls Wilder, grew a love for all things pioneer. This book combines that passion with a love for cooking, and the result is delicious! Very easy, very cost effective pioneer recipes fill this book. Each savory dish uses five ingredients or less, and can be made without any expensive or complicated equipment. So step back in time and taste a little history!

Super Simple *Sweet* Pioneer Recipes (five ingredients or less!)

Just because something is easy to make, doesn't mean it isn't delicious! The pioneers knew this well and managed to create, with few ingredients and some simple steps, some absolutely delectable treats. This is a collection of authentic pioneer recipes that are as tasty as they are easy to prepare. No fancy or expensive ingredients, no complicated equipment, and yet some wonderful results. Laura Ingalls Wilder's *Little House* books mention one or two of these treats, and it's likely they ate many of them regularly. So, bring out your inner "Ma" and give them a try!

By Marilyn Siden & Robynne Elizabeth Miller

Finding Common Ground: One Octogenarian's Quest to Help our Nation Heal

Why would a feisty almost-eighty-year-old grandmother slip into her Birkenstocks, throw a sleeping bag into the back of her Subaru, and set out across America? Because she'd had enough. Enough anger. Enough hatred. Enough division.

Marilyn Siden has lived through much: the aftermath of World War II, Korea, and the horror of Vietnam. She's navigated good political administrations and struggling ones, a thriving economy and want. Her eight decades of experience living in the US have shown her the best America has to offer and, unfortunately, the worst. But she never thought America would become a place of vitriol and despair. So, she decided to do something about it.

Through a series of epic journeys across America, Marilyn discovered what she was after: practical advice on how to help our nation heal. But she found something she wasn't expecting ... something far more powerful.

Marilyn found our common ground.

Made in United States
Troutdale, OR
10/14/2023

13714984R00181